THE PYJAMA PARADE

THE PYJAMA PARADE

Steve Gilhooley

LOMOND

First published in Great Britain in 2001
by Lomond Books
36 West Shore Road, Granton,
Edinburgh EH5 1QD

ISBN 1-84204-035-9

Designed and typeset by Cutting Edge Design & Print Ltd.
Printed and bound in the United Kingdom.

THE PYJAMA PARADE

By Steve Gilhooley

'For our lack of facing the truth regarding abuse by clergy and others, for our tendency to retreat into denial and self-protection in the face of such abuse, for our response of fear and avoidance rather than of care for the survivors of clergy sexual abuse, we ask pardon and forgiveness.'

Bishop John S. Cummins,
Oakland Diocese, California

MY THANKS...

To my Uncle Tommy for gently encouraging me to write all of this down
To Fran and Dougie for getting it published
To Clare for attempting to edit it
To my Mum and Dad for sharing the pain
To Fr John Scally for having the courage to put his name to it
To Joe in the hope that his hell will now come to an end
To George who took the risk of backing me
To Keith for his friendship
To all my family and friends who stood by me when I felt ridiculed, discredited and isolated

This book is dedicated to all those who have been abused in any way in the Church, but especially to those who are being abused all over again by people who have chosen to walk by on the other side. It is written in the hope that an air of honesty and openness can take hold in the Church.

Foreword

'Self-reflection is about the hardest and most repellent thing there is for man, who is predominantly unconscious. Human nature has an invincible dread of becoming more conscious of itself.'
Carl Jung

In counselling there is the phenomenon of the 'gallows laugh'. This is when someone relates a tragic story, situation or event and laughs out loud while relaying the details. The listener is encouraged to see the funny side of the tragic or cruel. The laughter hides and betrays a labyrinth of emotions suppressed deep inside. For the client, the laugh is indeed a 'gallows laugh', for he is dying, and being killed emotionally by the reality of the memory. Many, if not most of us, have a 'gallows laugh' story to tell. Most of us prefer to laugh rather than face the frightening emotions that could be unleashed if we dared to stop laughing and feel the emotions – and then face the consequences. This kind of self-knowledge is painful and will entail suffering. Most of us choose to avoid the pain.

In Steve Gilhooley's book, we laugh with him at the many hysterical moments of his life, as we view situations through his eyes and listen to his mind. Beginning as a child in the mining village of Loanhead in Midlothian, we journey with him to junior seminary when, at the age of twelve years, he thought he wanted to be a missionary priest when he grew up. Growing up became something very different to what he had expected. We are given vivid details of his time spent in the seminary, as he recounts his journey from boyhood to young adolescence, through stories and descriptions of what life was like for the young trainee priests and how they were exposed to the rigorous regime of study, prayer and preparation for priesthood. The teachers are all priests, all men entrusted with the care and well-being of young boys whose aspirations, dreams, prayers and human development lie in their hands. These priests fail dismally in their task. Brutal beatings, perverse rules and regulations, damaging mental guilt and abuse pervade the system as do silence, fear and 'gallows laughs'. These are the repressed memories, buried deep; buried deep for God knows how long and for how many generations.

Steve began this book as a cathartic exercise for himself and to try and understand why one of his best friends tried to kill himself. This journey of self-recollection has, I know, been painful and slow, as he has awakened and exposed deep memories that were trapped very efficiently and safely in his mind.

He has been encouraged to record his experiences for others. It is Steve's hope that others will find the strength to become conscious. In his analysis, Steve poses very difficult and uncomfortable questions and observations; if the majority of parish priests have experienced junior seminary training, then maybe there are many priests who have experienced the same as Steve? What about the many 'failed' trainee priests who left seminary or were kicked out? Are they, too, survivors? How are they coping with life after junior seminary? And if there are casualties, what pastoral response can, and does, the Church give?

If one man is given strength to admit his need for help, to acknowledge his fears and nightmares, and seeks help, then Steve's book has achieved good. Steve started this book for himself, but now it is for the many, a fact that, sadly, is proving only too true.

'There is no higher aim than to reclaim another,
blinded by life's pain, to help him see and live again.'
Carl Jung

Fr John Scally

Introduction

I have now been an ordained priest for just under ten years. At this moment, I could count on one hand the number of priests I could call 'friends'. Since the age of twelve, I held a dark secret deep within me, so deep that I wasn't even aware of it until well into my adulthood. When I eventually blurted out to another human being what had been unconsciously menacing me, there then began a long and painful process of self-discovery and healing. Someone advised me to write it all down for therapeutic purposes. This I did and I found it of tremendous help. However, what I wrote down also challenged me to look more honestly at the nature of the priesthood and the Church.

Over the last decade, I have been in the privileged position of being given a microphone not only to preach from a pulpit on a Sunday, but also to contribute regularly to a variety of media outlets. I have written weekly columns for the *Edinburgh Evening News* and the *Scottish Catholic Observer* and I have presented BBC Scotland's 'Thought for the Day' as well as Radio Forth's 'View from Earth'. In all of that, I tried to take the risk of speaking openly and honestly, whilst also trying to maintain a sense of humour.

The reaction, as would be expected, has been mixed. Some have described my outpourings as refreshing, others have called me Satan's reincarnation and have actively tried to get me out of the newspapers and out of the Church. However, one event made me decide that I was not going to leave what I had written buried in the bottom drawer of my desk. I have broadcast and written about many subjects which some would call controversial: women priests, the relaxation of the celibacy law, the abusive asylums in Ireland, the role of the Vatican in World War II and so on. In all of that, very few of the clergy made any comment to me, although plenty was said behind my back. (One newly ordained priest told a senior clergyman to 'Make sure and give Gilhooley a boot up the arse.' The oil of chrism was hardly dry on him yet! In the past I would probably have confronted such puerile arrogance. Now, I just pity such people. They'll wake up when they're old and wonder what they have been doing with their lives.)

But one particular week, I decided to write about my junior seminary for the *Scottish Catholic Observer*. I didn't give very much detail about what had happened there, but merely hinted from that all had not been well. I didn't name the place because it is not important.

I realised that I had been severely scarred by my experiences there and I was trying to invite all men, including the majority of Catholic clergy in Scotland today, who had attended a junior seminary, to reflect on the possibility that they too might have been adversely affected by their experiences in such institutions.

The newspaper had hardly landed on the tables at the back of Scotland's churches when my phone started to go into meltdown. Some priests began to cancel their parish subscription to the newspaper until such times as I was removed from my column. Other priests called me a traitor and accused me of 'letting the side down'. A few days later, the letters began to arrive. A senior priest in Glasgow wrote a venomous letter to me, telling me to apologise to every priest who had worked at a junior seminary, and to beg forgiveness from God for what I had written in the article. I wrote back to this priest and told him some of the horrific things that had happened to us at his 'beloved' junior seminaries. To give him his due, he wrote back to me by return of post and apologised when he realised the gross way in which we had been treated. He said that he had been unaware that such things had been taking place. I simply do not believe that you can be a priest for forty years and not know what has been going on.

The priest ended his letter by saying that he would burn my letter so that the contents would never be known by anyone. It was this statement which finally made up my mind to publish. There are young men who no longer walk this earth because of what happened to them at junior seminary. There are others who have had nervous breakdowns, become chronic alcoholics or whose lives lie in ruins because of what happened. I am not keeping quiet about it any more. The consequences for too many young men, and for the Church in general, have been too serious.

Personally, I cannot leave my past as meaningless pain. I believe that something good and positive can come out of what many of us suffered. If even one person who has suffered in the same way can be set off on the road to healing, this book will have been worth all the criticism it will no doubt provoke. I have deliberately not given the names of certain people and places. The names of fellow students at junior seminary are fictitious. So often, the reaction of society is to visit its anger on individuals who have transgressed, once they are identified, to the detriment of looking at why the person transgressed in the first place. The Catholic Church has a huge problem. Until we begin to address structures and have the willingness and honestly to admit who we are – and change – we will continue to see priests on the front pages of our national newspapers, for all the wrong reasons.

As you will see, I am not a journalist, an intellectual, nor a particularly gifted writer, but I only hope that what I am trying to say, gets across. Someone who read the book before publication asked why I had written so much about my visit to the World Cup in Spain in 1982. The simple answer is so much of the book was painful to write; I was dredging up memories that I had long since buried. On a number of occasions, I had to switch off the computer and just walk away, I felt so upset. On the other hand, it was a delight to recall events like the World Cup, one of the happiest times in my life, so it was easy to write. But even that wonderful time was still tarnished by thoughts of the junior seminary. I hope the reader bears with my self-indulgence. In any case, as I now know, everyone's life is a mixture of the good and the bad, the happy and the sad. I believe it is just as important to recall the smiles as it is to remember the frowns. All of it together goes to make up who we are and who we will become.

Chapter One

The groans from the other cubicles became muffled and distant as the morphine kicked in. Normally, this powerful drug is injected into the muscle area surrounding the hip. On this occasion though, the young doctor took pity on me after listening to my pathetic whimpers for over half an hour. He administered the painkiller straight into a vein in the back of my hand. Within seconds, the excruciating agony that had racked my body since the previous evening began to fade. Suddenly I began to understand the film *Trainspotting*. I understood why so many young people turn to drugs to ease the pain of the dreadful disappointment of existence. I lay back on the hospital trolley and exhaled every drop of breath from my lungs. The morphine provided me with the illusion that all my troubles were gone. In the few seconds that it took the doctor's thumb to travel the distance of one inch to release the drug from the syringe into my welcoming bloodstream, the delusion set in that my physical pain – and everything else that had been mentally crushing me – had totally disappeared.

Accompanying that feeling of almost cosmic relief came tears. My body shuddered as I wept silently. The lines from the drips into my arm tangled as I raised my hand to cover my eyes. Crying has always been a very private affair for me. I was in no position to seek out a room where I could weep on my own so I did the next best thing. I covered my eyes. It was like the child playing hide-and-seek. He doesn't know where to hide so he just shuts his eyes. The logic being, if I can't see them, they can't see me. It was weird, saline was going in one end and tears were flowing out the other.

Carl, an older man with whom I would have entrusted my life, stood beside me, gently and soothingly rubbing my arm. He tried to console me: 'Just relax, Father Steve, everything is going to be okay now.' I realised something in that morphine-induced, enlightened moment. It is only at times of total helplessness that I allow anyone near. It was Carl who had brought me to the Accident and Emergency Unit. He and another parishioner, Joan, had found me in the church house in a state of near collapse.

I was in so much pain, I couldn't even speak to them. I had spent all morning spewing the bilious contents of my stomach into the bathroom sink. When there was nothing left to spew, I just retched.

As the porter wheeled me off to the Special Care Unit, I saw my face in a mirror in the hospital corridor. I was white. My lips were purple and parched. I felt as though I had not a drop of liquid left in my body. I was to find out later that when Carl left the hospital, he had broken down in tears in the car park. My parents arrived having just been told that I had been rushed to hospital. They saw the state Carl was in and, panic-stricken, assumed I was dead. Carl told them that he was just upset to see me at such a low ebb.

I was in St John's Hospital, Livingston, on the west side of Edinburgh. I was glad I was there and not in the Western General or the Royal Infirmary. Nothing against the other hospitals, it's just that, being a priest, the 'Saint' bit accorded me some sort of spiritual or maybe even superstitious reassurance.

There was room for four beds in the unit. The porter parked me at trap one. I noticed the wooden locker at the side of my bed. Having lived most of my life in institutions, such Kentucky fried furniture seemed to follow me around everywhere. There must be millions of these wooden lockers all over the country, but you'll never see them on 'The Antiques Roadshow.' There aren't any Edwardian or Tudor lockers. I think they must have been invented by hospitals, borstals or army barracks. They are there to remind you that you are away from home and the people you love. You are just a number in a system, an item to be processed. And you are transitory. Even the grapes which were to adorn the top of the locker later in the week never made it feel more homely. We never had grapes in our house. Or at least, not for very long anyway.

A nurse gently woke me from my thoughts and set about the routine of blood tests, temperature and pulse taking. She was very kind and gentle and treated me as if she really cared. She asked me if I was able to give a urine sample yet. Being totally dehydrated, I informed her that if she came back next week I might be able to assist her in that department. She responded that either I'd provide a sample or the doctor would come and take one. I immediately conjured up an image of a doctor with a syringe and needle setting about my private parts. Suddenly, the dehydration seemed to dissipate somewhat. As if she could read my mind, the nurse told me that there were cardboard bottles in the toilet when I was ready. Bent over double, and trailing my drips on a wheeled gantry behind me, I made my way to the toilet and did the necessary – all 5 ml. of it. It was almost Churchillian: Never had so little been achieved by so few…for so much effort.

Once back in bed, the chronic pain in my belly began to return, accompanied with the feelings of anxiety and distress. I didn't want to bother the nurses or doctors so I suffered in silence. A rough-looking man was then wheeled into trap two. He was obviously in agony and demanded a painkiller. The nurses first had to complete his check-in formalities and as they did so, he gave them dog's abuse. Eventually, they relented and gave him a shot of morphine in the backside. It had the desired effect – the guy shut up. The cursing and swearing died down as he was given the same dire warning as me – a sample would have to be provided whether voluntary or involuntary. The geographical location of the toilet was pointed out to him. I drifted off to sleep again, thankful that 'heid the ba' in the next bed had quietened down.

I woke up to find him struggling towards the loo, drips in tow. He seemed to be in there an age and when he finally emerged triumphantly, he was carrying, no, wielding a round cardboard sick bowl. The nurse shouted across the ward at him, 'Excuse me, Sir, you don't do your urine sample in those. There are cardboard bottles in the toilet.' I let out an audible groan as he replied, 'Nurse, it's not a urine – it's a shite!' Oh God ! I tried to turn over in bed to face the wall, but the pain wouldn't let me. The nurse dashed across the ward and removed the offending bowl from him, trying to appear as professional and nonchalant as she could. It was obvious though, she wanted to puke. The patient hobbled back to his bed looking quite hurt and offended, obviously alarmed at the prospect of now having a urine sample extracted from him, rather than provided by him.

By now, I was again in some distress. The nurse asked permission from the duty doctor to administer another dose of morphine. I floated off into the ether as the drug performed its task. Seemingly, Panda, a priest mate of mine, George, the chaplain to the hospital and Harry, my friend and former boss at work in another life, all visited me that night. I remember very little of their visits, which probably had more to do with the morphine than the quality of their conversations. Tomorrow would bring the results of the tests and I would then discover what awaited me. Surgery, chemotherapy or whatever. Who cared? I certainly didn't. I don't wish to be over-dramatic or over-theatrical, but I really didn't care any more. I was tired of the stresses and strains I had been living under for a number of years now and I wanted it all to end.

The consultant strutted into the unit the next morning followed by a brood of overworked junior doctors. I couldn't help thinking about Frankie Howerd and Barbara Windsor. I remembered an incident when I had gone to visit a sick parishioner in hospital. I would normally always ask permission from the staff nurse to go into the ward but on this occasion there was no one to be found. I saw the lady I had come to visit through the ward door windows, so I went in and sat on the edge of her bed. There was no chair, but even if there had been, I still would have sat on the bed. As we sat chatting quietly, a shrill voice pierced the sedated atmosphere of the ward, 'Get your arse off that bed and anyway, who gave you permission to be in here?' The staff nurse stomped towards me very threateningly. The patient burst into tears pleading with her that I was her priest and had only come to visit her. By now every patient in the ward was staring at us. The staff nurse's way of mellowing her attitude, once she realised the upset she had needlessly caused, was to bark, 'Well, at least find a seat to sit on, it's against the rules to sit on the beds.' My God, it's not just the Church, the NHS provides a platform for these uniformed tyrants too. I stood up and walked towards the exit door. Just as I was about to leave, I turned and said loudly to my parishioner, 'I'll come back later...' Then to the immense hilarity of everyone on the ward I added, '...when Hattie Jacques yonder has finished her shift!' I left the ward to howls of laughter. It was obvious that this nurse had been bullying everyone in that post-war, eat-your-brussels-sprouts-or-there'll-be-no-pudding-for-you-my-lad type of way. Nowadays in hospitals across the land, no pudding is considered a reward for good behaviour.

Anyway, on this occasion, I was the patient. The consultant standing at the end of my bed demanded to know what the problem was with me. I remember wishing that he would lower his voice to a roar. I didn't want my business being discussed so publicly. The junior doctor who had admitted me stepped forward and stated much more sensitively and quietly that I had pancreatitis. He explained that he thought it could be drink related. To my extreme humiliation, the consultant swivelled round on his immaculately polished brogues and made for the next bed, stating dismissively, 'Well, I think we'll just leave him to Doctor So and So.' I was devastated. The contents of the next patient's grey cardboard bowl the day before, had been treated with more respect than I had been. I think that was the lowest point. I really did feel like shit.

Whether the junior doctor sensed this, I don't know, but he returned to me after they had finished their rounds. Funnily enough he sat on the end of my bed. He did that for the same reason that I always did it when I was visiting patients. It gives a sense of informality and intimacy. It provides reassurance. The young man explained that tests had shown that I had a problem with my pancreas. He told me that such problems had one of two causes. Either a stone from the gall-bladder had slipped towards the pancreas, or the pancreas was damaged by over-consumption of alcohol. He said that I would have to go for a scan to find out which it was. I told him that he could save himself the bother. I admitted honestly to him – and to myself – that alcohol was the direct cause of my ailment. I say 'direct' cause because there were certainly many reasons why I had sought comfort in alcohol. The doctor told me that it was good that I openly and honestly admitted what the cause was, but it would still be necessary to go for a scan. This I did, and as suspected, there was no gallstone. I was in hospital because I had been drinking too much.

All the jokes I had heard about clergymen and drink were no longer funny. I had heard the story about the man running up and down the train shouting, 'Is there a Catholic priest on board?' There wasn't. A minute later he was shouting, 'Is there a Church of Scotland minister on board?' None. Eventually, one man stood up and said, 'I'm a minister of the Free Presbyterian Church, can I help?' The guy replied, 'No, I'm looking for a bottle opener!' I had used the story in many an after-dinner speech, I suppose to display an air of self deprecation, but I knew only too well that the joke was hinting at a very tragic reality. Clergymen see and experience so much suffering, that for many of them, alcohol becomes a welcome, if ill-advised, escape. Ironically enough, one occupation which has a higher incidence of alcoholism is the medical profession.

The junior doctor asked me if I knew the reason why I sought solace or escape through drink. I pointed to the television at the end of the ward and to the newspapers on top of my locker. The headlines in both were about a nun who was in court for abusive behaviour towards children in her care over three decades ago. The doctor seemed perplexed. I explained that there was another court case coming up regarding a priest who had sexually abused youngsters under his care. I had been one of those youngsters. I would soon be called to court to give evidence against him. To my knowledge, it would be the first time a priest would be giving testimony against another priest in such a case and I knew the media wouldn't be turning a blind eye to this fact. I feared I was going to be under intense media scrutiny, probably more than the abuser priest. I was genuinely apprehensive, to say the least. This was not the only reason alcohol had become my treacherous friend, but it certainly was the thing that had been uppermost in my mind since that matter had come to the attention of the police a few years previously.

I don't know whether the junior doctor informed the consultant or not, but during the next tour of the wards, the consultant did ask me how I was. I told him straight that I had been hurt by his dismissive attitude towards me. He too then sat on the end of the bed. I explained something of the situation and suddenly his attitude changed. He asked if I was receiving support from the Church. I told him that there was no official support network but that my Archbishop, my family and my parishioners were very supportive. However, the Vatican, the majority of the hierarchy, most of the clergy and many churchgoers had treated me like a leper and wanted me silenced. I was being treated as if I was the perpetrator instead of the victim. The consultant said to me sternly, 'If the Church will not provide ongoing support for you, we certainly will.' I was touched by his concern. Initially, I think he had read me wrongly. I then realised that I had read him wrongly too. He left me with the impression that he did care.

Throughout that week, I was given morphine four times a day. Towards the end of the week, the consultant decided that I would have to go for a CT scan. By now, I had regained the will to live and I feared what the results of the scan might be. Given the pain I had been in, I suspected that cancer might be found. On the evening after the scan, I sat in the ward with five others who had undergone a CT the same day. We waited for the consultant to arrive with the results. The atmosphere was so heavy that had the grim reaper walked in, no one would have been too surprised. I was first. An audible hush shrouded the ward. The doctor informed me that my scan was completely negative. I had pancreatitis and time would heal it. I was told to stay off the drink for the foreseeable future and if I did drink again, to do it in moderation. He made reference to the pressures on me as a priest and stated that I really had to take steps to deal with what lay behind my alcohol dependency. It was a yellow card instead of a red. I was happy to be given a second chance. The consultant then moved to speak to the other five guys. Four were fine and were discharged. One was told that an appointment had been made for him for the Monday morning in another hospital which I knew, specialised in the treatment of cancer. The poor man's jaw dropped; I felt sorry for him. I said a silent prayer that he would be okay.

The morphine was stopped and painkillers in tablet form replaced them. The drips were dismantled and taken away and I was left to contemplate with a more sober head all that had happened. I had to ask myself honestly how I came to be in a hospital bed suffering from a condition which has killed stronger people than me. I knew that my time as a young boy at junior seminary from 1974 to 1979 had disfigured me terribly. That realisation only began to surface in 1982 when I had been working as a lab technician for three years. As I entered adulthood, disturbing signs soon began to rear their ugly heads. The following is my story detailing what happened to me and to others. I hope it helps those who have suffered the same, especially those who have been unable to verbalise the trauma they endured and are still enduring. You are not alone. I also hope that it embarrasses those who, under the banners of loyalty and obedience to the Church, have treated the abused so appallingly, while offering holocausts and babbling religious formulae each Sunday morning. To describe such people's loyalty as 'misplaced' must be the understatement of Church history.

Chapter Two

The work was finished for the day. We lazed about in a smoke-filled office, talking about nothing of any consequence. We never talked about anything at a deep level; it was like an adult version of the school common room. I was to find out later that some people there were carrying their own terrible burdens – but the conversation was about T-shirts. I too was carrying an awful secret. It was so secret that I had hidden it from everyone, including myself.

Anyway, the idle chatter subsided when Harry shoved the door open. It clattered off the knee of the guy who was sitting in Harry's chair. He grimaced in irritation more than pain. Harry muttered something about getting the work done. I told him that it was all done. 'Look at the state of this place! You could cut the bloody smoke in here with a knife!' he continued, totally ignoring me. We were getting a row for something, for anything. Harry was in a bad mood.

Harry's bark was worse than his bite...unless he bit you. He was one of those people whose words you had to read between the lines. Some utterances were to be listened to and acted upon. Others, spoken in the same serious tone, could be nodded to and then totally ignored. The secret to a happy existence was in knowing the difference.

The moaning about the smoke-filled office was category 'B' stuff. You could tell this by the way that everybody lit up another cigarette as he was talking. He waved a glossy magazine at the smoke and then threw it with a slap on the desk. It was a holiday brochure for the Costa del Sol. 'Right, ya muppets,' he said, in a voice which was as near to politeness as Harry could muster, 'who wants to go to the World Cup in Spain this June?' Raymond and Shug fidgeted in a macho acknowledgement that the proposal might, indeed, be of interest to them. Harry stated that the downside was that the trip would cost at least six hundred quid. That was well beyond my means, so I immediately volunteered, 'Aye, you can count me in as well.'

The prospect of going to Spain gave me a buzz for the next few months. I had been falling into inexplicable depressions over the last couple of years. I constantly had a knot in my stomach and couldn't understand why. I didn't tell anyone about it because I didn't know what to tell. Alcohol helped, until the following morning. I do

10

remember Frank Sinatra's comment about people who never drink. He said, 'When they wake up in the morning, that's the best they're going to feel all day.' I knew what he meant.

Finances had to be found for the trip, as I certainly was not missing this chance of a lifetime. I had heard about all the stories of Celtic and Rangers supporters travelling to the European Cup finals in the sixties and all the weird and wonderful events which had befallen them. This was my chance! Given the fact that my wages at the time were a pittance, a pilgrimage to the bank manager for a loan had to be undertaken. The World Cup wouldn't wait for promotion and a better wage at my work.

I put off the visit to the bank for as long as possible, justifying my procrastination with the thought that if I got the money too soon, it would be spent before we went to the tournament. I delayed and delayed until eventually, the morning of the day of departure arrived. I phoned from work and asked for an appointment to see the bank manager late that afternoon. Looking back now, it was unbelievable that I left things so late, but that's the way I was then. I'd put off anything negative until the last minute.

As I sat in the small waiting-cupboard outside the manager's office, I began to panic. What if he says no? His door creaked open at precisely 6.15 p.m. and he ushered me into his den. I expected him to be very businesslike and aloof, but he wasn't. He was a very pleasant wee guy with half-moon specs and a chubby red face. He enquired about my health and how I was getting on at work. I wasn't at all used to this scenario so I asked him how he was getting on at his work, out of politeness. I thought it was the done thing. He said that he was getting on fine and laughed heartily in a way that told me that asking the bank manager how he is getting on at his work is not the done thing.

We twittered away for about fifteen minutes and then he popped the question, 'Now, Mr Gilhooley, what can I do you for?' I noticed two things about his question. Firstly, he had called me 'Mr Gilhooley'. My teenage years had only just ended and I wasn't used to being talked to as an adult. I still felt somehow inferior. But, mind you, maybe that's just bank managers for you. Secondly, I noticed he had said 'do you for', instead of 'do for you'. Lots of people said the same thing at my work when they were answering the phone. I made a mental note that I would have to do the same when I returned from my holiday. That may seem insignificant but, in fact, I did that constantly: listened to what adults said, or did, then copied it. I was trying to find out how to be an adult.

In an attempt to be as professionally friendly as he was, I answered his back-to-front question, 'Eh, will Wall Street come crashing down again if I was to get a small overdraft?' I think he appreciated my approach. The friendliness continued. 'I hope you don't think that I'm prying,' he pried, 'but it is normal procedure to enquire as to why you want the money.' His intention was not to educate me on banking procedures. He wanted to know why I wanted the money. 'What's it fur?' would have sufficed. I informed him seriously that I wished to travel to the World Cup. He seemed delighted to hear it. 'Ah, you're a football supporter?' he ventured. 'I replied, 'No, I'm a Scotland supporter.' My answer worked a treat. He stated, almost gladly, that he would loan me three hundred pounds and that he would pay the money into my account, where I could withdraw it from the cash machine at my leisure. I told him that I didn't think that he could do it that quickly. 'Why?' he mused, 'When are you going to Spain?' I looked down at my watch and said sheepishly, 'Eh, in about half an hour!'

Since that day, I have never again heard a bank manager swear. It was a unique experience in my life. The placid, grey-suited veneer suddenly vanished. He bustled around his office trying to work out what to do, saying out loud 'But all the tellers have gone home, I don't have access to that amount of money...' Then he came out with one of the nicest things anyone has ever said to me. He said, 'What are we going to do?' Wasn't that nice? We were in this together; my problem was his problem.

Believe it or not, he ended up borrowing the money from behind the bar at the local Miners' Club, five minutes later. In this world of global financial transactions, it was touching to realise that the bank manager could still nip up to the local pub for a sub. I thanked him heartily then headed off to pick up my suitcase and meet up with the other three to leave for the sun.

Harry sighed with relief when I told him that I had got a result at the bank. He could now rest easy for at least a couple of days knowing that he wasn't going to get stung for money. We made our way to the Illicit Still, a pub in Edinburgh, to meet up with Raymond and Shug to congratulate ourselves, with a few beers, for having started our holidays successfully. When we got there, my dad walked in. I couldn't believe it. How did he know where we were? The truth was he knew that I was skint and had come to give Harry fifty quid to give to me if I ran short. For me it was like the icing on the cake. We went for an Italian meal and washed it down with a gallon of Chianti. We jumped into the car, now affectionately christened 'The Spainmobile', and began the long journey south to witness the latest Scotland tragedy. I settled into the back seat of the car. I could not recall ever being any happier in my life. It was June 1982 and I was twenty years old. Well, at least physically I was twenty years old.

Raymondo (we were now speaking our best, fluent Spanish) had brought a tape of Monty Python with him. I hadn't really heard them much before but by the end of this holiday I knew every sketch back to front. We hit the motorway singing 'Eric the Half-a-bee' and sped towards the north of England. The journey began like all Tartan Army epics: 'Harry, can we stop for a pee?' Normal people do all that kind of thing before they set off. Not us. Harry obliged, we all re-embarked and soon we were near Lancaster. Suddenly, the sound of Michael Palin and Eric Idle, the shrieks of laughter, all became distant to me. I recognised some of the names on the signposts and I could feel myself withdrawing into myself again; my stomach muscles tightened up and I began to feel nervous. There was an internal battle going on in me. Horrible memories were trying to surface but I was desperately trying to suppress them. To this day, I hate that part of England. If I ever have to go to Manchester or Liverpool, I prefer to travel via Leeds.

As a twelve-year-old, I had attended a junior seminary boarding school in Cumbria. It had been a nightmare. Even being in the area again made me more than uncomfortable. It must have been a couple of hours later when I heard a voice shouting, 'Is he sleeping or what?' I came to, and made a vain attempt at joining in the banter in the car again. We were passing through Birmingham. I hadn't been sleeping, nor had I been reminiscing about the past. I can't explain it; I was kind of 'unplugged' for a couple of hours.

We arrived in Portsmouth, boarded the ferry at sunset and drove on to French tarmac at about eight o'clock the following morning. It was the second time in my life that I had been abroad. I must have given off an aura of being a seasoned traveller because Harry flung the map at me and barked, 'Right, you're the navigator.' I had cracked it! Front seat! My delight was somewhat previous. The first major domestic was just around the corner.

We had written to a motoring company before we left, asking them to outline the best route to Malaga. They sent us a map of Europe with a straight line from Edinburgh to Malaga drawn in crayon. I knew we had to come off this motorway and get on to the main road heading south. El Shuggie and Raymondo began to make noises in the back of the car to the effect that we should have come off the motorway at the last exit. With an air of self-assurance which in no way could be justified, I reassured Harry that it was definitely the next exit at which we were to come off. Harry swithered. He decided to follow my instructions; I had the map after all. We exited the motorway and began to drive along a road that got narrower and narrower until it became almost a dirt track. Road markings ceased; we were in a country lane. The protests from the back seats started again. I dismissed them and ordered Harry to drive on. 'It's the correct road according to the map,' I stated authoritatively. Harry shook his head in frustration and muttered something about me being insured for French hospitals. We turned a sharp bend and then suddenly came to an abrupt halt. The road in front of us went straight into a huge lake. Harry's face began to turn purple.

There was an awkward silence for at least two seconds. I think we were trying to work out what form Harry's self-combustion would take. I've never liked silences so I broke this one. 'Are you sure this isn't an old map, Harry?' Harry erupted as I dived out of the car and scampered. There was a lakeside cafe nearby so I made for it. Given the level of frustration I had left in the car, it would not have surprised me if they had just driven off and left me. I knew they wouldn't though. I went inside the cafe and ordered a beer, waiting for the inevitable to happen.

A few nervous moments elapsed and then the cafe door flew open.

Harry entered first, shaking his head like a donkey with a dried pea in its ear. Shug and Raymond followed at a discreet and safe distance. 'Can I get you a beer?' I said to Harry. Ignoring the offer, he bellowed, 'Shug, keep me away from him!' He was inarticulate with rage. I think I understand why, at funerals, priests always say, 'On an occasion like this, words are inadequate.' But I hadn't killed anyone. I had merely taken a wrong turning.

After half an hour, we were ready to get going again. I knew this because Harry screamed, 'Right, ya eejit, get in the bloody car!' I was informed that I was no longer the navigator and that I was to sit in the back of the car because the roof-rack was full of cases. I was also invited to maintain a silence for the rest of the journey. We had travelled about one mile, trying to find the motorway, when Harry decided to switch on the radio. Bonnie Tyler's song, 'I Was Lost In France', came on. I couldn't hold it any longer. I burst out laughing. The car ground to a second impromptu stop. Harry tried to be angry but he creased himself laughing as well. It was so funny I was in pain. He started up the car again and ordered Shug for a second time to 'Keep that eejit away from me.' The heat had been taken out of the situation. Thanks, Bonnie. We soon found the motorway and sped off to the South of France.

It was a long journey through France but I enjoyed every moment of it. I remember stopping at cafes in the countryside and tucking in to French bread and cheese, washing it down with red wine. Harry was the only driver and as evening crept up on us, he fell asleep. Luckily, Shug was awake as Harry was at the wheel. I remember being jolted out of a slumber by his panicked shout and realising that we were careering towards a forest. Harry woke up and grabbed the steering wheel. We skidded on the hard shoulder for a few moments and then eased back on to the motorway again. Shug opened the window to clear the smell in the car. We decided that we would have to stop soon or we'd all be dead. We made for San Sebastian just across the border.

After spending the night there, at seven o'clock the next morning we were Madrid-bound. We had intended to bypass the city but, somewhere along the line, Harry had made an unforced error for which he blamed Shug, who was now the navigator. We ended up slap bang in the city centre. I deliberately moved my head across a bit so that Harry could see my smug face in the rear view mirror. We were in the middle of a six-lane road surrounded by mad kamikaze drivers who went from lane to lane without indicating. I had never seen so many dead Alsatians at the side of a road in my life. Suddenly Harry slammed on the breaks, took the keys out of the ignition, got out, dodged the traffic and went into a bar. A minute later he reappeared with a glass of beer and sat down at a table under a tree. He took a huge swig from the glass, burped and then glared across the road at us. 'I think we're stopping here,' Raymond said.

Back in the car, we looked at our map with the crayon line from Edinburgh to Malaga. It was at this part of the journey that the map was to cost us dear. A new motorway had indeed been built from Madrid to Malaga. We were totally unaware of this, though, so we headed off south on the B route towards the mountains of Granada. Big mistake. We soon found ourselves driving at twenty miles an hour round the never-ending twisty roads, miles away from anywhere. We could have been on the surface of the moon.

Had we followed the motorway, we would have been in our villa by seven o'clock in the evening. As it was, by ten o'clock, we were still twisting and turning on dirt tracks high in the mountains of Granada. Harry's mood was foul. He wanted to kill the guy who had given us the map. We were all too tired to afford the luxury of bickering and fighting. We had to take it in turns to stay awake to keep Harry awake at the wheel. Suddenly, we came round a bend and there was the sea stretching out in front of us. Well, we thought it was the sea because the land had stopped. We found the village where we were staying and located our villa. We were delighted at having arrived, but you wouldn't have known it had you looked at Harry's face.

Suitcases were unceremoniously dumped in the upstairs rooms. Harry chose the best bed and collapsed face down on it. Tired or not, we were for going out and checking out the lie of the land – well, finding the nearest bar. We left a note for Harry telling him that we would be in the German pub up the road. We stepped out into the warm Spanish night, breathed in the fresh sea air…then ordered up the beer.

As we sat in total bliss in the pub, and the alcohol began to take effect, we all agreed that we forgave Harry for his outbursts. He was, after all, the only driver and it must have been a hard shift doing three days constant driving. We were just ordering another round of drinks, to congratulate ourselves on being so compassionate to Harry, when, suddenly, the door burst open and in he breezed, all showered and shiny. His mood didn't match his personal hygiene. He started moaning on and on about how long and difficult the drive had been, how his limbs were aching and how we wouldn't understand because we weren't drivers. I cut in abruptly. 'Look, Harry, what do you want? A round of drinks or a round of applause?' Rarely stuck for words, he retorted in a growl, 'What I want from you is a pint of lager and less of your smart-arsed comments!' Good, I thought, he's getting back to his normal self.

The scene had now been set. This was not going to be a holiday for the faint-hearted. The next morning they all agreed that I should be sent to the supermarket for some solids. I was handed some pesetas and ordered to get 'breed (bread), butter, eggs and bacon, coo (milk) and sugar, coffee and tea'. As I wandered aimlessly around the shelves, trying to keep the trolley going straight in spite of its buckled wheel, I breathed in deeply the rich mixture of aromas which pervade the Mediterranean supermercados. I came upon the drinks department. I was astonished at how cheap everything was. It was like a liquid Aladdin's cave. I filled the trolley with vodka, brandy and cases of lager. By the time I had finished, there was no room for non-essentials like food. I wheeled the trolley back to the villa in a zigzag fashion over the cobbled street, thinking that the guys would be really chuffed with my inventive and thrifty spending. I rang the doorbell and hoped that Harry didn't answer. Harry answered. He looked at the trolley then proceeded down the steps for a closer inspection. 'What's this?' he muttered, rattling a couple of the bottles. 'Where's the breed?' I tried to tell him how cheap the drink was but he yelled, 'Raymond! Shug! Get oot here now and take a look at this!' A few heads appeared above the sun lounges around the swimming pool to see what all the commotion was about. Shug and Raymond took one look at the trolley, then began to fall about laughing. Harry wasn't amused, which made us laugh all the more. Harry disappeared back into the shade inside the villa, shouting things which are better left unprinted.

When normal people go on holiday to one of six villas surrounding a swimming pool, they may look out of their window and say, 'That's our swimming pool.' We didn't. Our attitude was more along the lines of, 'There's our swimming pool and our other five villas.' We were never out of the other villas. It was like Hogmanay, but in June. Our nearest neighbour was a guy from Scotland who introduced himself as 'Ian, a retired house-breaker from Castlemilk'. One day we locked ourselves out of our villa, so I called in the expert. It took him about thirty seconds to get us back in. It was so nice to see a reformed character putting his skills to good use for a change.

Ian had told us that there was a nice wee pub down the road called Los Piratos. We decided that we would go there that evening. As we walked down the leafy lane towards the bar, Harry started lecturing us about not talking to the locals or we would just end up getting into trouble. He seemed to be concerned that, since the Falklands War was going on, some Spaniard with a cousin in Argentina might want to do his part for the war effort – on us. It was not the most popular thing at the time, to be English and in Spain and as far as anyone else was concerned we looked English.

I bought a pint for a wee Spanish guy who was wearing ripped jeans and broken sandals. From what he said, I made out that he was either a fisherman or a bullfighter. Buying him a pint was the best thing I did that night. A while later, a guy came over to me and started muttering something about the Malvenas. I realised he was going on about the war. He mentioned Thatcher so I told him that I had never heard of the guy before. The Spaniard looked as if he was coming off a drugs trip. He looked dangerous. Suddenly, without warning, he pushed me and made gestures to have a go at him. I braced myself to fend off any punch he might throw. He didn't. What he did was far more sneaky. He stuck two fingers in my eyes. Everything went fuzzy and I bent over to cover my face. I thought my eyes had popped out. I put my hands up to my face then he punched me in the Adam's apple. I couldn't see and I couldn't breathe. I could, however, hear, and what I heard sounded like tables overturning and glass smashing. I thought he was going for Harry, Raymond and Shug now.

It turned out that my wee friend for whom I had bought a pint had intervened. He was now decorating the pub with the maniac who had attacked me. I was grabbed and pulled away. I couldn't see anything. I thought I was blind for life. Then a light was switched on. The four of us were in a cupboard behind the bar. I wasn't blind after all, the cupboard had just been pitch black, that's all. The barmen had ushered us in there for safety. The mad guy had seemingly had a knife at Harry's throat.

The barman eventually opened the door and said in broken English, 'Right, the coast is clear, you can come out now.' We wandered back up the lane towards our villa, being lectured at by Harry who wouldn't accept that what had happened was not my fault.

We had been together for three days now and our capacity for arguing and fighting with each other, never mind anyone else, was quite evident. Another addition to the volatile mixture then arrived on the scene. Jackie, a mate of mine, and someone who would have pulverised the troublemaker in the pub, was to be picked up at Malaga airport the next morning.

We found Jackie at the airport then headed to a hotel where we were to pick up our tickets for the Scotland matches. The tickets were at an inflated price but we didn't mind paying the extra to assure us of Brazil tickets. Jackie did mind. He refused to pay extra and told the salesman where he could stick his tickets. He claimed that he would get tickets 'no problemo' at the ground. Later, as we went to the Brazil game, he still didn't have a ticket, so we poked fun at him. Right outside the ground he spotted a guy he knew who used to work with him down the pit. The guy gave him a ticket for thirty bob. We had paid sixty quid each for ours. That's Jackie for you.

After a night out to welcome Jackie, we returned to the villa for a quiet game of cards. We had no sooner started when the front door bell went. Nobody said 'Now who the hell can that be at two o'clock in the morning?' Everyone just sat there and continued to play cards. Harry glared at me. 'Well, the door won't open itself.' I took it as a personal invitation to answer the door. When the door swung open, there was a rather worried-looking lady standing there, out of breath. Before I could ask her what she wanted she yelped, 'It's the Germans. Quick, the Germans are throwing bricks at Ian.' I recognised the Castlemilk accent.

Jackie and I accompanied the distressed woman to the scene of the brick throwing, down the lane and in and out of a few hedgerows. We came to a fence, behind which was a swimming pool and a villa. We saw a figure on the far side of the swimming pool. I asked the woman if that was the Germans. She said, 'Naw, that's my husband Ian.' As we approached, she filled us in on what had happened. They had been returning home from Los Piratos when Ian had received a call of nature. Minding his own business he had innocently climbed the fence and proceeded to pee in the German guy's swimming pool. The German guy was unreasonably upset and had started lobbing half-bricks at Ian from his second floor balcony.

As we reached Ian, I noticed that his head was split open and blood had saturated his white T-shirt. He picked up a rock; we tried to stop him but – too late; he threw it at the German, who quickly ducked for cover. We watched as the brick sailed through the Mediterranean night sky...and crashed through the patio window of the villa. The German guy was so angry he did a kind of dance then, looking as though the situation was not yet finished, he climbed through the hole in his window – it was a big hole. Ominously, the downstairs lights suddenly went on.

We attempted to get Ian to come away but the man was not for turning. The front door of the villa opened. I expected to see two Doberman Pinschers come bounding out at us. They didn't. Instead, the German guy appeared brandishing a sword in each hand. He ran for Ian – who promptly took off round the swimming pool. It was like a scene straight from *The Keystone Cops*. After about three laps of the pool, Jackie said 'Oh, I've had enough of this!' He stuck out his leg and kicked the German into the swimming pool. We grabbed Ian, who was now much more open to the suggestion of going home, and ran for it. We took them home, made sure they were okay, then went back to our residence. When we got in, there was a note on the card table from Harry. It read: 'Where have you been? In your absence, I played your hands. You lost and I've got all the money.'

If anyone had stopped me at that point of my life and told me that one day I would be a priest, I would have laughed them out of court.

The highlight of the holiday was without a doubt the Scotland versus Brazil match where we were only defeated 4-1. A moral victory for Scotland as far as I was concerned. There was a carnival atmosphere with the Brazilian supporters before the game, which made a change for us. Jackie was wearing an old dark blue, beer-stained sloppy Joe. I couldn't believe it when he marched up to this beautiful Brazilian goddess, who was wearing a gleaming, brand new Brazil top, and enquired, 'Hen, el swappo.' She immediately took off her top and handed it to Jackie, to the cheers of a now growing band of supporters round about her. Jackie peeled off his manky T-shirt and handed it to her. Jackie would come home to Scotland with an expensive, golden shirt. She would return to Rio with a dishcloth.

The match was to provide us with our best memory. David Narey smashed the ball into the Brazilian net in a shot which was to be described by Jimmy Hill as a toe-poke. The Scottish support went crazy. Brazil simply felt a minor irritation and moved up a gear to completely slaughter us. We didn't care. For a few moments we had been on top of the world.

The tranquillity between us was as short-lived as Scotland's lead over Brazil. When we returned to the villa, the cards came out. So did the tempers. Having only just learned to play, I was not aware of the subtleties and nuances of the game. During one game, for a pot of pesetas, I declared my hand. Harry was left with all his cards counting against him. Too many, he was out. He started yelling that I was hopeless and couldn't even play the game. I mused out loud whether there was any relationship between Harry's moaning about my inability to play the game and the fact that he was out. Harry went over the score this time though. I was beginning to get hurt by his comments. Ever since my days at junior seminary, I had developed the ability to shut down emotionally. When something hurts, you just build an invisible, internal wall to stop the pain. You just blot it out. Shug, I think, could see what was happening and he took Harry aside to tell him to cool it. Much of the arguments and shouting was a lot of play-acting and made me laugh. This had gone over the thin line. Harry laid off.

The holiday was drawing to an end. I recovered from my hurt feelings and Harry returned to playing the role of grumpy grandad. We each chose a set of travelling clothes for the journey home on the basis of which items were the least nasally challenging. The cases were filled with three weeks worth of dirty laundry. I secured them on the roof-rack with treble knots, to try to dissuade the customs officers from having to perform the ordeal of raking through the smelly clothes. I reassured the guys that no way, baby, would they choose to search our cases. I had completely forgotten that we were going to need to take the cases off ourselves when we stopped at a hotel that night, as we wouldn't be sailing for two more days.

Departure time arrived. I looked on it as another three days holiday although there was the feeling that we were heading back to work. As we were getting into the car, Harry ordered me to sit in the back and to shut my face until we were back in Scotland. 'Aye, have a pleasant journey yourself, Harry,' I muttered. The car moved off. As we neared the supermarket, I wished that we were back at the start of the holiday again, when I was sent to get the 'breed'. As we drove past, something clattered off my window. 'I think something has just fallen off the roof-rack,' I volunteered. Harry cracked. He slammed the brakes on and ordered me out of the car. 'Right, get oot on to that road and you better find something. If you come back here with nothing you're gettin' left behind.' I climbed out of the car to howls of derision. I prayed that I would find something, wondering if there was a saint that you pray to for finding bits that have fallen off cars. Bingo! There in the middle of the road was one of the clamps which secures the roof-rack to the top of the car. When I looked back at the car, there was even more compelling evidence. The cases were lying all askew and were just about to fall off. Harry surveyed the damage, then barked, 'Right, gerrit fixed then get your arse in the car, pronto!'

I have no recollection whatsoever of where we stayed that night, except Harry going mad when he couldn't undo my treble knots. I think it must have been the South of France somewhere. The next evening, we arrived at the port of St Malo ready to board the ferry. I hadn't got into any trouble all the way there so I was in a confident mood. I suggested to Harry, as the cars were boarding the boat, that we hang back. I was following my 'last on, first off' theory. Harry had also warned the guys not to tie the cases too tightly on the roof-rack in case we got searched. I had ignored him and told the others, 'Just tie them tight, we'll never get stopped coming back from the World Cup.' We secured the cases so tightly that Houdini wouldn't have got into them, never mind out of them.

Both my theories slipped up a treat. We were last on the ferry…and last off it. And to pour salt and vinegar, mustard and Tabasco sauce on the wounds, we were stopped to be searched. The female customs officer ordered us to remove our cases from the roof-rack, to place them on the bench and open them. I enquired sceptically, 'Are you really sure you want to do this, Mrs?' She motioned for us to get on with it. Harry was mad enough at that, but you should have seen him half an hour later when I was still trying to undo the knots. He was beginning to tremble. None of us had anything illegal in the cases so we weren't worried about that. But the smell coming from the cases should have been against the law. When the customs lady opened the lid of my case, she had an expression like a grave-digger who's just put his foot through the lid of an old coffin. She prodded about in the case very tentatively wishing she had never stopped us. Suddenly she let out a scream and demanded, 'What on earth is that?' Harry, Raymond, Shug and two other customs officers gathered round my case. There, in the middle of my crumpled clothes, were the remains of the biggest bee I have ever seen in my life. It was nearly the size of a sparrow. I don't know if it had crawled into my case and had been killed by the smell. When I closed my case I must have inadvertently sliced the poor thing in two. All that was left was a head, part of its body and a wing. She asked again, 'What is it?' Raymond and I answered at exactly the same moment, 'It's Eric the half-a-bee!' Harry sprawled out over the bench, roaring with laughter. The lady stated curtly that she didn't appreciate Scottish humour. I didn't have the heart to tell her that, in fact, that humour had been born in Oxbridge, actually.

We put the Monty Python tape on again as soon as we got back into the car. As we drove up the motorway, the conversation was about all the things which had happened on the trip. Harry was now laughing at the various episodes which, at the time, he had shouted about. I felt myself drifting off again and feeling depressed. We were passing through Cumbria once more. Again, memories were trying to surface but I fought to bury them. On the way to Spain it was easy to put them to the back of my mind; the prospect of the World Cup was much more immediate to me than experiences from the distant past.

I didn't know it then, but those distant memories were about to come back and haunt me big time.

Chapter Three

The return to work was difficult. With the World Cup over, there was nothing to look forward to, nowhere to escape. The first few years at work had been a bit of a novelty. The novelty was now wearing thin and I was increasingly finding myself asking, is this what I want to do with the rest of my life? On numerous occasions, I fell into depressions and couldn't understand why. I still tried to be happy at work, to find good laughs, but it was progressively sapping my energy.

Harry encouraged me to go to night school to attain an O-grade in Biology, which I needed if I was to progress as a technician. Deep down, I didn't want to be a technician. I had never been very technically orientated at school. I was totally uninterested in the sciences. My talents lay more towards English and so on. But I carried on, not wanting to let Harry and the rest of the management down.

Harry used to organise weekends away, to watch Manchester United. These weekends served as momentary breaks from the monotony. I loved them. A company which used to sell equipment to the Blood Transfusion Service invited us to watch Luton Town versus Manchester United. Four of us travelled south for the game. It was the same story as we travelled through Cumbria; I felt sick as we passed by some of the towns where I had been as a youngster.

When we got to Luton we were treated like kings. Champagne and snacks in the hospitality suite before the game. I always thought that the definition of a posh party was if the chicken drumsticks were wearing tiny chefs' hats. Well, they were, here. I felt that I had arrived. George Best was there. It was the first time I had met him, that he was aware of. We got to take penalties against one of the reserve keepers. As usual, I made a hash of it. I was wearing slip-on shoes. As I ran to strike the ball, I moved my body to try to send the keeper the wrong way. The ball sailed over the bar and into the crowd. My right shoe nearly burst the net. The goalkeeper and the crowd burst out laughing. It was the most public red face I had ever had. I've heard players saying that when they get sent off, the journey from the pitch to the tunnel is the longest walk in the world. I think they're wrong. The West Highland Way is longer, but the journey across the pitch that day was pretty long.

We returned to Edinburgh and went to work on Monday morning. I wasn't conscious of it at the time, but the trips to the football, the weekends away, were beginning to lose their 'opium' value. By that, I mean that they were painkillers. When Karl Marx said that religion was the opium of the people, his words were construed as meaning that religion helped people avoid the awful possibility that there might not be a God, that death meant death. Religion gave people pleasant feelings and acted like a drug for the masses. The truth is that, in Karl Marx's time, opium was used when patients had to have limbs removed. It wasn't just a feel-good drug, it was a killer of pain. The holidays and weekends were acting just like that for me. They were helping me to avoid what was menacing me.

One morning back at work, Harry shoved his office door open abruptly – as always. The guy sitting on Harry's seat grimaced as the door connected with his knee – as always. He announced that the work had better be finished and that he was going off for the afternoon to speak at a union meeting. We all looked at each other and smiled. The reason for the outbreak of mirth was that everyone in the laboratory knew that I had just inserted a tiny banger into one of Harry's cigarettes – everyone except Harry, that is. After he left, we creased ourselves laughing, imagining Harry standing up to address the meeting. 'Brothers, sisters, comrades…' then taking a draw from his cigarette and 'Boom!' It didn't quite work out that way, unfortunately.

I came in to work the next morning, taking a short cut through the Accident and Emergency department. An old man was being carried from an ambulance and was in a state of shock. He was screaming for his mother. The scene disturbed me. As I walked up the corridor, a couple of porters were making a joke about the situation. I was angry at them for their insensitivity to the poor guy. I realised later in life that the two porters were simply protecting themselves; they see broken people being carried into hospital every day. If they were to get emotionally involved in every tragedy they saw, they would crack up. The jocular comments were simply a defence mechanism to protect their sanity. I was later to realise that all my 'laddish' behaviour was serving this exact same purpose for me.

I turned into the Blood Transfusion corridor. A workmate passed me, trying to struggle into his lab coat. He began to snigger when he saw me and warned me that Harry wanted to see me. 'You're in deep shit,' I think were his words. I immediately thought of the banger in the cigarette. I wasn't unduly perturbed. For all his gruff exterior, I knew that Harry had a sense of humour. If the banger had gone off at the union meeting, Harry would shout and scream about it, but deep down, in the end, Harry would see the humour in it. It would be another story for him to tell.

I wrestled my way into my lab coat and entered the laboratory. Harry was sitting at the far end, leaning over a bench holding his head in his hands. I expected him to start shouting but he didn't. In a very low, serious voice he told me to come over to him. His face was purple and there was a hole burned into his fresh white shirt. He motioned for me to stand still then, in the same voice that you would use to ask someone if they had turned the light off, or if they had closed the door behind them, he asked, 'Did you put a banger in one of my cigarettes?' I tried my best to look as if I didn't have the faintest notion what he was talking about. I pointed to the hole in his shirt and asked, 'What happened to your shirt, Harry?' He pushed my pointing finger down and asked again, in a more threatening tone, 'Did you put a banger in one of my cigarettes?' I toyed with the idea of lying, but decided to come clean, smiled and said 'Aye, it was me. Did it go off at the union meeting?' Harry nodded knowingly, totally ignoring my question. 'I thought so. It couldn't have been anyone else.' He informed me that I had nearly killed him. Still trying to be upbeat, I asked him again what had happened.

Harry had driven to the meeting the previous day. When he had been getting out of his car, he reached for his cigarettes. There were only three left, one of them – unbeknown to him – loaded with a banger. Since the meeting was going to last for a few hours, he had left that packet in his car and opened a fresh packet. After the meeting he had gone home. The next morning, as he was travelling at a fair rate of knots along the motorway on the way to work, he remembered about the three remaining cigarettes in the old packet. He casually extracted one from the packet and lit it. It blew up, sending the lit tip of the cigarette flying against the windscreen, then it bounced back and landed in his shirt pocket. In his panic to quench the burny bit, he lost control of the car and hit the central reservation of the motorway. The car was now in a garage being repaired to the tune of six hundred pounds.

Harry informed me that I would be on labelling in the cold room – the worst job at work – for the next month. I was getting let off easy. Harry told everyone at work about his escapade. People smiled as they passed me in the corridor. Some people even came up to look in the wee window in the cold room to see me doing the labelling. They tapped on the window and made a 'thumbs-up' sign. I made a different sign back to them. Harry was telling everyone that the incident had cost him six hundred pounds. When people asked me about it, I said that it had cost him six hundred and five pounds. When he heard about this, he called me into his office again and asked why I was saying six hundred and five instead of six hundred. I said, 'Did you not have to buy a new pair of pants, Harry?' My comment earned me another week in the cold room.

By now I was on a day-release course to a college of further education doing an ONC in Medical Laboratory Sciences and Blood Group Serology. My college day was a Friday. I hated it with a vengeance. It was like watching paint dry. The lecturers were speaking English but, for all I cared, they could have been speaking Chinese. I just didn't care. I also missed my mates at work for that day each week. I even missed Harry's ranting and raving. It became clear that I was not cut out for the intricate life of a technician. I didn't know what to do.

I drifted along seeking a good laugh at work and dodging college as often as I could. The laughs at work, which were instigated mainly by me, became fewer and fewer. Yet again I fell into a depression. The practical jokes and the banter just dried up. I couldn't understand what was happening to me. One day, at the morning break, I went to the canteen and asked for a coffee. I used to always enjoy the crack with Jenny, the lady who poured the coffee. I hadn't realised it, but for months now I had hardly said a word to her. This morning she pushed the coffee over the counter to me. I went to lift the cup, but she kept her hand on it. I was a bit startled and looked at her. She looked at me sternly and asked, 'Are you going to tell me what is wrong with you?' I was puzzled and muttered that there was nothing wrong. She pushed her face forward and said forcefully, 'Aye there is, son. There's something up with you and, for your own sake, I hope you get it sorted out soon.'

I was really touched by Jenny's concern. I think she saw a happy-go-lucky young man struggling, and she wanted me to be happy again. Her kindly reproach stayed with me and for the first time I decided that I would have to do something. I paid a visit to the doctor. I told him that I just felt constantly down in the dumps. I had butterflies in my stomach and had broken down crying, on a number of occasions, for no apparent reason. He asked a variety of questions and then gave me a prescription, signing me off work for two weeks.

My mate, Jackie, noticed that I was off work and asked what was wrong. I told him that the doctor had said I was suffering from depression. Jackie told me that a year before he had gone to his doctor and that the doctor had diagnosed depression for him. He handed him a prescription for Valium. Jackie had told him that if that was all that was wrong with him, he didn't need the Valium and would simply give himself a 'good boot up the arse'. Jackie's comment made me laugh. It didn't matter what you were talking about, Jackie had been there, done it, got the T-shirt and eaten the pie before you. (Or in this case, had the prescription.)

Anyway, I ignored Jackie's advice about not taking the medication. I was soon back at work but the depression was not lifting. I was to find out later that there were other young men who were going through the same as me. We all had one thing in common. We had all attended the same junior seminary.

Chapter Four

I had been brought up in a very Catholic family and had enjoyed an extremely happy and carefree childhood. We lived in Loanhead, a mining village on the outskirts of Edinburgh. Over two thousand of the local men were employed in nearby Bilston Glen Colliery. The pit left its mark on almost all aspects of the town's life. So much of the town's social life was organised through the pit: summer trips and picnics at the seaside, and, the highlight of the year, the Gala Day. On that day there was the ceremonial crowning of the school queen, a handout of money and buns to all the local children, a sports day, fancy dress, and the shows came to town. I always remember the parade, with pipe bands and colourful floats containing people I knew, but they were dressed up in fancy clothes and were acting daft. I always admired those people who were willing to make eejits of themselves to entertain the rest of us. The priest and ministers were always invited to take part in the parade. One year, they were marching behind the horses from the local riding school. At the main crossroads in the town, one of the horses had a call of nature and a huge deposit of steaming dung was left in the middle of the road. The priest and ministers were so busy waving to the crowds that lined each side of the street, that they didn't notice the obstacle in front of them. They walked straight into it – to roars of laughter from the onlookers. It was a hilarious scene.

There was a tremendous community spirit which I always remember with great pride and fondness. Under the surface there was a Catholic-Protestant divide, but it wasn't overt. The best way I heard it described was that there never was a fight about religion, however, everyone knew which side their bread was buttered on. The only time I ever saw trouble stemming from religion was at the primary school, where it was all very harmless. The Catholic school had about eighty pupils, the Protestant school over two hundred. I remember that, at one stage, trouble between the two schools got a bit out of hand, so the two headmasters got together to find a solution. It was decided that our school would be let out ten minutes before their school so that we could get home safely before the other kids hit the streets. It didn't work. Some of our kids fixed up a fight with the 'Pea-Pods' as we affectionately called them. (They referred to us as 'Cackies'.) We were to go up to the park after school and wait for them getting out of their school. I'll never forget that day. We waited nervously. I kept going to the park gates and looking down the main street to see if they were coming. Suddenly, I heard a noise in the distance. Then, at the bottom of the street, hordes of them came running around the corner, heading straight for us. I can never watch *Schindler's List* these days without thinking of that event. In the black and white film there is only one splash of colour, the little girl with the red coat. This was something similar. In the middle of this crowd who were after us, there was a shock of bright ginger hair belonging to a guy called 'Dicey'. He was a right wee hard man. I ran back to the park and, with all the courage I could muster, I shouted, 'There's hunners o' them! Run for it!'

It's strange how life works. I spent years running from Dicey and his mates, yet, as adults, we're the best of friends. Recently, a drunk anti-Catholic guy was having a go at me in a pub for no other reason than that I happened to be a priest. I went to the toilet and the guy followed me. He began to get aggressive and, just when I thought he was going to throw a punch, the door burst open and in came a shock of ginger hair that pinned the guy against the wall and left him in no doubt that it would not be a good idea. I was touched by Dicey's concern. As I say, fighting because of religion was a childhood thing in my town. Among adults, overt bigotry was put to bed.

My family attended Mass every Sunday without fail and often went to the weekday evening Masses. As a child I remember asking my dad why we had to go to Mass. We were told that it was important. It was a fairly major sin to ever miss it on a Sunday. I tried to find instances where something would override the obligation to attend. For example, an old lady always used to walk down the street to church in front of us. I asked my dad whether, if she suddenly fell off the kerb and broke her leg, we would stop and help her or we would have to go to church. My dad said that of course, we would stop and help her. It was more important to help your neighbour than to attend Mass at that particular moment. He added, much to my dismay, 'In any case, there's Mass in Dalkeith this evening.' I wanted to put my newly discovered morality into practice. I spent the next few years going to church behind the old lady, hoping that she would fall off the kerb and break her leg – so that we could help her.

The local church and the primary school worked together closely. I remember my first day at school. Some kids were crying for their mums. Others just got torn into the plasticine. I did neither. I just watched them. People sometimes say that they remember the priest from their childhood, that they were frightened of him. We weren't; he was friendly and used to constantly wind us up about the football team we supported. We were, however, petrified by our first teacher. She was an ogre who constantly screamed at us. She also had a wooden hand which she disguised with a hand-coloured glove. But we all knew. If she came near you, especially if it was to give you a row, you didn't look at her face. You kept your eye fixed on her hand in case she swung it at you. It was a lethal weapon. A smack from this teacher could mean hospitalisation. Thankfully, she never swung it in my direction.

I meandered my way through primary school relatively unscathed. I can remember enjoying both school and the holidays, especially the summer ones. My grandad had spent all his younger years, and all his free time as an adult, camping and fishing at St Mary's Loch and on the banks of the Rivers Yarrow and Ettrick. That influence had been passed down through the family. My dad would often take us to the caravan opposite the Gordon Arms Hotel, next to the River Yarrow, or he would set up camp with an old army tent, which he got from God knows where. It holds wonderful memories for me. Waking in the morning to hear the river flowing through the rounded boulders a mere ten feet away. The excitement of being on holiday in this magical place will always remain with me. I remember going to the farm to buy milk and eggs for breakfast, flat hedgehogs on the road and hairy caterpillars on the fence posts. I recall catching my first trout. If I had caught another six the same size I could have had them on a sandwich. I remember a group of fisherman, from my home town, visiting us for a day's fishing. One of them had me in stitches when he pointed out a young sapling which had just been planted. There was a small wooden cross in front of it which read 'Spruce.' He said, 'God, what a long way to come just to bury a dog.' The happiness and peace that this place held for me in my younger life was to become a healing factor in my later life.

I arrived at primary seven, the last year before we were to go to secondary school. It had been a very positive and happy experience. The teachers were excellent and cared for us as if we were their own children. But something was to happen in that last innocent year which would change the course of my life forever.

Older kids at the secondary school used to enjoy impressing us by telling us frightening tales of the things which would befall us when we arrived there after the summer. We would get our heads shoved down the loo and so on. We went on a day trip to the secondary to be introduced to where we would be spending our teenage years. What I saw didn't augur well for my future. I saw a fight between two older guys. One guy smashed his fist into the other's face. I wasn't accustomed to such violence. The most I ever saw at the primary was a hard push. This was the big league.

It has always struck me as strange that the Mary Whitehouses of this planet tell me that I shouldn't be allowed to watch violence on the television, presumably because it might encourage me to become violent. Witnessing violence has always had the opposite effect on me. When I see it, I want to stop it. I wish Mrs Whitehouse had spent her life campaigning that war should be shown in all its horror, then maybe more people would be moved to stop wars.

Anyway, the picture being painted of the secondary was not a pleasant one. I got a mental picture of me lying in a hospital bed, recovering from being beaten up, trying to get my homework done while the teacher came in to belt me. I was glad when the day visit was over and we were back in the safe haven of the primary school. I was now dreading my move to the secondary. In fact, the secondary school concerned was, and is, an excellent school, filled with very committed and caring teachers. As an eleven-year-old, I didn't quite see things that way though.

At this point, a missionary priest, who had been working in some far-off exotic land, arrived in the highly fertile soil of our school to encourage some of us to give up the delights of secondary and go off to junior seminary to train to be priests. After the trauma of my visit to the secondary, I, for one, didn't need much convincing to seek other options. To this day I feel it is wrong that a guy like that could just waltz into a classroom of impressionable youngsters and peddle nonsense to us. I speak as a present-day chaplain to a school.

The priest wanted to speak to us about 'black babies'. (Political correctness was yet to be invented.) However, the hidden agenda of the priest was not to inform us of the missionary work being done in Africa. The real agenda was to recruit us to go and train to be priests to work there. As I recall, he said very little about the Dark Continent. Instead he told us about how wonderful junior seminary was. 'You get to go hill walking, tree climbing, canoeing, football and cricket…' Okay, I could endure the cricket for the sake of the other things. I decided that I wasn't going to a place where you get beaten up, your head stuck down the loo and stacks of homework – I was going to Butlins!

I ran home that afternoon to inform my mum and dad of my intentions. I was going to be a priest. They didn't share my enthusiasm. Apart from the fact that the fees for the junior seminary were way beyond their means, they were unhappy about me going to a school so far away from home. They told me that I would be going to the normal secondary and that if I still wanted to be a priest when I was older, I could go ahead. I was disappointed but I continued to beg them to let me go. I could see the big picture, me cutting my way through the jungle, baptising as I went, stopping off every now and again for a game of football, of course. Eventually, my parents agreed to let me go on a 'come and see' week which was to be held at the seminary that summer. My dad would drop me off at the college then take my brothers to my uncle's in Yorkshire. Everything was set. I passed the few weeks until departure time going over the brochure the college had sent me, time and time again. I especially liked the section on our social welfare. Wednesdays were half days, according to this, so there were to be no classes. Football would be provided instead. There were facilities for fishing and the college was set in the magnificent surroundings of the Lake District, so we would be taken hill climbing regularly.

When I think back now to what I was feeling at the time, I feel embarrassed. I was eleven years old and could hardly contain the excitement I was experiencing. I lay in my bed at night, picturing this wonderful, idyllic place. I actually felt sorry for the other kids who were having to go to the normal secondary. Little did I know it, but I was about to embark on a nightmare.

My dad drove me to the seminary at the beginning of July. I talk in terms of months because my dad is a slow driver. He had driven the scenic route through the Lake District instead of taking the motorway. I liked the Lake District. I didn't know it then but I would grow to hate it. We eventually found the driveway that led up to the college. As always, the place in no way resembled the pictures in the brochure, or the pictures in my imagination. I won't say I was disappointed when I clapped eyes on the place for the first time, but, suffice it to say that huge flashing lights warning 'BIG MISTAKE' appeared before my eyes.

The place was a dump. It consisted of an old spooky-looking building which was where the priests stayed. It had been built in the last century and certainly looked like it. At some later stage the main college building had been added on. It contained the church and crypts, the refectory, the old library, the dormitory and a few classrooms. Across the quadrangle from this building were the rest of the classrooms and a large gymnasium. The college was not, in fact, set in the Lake District. It stood beside a stagnating canal, by a forest on a hill. A mile or so away was Morecambe Bay and a sleepy village called Grange-over-Sands. On a clear day you could see a strange-looking building on the far side of the Bay. Someone told me that it was Windscale, the nuclear power plant. Meltdown would be the least of my worries here.

There was something menacing about St. Mary's College, which I perceived immediately. When we arrived I was desperate to tell my dad just to keep on driving to Yorkshire and take me to my uncle's as well. I didn't want to stay here for one week never mind six years. I said nothing. I knew that my mum and dad had gone without in order to pay for my stay there for the week. I decided that I would endure the week then tell them when I got home that I didn't want to be a priest after all and that I would just be going to the secondary school. It might seem that I was hardly giving the place a chance, but that is how I felt. The place looked nothing like I had imagined and I just didn't want to stay there. I watched my dad's car winding its way down the driveway then out of sight. I was alone…in England.

There were over sixty children on that 'come and see' week. Most were from England and Wales. Three of us were Scottish, me and two guys from Glasgow. I picked up immediately that my two Scottish pals were not interested in training for the priesthood. When they passed a huge crucifix, one of them looked up and said, 'Heh, look. Jaggy bonnet.' It was a reference to Billy Connolly's sketch about the crucifixion.

The innocence of my childhood was about to disappear forever. I was soon to learn that racism is not just about the colour of skin you have. My accent was to be the cause of untold misery that week. A priest, dressed in a black cassock with a tattered black cord hanging down the side, marched around the building ringing a big bell and ordering us into the hall. When we were all together he stepped forward and shouted that this was not a holiday camp. Another man warned everyone not to pick on 'the Jocks'. I couldn't believe it – the bloody fool had just drawn attention to us. To this day, I hate being referred to as a Jock, not because I can't laugh at myself, but because the word is filled with too many negative memories for me.

Our first character-building exercise of the week was to be a brisk, evening stroll over the moors which surrounded the college. We set off at about six o'clock. The anti-Scottish taunts started almost immediately. Some of the guys would constantly clip your heels in an attempt to trip you up. I moved away from the main group to try to avoid more hassle. Before long I began to lag behind. I came over the top of a hill to find that everyone had disappeared. I ran forward to try to find them, but they were nowhere to be seen. Darkness fell and I was hopelessly lost. Somewhere, in the darkest recess of my mind, I remembered that children had once been murdered on the moors. I wasn't to know that it wasn't these moors. In panic, I began to cry. I had just turned twelve years old and I was lost in the pitch darkness on a moor, hundreds of miles away from home.

Nowadays, when I think about the measures which are required by law for the supervision of children, I shudder in disbelief about that situation. Sixty children taken out on to the moors, at night, with one adult supervisor. Not only was the Church woefully inadequate with regard to political correctness, where was it when the health and safety lectures were being given? Months later, I would endure another character-building stroll, this time up the highest mountain in England, in the middle of winter. I was wearing a tracksuit and plimsolls for that one. I would normally say training shoes, but these weren't. They were those horrible, old, black plimsolls. I can vividly remember crawling through the snow, above cloud level, whimpering like a child – I was a child for God's sake. I had to be carried back down the mountain to get below the snow line to defrost.

Meanwhile, on this first jaunt, I was stuck on the moor in the dead of night. I was disorientated and seemed to wander around for hours. I guessed that the police would now be out looking for me. I would be in trouble, but who cares, at least I'd be safe. I saw some lights in the distance so I headed for them, falling into holes and clattering into God knows what on the way. I crashed into a fence and scrambled over it. My feet touched solid ground – it was a road. In my essays at primary school, I always used to use phrases like 'his heart was thumping like a drum' or 'he could hear his own breathing'. These were now true, not for some imaginary character I had dreamt up in the safety of my classroom. They were true for me.

The lights were from the local town, Grange-over-Sands, which I knew was near the college somewhere. I reached the warmth of a row of streetlights, which brought some comfort. A few bats fluttered around them. I had never seen bats before, except on vampire films on the telly. They gave me the creeps. After a while, the row of lights came to an end and I ventured back out into the dark road. The black silhouettes of the tree branches looked like tentacles ready to attack. Every ten minutes or so, a car would pass. None of them stopped to find out what the hell a twelve-year-old was doing in the middle of nowhere at such a late hour. I eventually came to the rear driveway to the college. I thought I would be relieved to get away from the shadowy trees, but I wasn't. The wide-open spaces contained their own mysterious shadows. I looked over to the far side of a field. I could see what I thought was a hooded, black figure walking slowly through the long grass. I froze. I looked down at my feet and increased my pace. I came into the quadrangle and made for the main door. I was frightened that the door would be locked and that I wouldn't be able to get in. I was to find out later that the doors were never locked. Anyone could have walked straight into the dormitory at any hour of the day or night. When I got to the dormitory, everyone was fast asleep. Nobody even knew I had been missing; they hadn't even bothered to count us. I was so relieved to get into my bed that night. I fell asleep for a short while, dreaming of my dad coming to pick me up and take me home.

Today when I hear people criticising the single status of priests, they say things like 'How can a celibate priest advise married couples when he has no experience of marriage himself.' I partly agree with their criticism. No parent or teacher would ever allow children to be put in that dangerous position. The priest who had taken us on the walk was culpably ignorant. On the humorous side, the argument that priests do not really understand everything that married life entails, holds some substance. Last year, after I had finished one of my Sunday morning Masses, I saw a mother carrying her screaming infant up the aisle, away from the altar. I asked her why the child was crying and she told me that he wanted to play on the Sanctuary. She had stopped him because she thought it would be disrespectful to God. I said, 'Nonsense, of course he can play there.' I put my hands out to take the child and I carried him back to the Sanctuary. I stood him on the floor and let him go. Suddenly, there was a loud bang as he clattered, face first, on to the floorboards. His mum rushed forward and shouted, 'Father Steve, what are you doing? He can't walk yet!' That kind of ignorance is laughable, I suppose. Other kinds of ignorance are far more serious.

Anyway, I got very little sleep that night after I returned from the moor. We were rudely awoken by a priest ringing a handbell. I remember dragging my towel behind me on the way to the washrooms thinking 'What happened to bedtime?' Once washed – I use the term loosely – we had to gather in the church for prayers. We sang some of those hymns which were obviously written in hippie colonies in the sixties, when everyone was on drugs. The pop world at the time was being infiltrated by such classics as 'Two Little Boys'. The Church was being flooded with religious equivalents: 'The Baker Woman', 'Bind Us Together', and the dreadfully dreary, 'There is a World where People Come and Go'. People claimed that these new hymns were better than the old ones. So they were – if you were deaf and dumb.

The day was filled with prayers and lectures; not a canoe in sight. Still, a barbecue was to be arranged for that evening. This was to be a barbecue with a difference for me. I never got there. We were told to gather in an old, dilapidated castle which stood in the forest on the hill behind the college. I made my way up a dirt track through the trees. The place spooked me. I kept hearing noises all around me, twigs breaking, leaves rustling. Before I knew what was happening, a group of guys jumped out and began pelting me with apples. One of them hit me full on the forehead and concussed me. I didn't have a clue where I was. I returned to the dormitory, climbed into bed and was totally miserable.

I mentioned earlier that there was an eerie dimension to the place. The next day, a very sinister event was to confirm my worst fears. There was a public phone down in what was referred to as the phone corridor. That evening I heard a real commotion coming from the corridor. It wasn't like the noise of a group of kids carrying on, this was a distressed sound. Upon investigation, I found a group of about ten kids clamouring to use the phone. They were screaming at their parents to come and get them immediately – not tomorrow – now.

Apparently, they had been fishing down at the canal when a mist had descended upon the water. According to what I could make out through the incessant whimpers, the figure of a hooded man had floated over the water towards them. We did find all their fishing gear abandoned at the side of the canal later, just as they had said. Judging by the state they were in, and the discarded fishing gear, something had terrified them. Every one of those kids left the college that evening. I would have left that evening too, but, unfortunately, I didn't have ten pence for the phone. There was a deathly hush over the dormitory that night. Not for the first time that week, I was sick with fear. I had convinced myself that the hooded figure I had seen in the field was someone taking their dog for a walk, or a shadow of a tree. Now I wasn't so sure. I was now very frightened.

I paid a lot more attention to the prayers for the rest of the week, for some strange reason. My prayers took the form of 'Oh God, please don't let anything awful happen to me. I'll be good from now on if only you'll let me get home safe.' I've found this form of prayer to be extremely common. I call it 'aeroplane spirituality'. It's where people get on a plane and once the doors are shut and it is about to take off, they begin to pray 'Please God, don't let the plane crash. I promise that I'll change my ways and I'll help senior citizens across the road from now on. Just don't let the plane crash.' Then when the plane arrives safely at the destination, the people who were praying hit the bars and get drunk. They forget all about their promises to God – until it's time to board the plane to come home again. 'Please God, I promise I'll be good if only…'

The last morning was the only one on which I woke up before the priest woke us. My dad was coming to pick me up to go home that day. I couldn't wait. There was not a snowball's chance in hell that I would ever be coming back here. I had seen more than enough to conclude that the priesthood was not for me. It seemed to take an age for my dad to arrive. Suddenly, in the distance, I saw my dad's car coming up the driveway. I knew it was his because it was going so slow. I had my kit bag all ready so we didn't have to hang about. I also had a speech ready. 'Dad, if Windscale explodes tomorrow and that place gets wiped out, can we have a party? Demolition would be an improvement for it.' I never got the chance to deliver my speech. As soon as we got in the car, he told me that mum was ill. He didn't tell me exactly what the problem was but I knew by his sombre tone that it was serious. He looked worried.

I forgot all about the college as we drove home. I was worried for my mum. When we arrived home, my mum was immediately taken to hospital. My younger brothers and sisters were shipped out to relatives and friends as my dad had to go to work each day. I was happy to be home, even under such worrying circumstances. My dad did the cooking. He always used to go to an Edinburgh butcher where he bought pies for Saturday dinner and sausages for Sunday breakfast. They were the best I ever tasted. Although, it has to be added honestly, that what he did with boiled cabbage was a mortal sin. He boiled it mercilessly until it was unrecognisable to the human eye. Never mind, it was so good to be home.

During all of this time, the question of whether I was to go to the seminary or not never cropped up. It just didn't seem to be on the agenda. I wanted to say that I wasn't going but everyone was concerned about mum's health. That was more important at the time. As usual, the longer you leave something, the more difficult it becomes to eventually deal with it. The date for the start of term was closing fast, time was running out and everyone just seemed to assume that I was going to go to college because I had attended the 'come and see' week.

Mum eventually got home from hospital. To welcome her home, dad got our first colour television. I was glued to it. I had always loved cartoons but now, in colour, they became my world. 'Scooby Doo', 'Catch the Pigeon', 'Banana Splits' and so on, were brilliant. I know the theme tune to 'The Pink Panther' off by heart to this day. My very, very favourite was, without a doubt, 'The Hooded Claw'. I escaped from my worries in these cartoons, but, one day, an episode of 'The Hooded Claw' jumped right out from the screen and faced me with an image of what lay ahead.

'The Hooded Claw', my first experience of a misogynist, captured Penelope Pitstop and carried her off to a barn in the middle of nowhere. He tied her up and hung an anvil above her head. He then put a candle under the rope which was holding the anvil in the air. Then, as only he could, he described the mechanics of the dastardly deed. He would light the candle, the rope would burn through, the anvil would fall and it would be 'Penelope…Shmenelope!' I could empathise with her predicament; I shared Penelope's sense of impending doom. Fortunately, in the cartoon, everyone's superhero, Peter Perfect, arrived just as the anvil was about to fall on the hapless Penelope, and saved her. Unfortunately, there was no Peter Perfect to save me. I was going back to the dreaded college, this time it was for six years, not just one week.

The day which had menaced me for weeks, finally arrived. The pressure on me to go to college was immense. People had given me presents. Two of my favourite school teachers gave me two prayer books in the colours of the school teams – St Ninian's and St Andrew's. There was even a special Mass in the church and a holy hour to pray for me. It was a very exalted position for one so young. People began referring to me as the boy who's going to be a priest. In the bus on the way to one of the last football matches I would attend for years, someone swore. One of the men went berserk at him and shouted, 'Stop the bad language, there's a trainee priest on the bus!'

I felt that I couldn't let everyone down; I had to go. As I placed the last few things in my case, the song 'All the Young Dudes' came on the radio. It was sung by Mott the Hoople but it had been written by David Bowie. The song appealed to me. It spoke to me of liberation, of young people being free to live outside crushing restraints imposed by omnipotent moral busybodies. I knew that the world I was about to inhabit would be the exact opposite. I was to become an avid listener to Bowie's music. It was disturbing and tragic. I could escape into that world now that there would be no more cartoons. As we set off again for the long journey south, I kidded myself that the place wasn't so bad after all. I would become a world authority at that type of thing later on. If an experience was too painful, change it in your mind to something better. Delude yourself. So began my teenage years, supposedly the happiest of your life. They would not be for me; in fact, I would spend my adult life trying to come to terms with what was about to unfold.

Chapter Five

I had never suffered homesickness before and I didn't suffer it at first here either. Homesickness lurks in the background like a vulture waiting for the novelty value of the place to wane. The rabble who had infested the college during the 'come and see' week had long since dispersed. In their place were now the college students who ranged in age from twelve to eighteen. There wasn't much laughter about them those first few days. Most seemed resigned to the fact that they were there, and would just have to put up with it. I heard one guy walking up the stairs sluggishly, whistling the theme tune to 'Colditz', a TV series which was on at that time about the infamous prisoner of war camp. The whistling registered with me.

The first thing we had to do was learn the timetable for each day off by heart. That was a relatively simple exercise. You got up at 7a.m., you worked your arse off all day, then you went to bed at 10p.m. There was a slight change to the timetable on Monday nights, when an odious event called 'the pyjama parade' took place at 8.30p.m. This was where any student who had merited a sound thrashing had to go and get changed into his pyjamas and wait outside the rector's room. When the rector was ready, the student would be brought in and belted with a leather belt on the backside. The idea of it appalled me. I was to learn that you didn't have to do much to merit a good belting. I was told that the reason we had to wear our pyjamas for our beltings was that once, a cunning student had wrapped a towel around himself under his jeans to try and ease the pain of the blows. The rector discovered his ploy and promptly gave him six of the worst on his hands. He then ordered the student to go and change into his pyjamas and come back, whereupon he was given six on his now unarmoured backside.

Looking back, I am now convinced that there was a sexual motivation behind beatings administered in such a manner. One student, whom the rector privately called his 'favourite boy', claimed that the rector would always pull his pyjamas down and rub his buttocks, between blows. On one occasion, after this student had been belted, the rector comforted him and, unbelievably, handed him a birthday card with two quid in it. It upset me that some of the priests looked on the beltings with humour. I'll never forget one of them advising me that if I was to be belted on the hands, I was to rub sugar on them beforehand. I asked a senior student if this technique worked to soften the blows, but he shook his head. He explained that the priest was only taking the piss out of me. If you had grains of sugar on your hands when you were belted, the pain would be even more intense as the grains would cut into your skin. I felt confused by the priest's advice. Why would a priest tell a child to do something which would obviously cause such pain? (I was later to find out that the priest who had laughingly offered such advice was committing acts of gross indecency against many of the students, although, thankfully, I was never a victim of his.) Very quickly, I began to shed the childhood notion that every word uttered by every clergyman is to be believed and obeyed. Sadly, there are still many adults who haven't learned that lesson yet and who remain unquestioningly obedient to, at times, complete nonsense.

The first few weeks in my new 'home' passed slowly. I spent my time desperately trying to avoid doing anything which would land me up in the pyjama parade. It was ironic that one of the reasons I had gone to this place was because I was frightened of the belt in the secondary school. Here, the belt was used on us as often as it was used for holding up trousers. However, after about the second week, the bottom fell out from beneath my world. I was sitting in my mathematics class bored to tears – literally: I burst into tears. For no reason at all, I just wept buckets. Homesickness had struck. It wasn't a kind of 'Oh I don't half miss Tartan Special and the *Daily Record*' type of feeling. For a child, it was far more profound and disturbing. Someone once described Hell as being totally and irrevocably cut off from God. We're dealing with similar emotions here. Nothing could console me and I saw no end in sight for what was happening. I wanted my mum and dad.

The priest who was taking the class walked towards me. He put his hand on the side of my head and began tapping it against my ear. He was not trying to hurt me, I think he was just trying to cope with a weeping youngster and didn't know what to do. By mistake, he trapped the air between his hand and my eardrum. I had perforated my eardrum when I was five or six. The trapped air caused piercing pain to shoot through my head. I hit the roof. I was removed from the class and reassured 'If you can't even come down to England without all this carry-on, how will you ever manage in Africa?' It was a theological version of 'Ya big Jessie'. I told him that he had hurt my ear. He told me that he had merely hurt my pride. I wish I had a pound for every time I was to hear that statement in the future.

I think it was at that moment that I opened up my 'hurts file'. For the next two decades I just stored all the pain and hurt in that file, where it lay unresolved, undealt with. I was to find out as an adult that traumatic experiences in youth can have catastrophic repercussions in adulthood.

Into this dreadful chasm of homesickness, the first nightmare was inserted. I had tried to block off from my mind the incident where the kids had said they had seen a ghost at the canal. I wouldn't go near the canal on my own. The canal was not the only place supposed to be haunted, either. There was hardly a room in the college which didn't have some weird supernatural appearance accredited to it. Indeed, there had been a few well-documented tragedies in the place's history, according to what we were told. A maid who was murdered in the previous century, a man who had committed suicide by throwing himself off the bell-tower, and so on.

I was invited to go for a walk by one of the priests. Fair enough. Off we went. He seemed friendly enough. As he began to head in the direction of the canal, I was hesitant, but surely nothing would happen. Ghosts wouldn't appear in front of priests. As we walked past a particular part of the canal, the priest suddenly told me to remember in my prayers a religious brother who had been at the college. I asked why. He told me that this was the part of the canal in which the poor brother had drowned a few years before. I just about died on the spot. This was the part of the canal where the incident with the ghost and the young fishers had happened. This priest didn't know about it because he hadn't been at the 'come and see' week. In my, by now, extremely fertile imagination I immediately made the connection between the mysterious figure and the death of the brother. The priest then began to describe what had happened on that fateful day. The unfortunate brother had been swimming in the canal and had suddenly dived under the water. He didn't resurface. The alarm was raised and other priests desperately began to search for him. He told me that after about half an hour, a flock of seagulls began swooping down at that part of the canal. It was there that they found his body, tangled in the reeds. By this time my knees were knocking with fear. I was waiting for the priest to burst out laughing and shout 'Just kidding!', But he didn't. Instead, as we arrived at the back of the college, he pointed to a stone table at the back door. He said, sombrely and reflectively, like the menacing old Scottish guy from 'Dad's Army', 'This is where they laid his body when they carried him from the canal.' I think he was actually looking at the body in his mind's eye.

Shit! Did he have to be so bloody graphic? I was frightened enough listening to all of this during the day, but what would it be like at night in my bed, when all of this stuff came back to haunt me? I dreaded night-time. I could never get to sleep. Any normal boy lies in bed and dreams about playing football for his favourite team or how he's going to get off with the girl he fancies at school. I would lie there trying to fend off horrifying images which constantly tried to surface in my mind. I could see the drowning brother under the murky water, tangled in the reeds. I shivered as his breath ran out and he took in a lung full of the filthy, stinking water. The disturbance on the surface of the water his hopeless struggle had caused, began to level out and the canal went calm and lifeless again. My imagination could fill in all the details which the priest had left out. Why would a priest tell me such frightening information? What was the point? Did he seriously think that I would go to my bed that night and think about playing football?

One night, shortly after the Jackanory from Hell, I was lying in bed concentrating on not thinking, when suddenly there was an unearthly scream. One of the guys on the other side of the dormitory had gone berserk; he just wouldn't stop screaming. One of the priests appeared on the scene. His pyjama bottoms were showing underneath a hastily thrown on black cassock. He went straight over to the guy who was screaming and shook him. The screaming evolved into a pathetic sobbing. The priest demanded to know what was wrong. The shattered boy blurted out that he had seen – wait for it – a green face leering at him from the bottom of his bed. My bowels moved. As a kind of self-defence mechanism I thought to myself that it served the poor bugger right. If he had kept his eyes tight shut like I always did, he wouldn't have seen anything. My eyes weren't the only things I kept tight shut at night. I used to lie in bed with my bladder just about rupturing, rather than go along the dark corridor to the toilets. (Later in life I met up with a former student and I related to him how terrified I was at nights and how frightened I was of going along the corridor to the toilets. He said, 'You should have done what I did – I just opened the window and peed into the back garden!' I just about peed myself on the spot when he told me. Brilliant! Why had I never thought of that one? It would have eased so much suffering during those dark nights.)

The distressed young man across the dorm demanded to phone for his parents. They came and collected him the next day and we never saw or heard from him again. He went, but did the green face go with him, I wondered?

By far the most frightening room in the college complex was the old library. It was supposed to be haunted by a bright light which would suddenly appear and begin to move around. No student would ever be found in that library on his own. We would sometimes go in, in pairs, but only as a dare. The library had two entrances, one from the students' side of the college and another from the priests' house. Just outside the priests' entrance there was a bedroom where one of the priests slept. I was to learn that the library was not only to be avoided because of any supernatural presence, it was to be avoided because of its proximity to this priest's bedroom. If he was around, you stayed well clear.

There were hundreds of old leather-bound books, complete with dust and cobwebs, in the library. A strange musty smell also permeated the place. One night, after the usual struggle to find solace in sleep, I found myself slowly coming round. I had obviously been in a deep sleep. I was used to waking with a sudden jolt as our cassocked alarm clock entered the dormitory every morning. But this was different. Slowly, bit by bit, I regained consciousness. I became aware that I wasn't in bed, I was standing upright. I was aware of the cold floor on my feet instead of warm bed sheets. It was pitch black; I couldn't see anything. Suddenly, in an instant, I was in the wide-awake club, fully conscious. Where the hell was I? What was going on? I was totally confused and disorientated. A terrible thought suddenly pierced my confusion. 'My God, I hope I'm not in the old library!' I began to tremble. I slowly stretched out my arms in front of me to touch something, anything. My hands brushed against something…it was a book. In an instant my worst fears were confirmed, I knew exactly where I was. I just about passed out! I had to get out of there quickly. I banged into a shelf and I heard books falling to the floor. I bounced backwards and forwards until I hit something solid. It was the wall. I felt my way along it until my fingers touched the light switch. I flicked it on. My self-defence mechanisms were screaming at me, telling me not to be so stupid and that this was all just a dream. But it wasn't. I was in the old library. I burst through the doors, out into the dark corridor and up the stairs to the dormitory. I could hear the sound of my cold feet slapping against each stair. I bolted across the dormitory and threw myself at my bed and pulled the covers up over my head. My heart was racing so fast I thought I was having palpitations. I felt physically sick.

I had never walked in my sleep in my life before. What was happening to me? The thought that I would do it again tormented me. God knows where I would end up the next time – outside, down at the canal perhaps? The doors weren't locked so there was nothing to stop me sleepwalking to anywhere. Had some strange force drawn me to the library? When I look back now, I realise that this incident was the first physical sign of many, that something was wrong inside me. The stress we were subjected to was causing disordered behaviour in most of us. Something had indeed drawn me to the library that night, but it was no supernatural force. The cause was all too human, or should I say inhuman. This warped institution and the way that we were treated was beginning to affect our behaviour, even in sleep.

I didn't sleep for the remainder of the night. Every single noise registered with me as I pulled the covers tighter around me to seek solace. The next morning, one of the priests demanded to know who had left the light in the library switched on. I had begun to think that it had all been a dream. Now I knew it wasn't. I didn't own up. I feared that I would get punished for throwing the books around. Maybe I would be ordered to go back and tidy it up. No way, not on my own. Anyway, who would believe me if I told them the truth? What could I say – I was doing extra homework until three in the morning? Least said the better.

The time had come for us new first years to be welcomed officially into our new, loving family. The initiation ceremony. They were kind enough to allow us all to settle in to college life, our new home, before they deliberately scared the shit out of us. Also, it was better to keep the initiation ceremony back until the winter months when the evenings were dark and cold. It added to the effect. This event typified the institutional barbarism of the seminary. The senior students were given carte blanche to think up and execute ways of torturing us. These students had been in the college for five or six years by now, so some pretty fertile and warped imaginations were at work here. If I am welcoming someone into a new group, I do my utmost to make them feel at ease, to make them feel accepted and loved. This notion seemed to elude this lot. We were all nervous wrecks already because of the various weird things which had happened. It wasn't as if they would have to work hard to create a frightening atmosphere. But, I must admit, they did do their best. Many of them told us frightening stories about evil events which had taken place in the college in previous years. The night when it was all to happen was chosen deliberately to be after the clocks changed. The darker, the better.

After darkness had fallen, all first years were told to report to the gym, in our shorts. We kicked a ball about nervously, not knowing what to expect. Well, most of us didn't know what to expect. One first year had a brother further up the house who had informed him of exactly what was going to happen. He didn't share the information with us though. Suddenly, the lights went out and the front doors to the hall were opened. Ten shadowy figures entered wearing masks. Remember, this place was staffed by people who had been in Africa for years. When I say masks, we're not talking Donald Duck or Batman. These things were grotesque. They had obviously been used in a previous life to put the shitters up the most hardened Zulu warriors.

Up until that point, I hadn't really cracked up. I was always good with the wit and repartee, a gift born out of my unwillingness to engage in stepping outside with someone twice my size to get lumps battered out of me. The better option is to take the piss. The word is mightier than the sword. If a situation looks dodgy, if the guy is bigger than you, use humour. For this reason, I was looked on as a bit of a cheeky little git. I was also a 'Jock'. For both these reasons, I had been put at the top of the list for 'initiation'. The masks moved in; they were after me. I tried to run but they plucked me out of the first years like swatting a fly. Whatever light there had been coming from the front door, was suddenly quenched as they put a sack over my head. I felt my hands being secured behind me. Whatever bravado I had left in me dissipated as I was carried from the hall. No amount of muffled, smart remarks from underneath the sackcloth could get me out of this one. I felt the freezing cold air on my legs as they carried me out into the darkness of the night. I went berserk. I was later to find out that when they called back to the gym to collect another student for initiation, the poor guy lost control of his bladder and pissed himself there and then.

I never knew what concussion was when I used to see a football player getting carried off the park on the telly, and the commentator assured us all that this was what he was suffering from. I only found out what it really was when that guy hit me on the head at the 'come and see' week. That unreal 'where am I?' feeling. But I got it again this night as these people stole me away into the night. I'm convinced there has to be a medical condition called shock-induced concussion. You don't have to be banged on the head to get it. I didn't have the ability, at that time, to ask myself, where did I want to be? Here, on the verge of a nervous breakdown, or back at home, sitting in front of a warm fire, watching 'Star Trek', munching Milky Ways which my Auntie Anne had bought for us. Why did it take me five years to scream 'Fuck off!' to this nonsense? Why do I still have to put up with religious maniacs who bleat, 'Oh, did you hear that? Did you hear his language? And him supposed to be a priest as well.' Well I think that bad language will be at the end of the queue when God is counting up the sins – and, isn't it about time somebody bloody well said it?

My captors seemed to carry me for miles. They were chanting something which sounded pretty evil, probably Gregorian chant. Mind you, 'Twinkle, Twinkle, Little Star' would have sounded evil, the way I was feeling at that moment. Suddenly, the chanting stopped. They knelt me down on a cold floor. That was the only part of the proceedings which gave me comfort. I was well used to kneeling by now. The floor was soaking wet. They told me that it was blood. They unceremoniously ripped the sack from me but kept tight hold of my arms. The scene which confronted me was surreal. Fire and candles had been placed strategically and menacingly around a dark room. Staring straight at me was the ugliest witch doctor this side of the Zambezi river. A protective numbness settled over me again. In Accident and Emergency, I think they call it 'shock'. It was as if I wasn't really there. Haunting music was playing in the background incorporating that sound of a distant bell pealing and a diabolic voice uttering slowly, 'What is this I see before me?' It was actually a Black Sabbath record which I hadn't heard before. If you get the chance, buy it and listen to it with the lights turned out. You'll get the feel of just what was going down there. The masked figure in front of me found me guilty of some minor indiscretion which escapes me at the moment, and, in a gruff voice, passed sentence on me: 'Take him to the canal and hang him from the bridge until he drowns.' Jesus, these guys knew their stuff alright. Decapitate me, knee-cap me. Throw me in an acid bath, but please, not the canal.

Later in life, when I reflected on that moment, I thought that it was extremely insensitive from another point of view. It was common knowledge that a brother had drowned in the canal a few years before. Could they not have burned us at the stake up in the old castle or buried us alive down at the farm? What would the family of the drowned brother say if they knew that drowning in the canal was part of the initiation? The sack was thrust over my head again and, to roars of approval from the torturers, I was carried off again – for execution. Four months earlier I had been sitting in my primary seven classroom on a sunny afternoon, talking to Maggs, Jacqui, Brendan, Joe and Nige about whose house we would congregate at that night to watch 'Top of the Pops'. Now I was stuck in this hell-hole and I was absolutely powerless to do anything about it.

As we headed for the canal, I could hear one voice above the others, not because it was louder than the others. Quite the opposite. This voice was the most quiet, but it was the most menacing. Whoever it was, he was speaking close to my ear and whispering. He obviously didn't want the others to hear what he was saying. I found out later that it was a third-year guy from London called Peter. He hated

54

Scottish people with a vengeance. I realised this by the way he hissed, 'You're a Jock bastard and now you're going to die.' This was accompanied, not by a dig in the ribs, but by him grabbing a handful of my skin and twisting it until I let out a scream. He also called me a 'Fucking prannock'. Sorry, Mrs, but those were the words he used. I have since travelled the world, to Africa, India and Latin America, and I have never heard that particular phrase again. Maybe it's a lack in my vocabulary. But anyway, I think it was an insult because the words were accompanied with another Chinese burn as he tried to rip the flesh from my ribs. This maniac was actually enjoying it. (This guy was not only a bully, he was also a pervert. He would sit in front of junior students and openly masturbate, grinning at them. He forced young guys to perform oral sex on him. When he was bullying youngsters, it was extremely violent and harsh. He had a glint in his eyes as he did such things.)

Someone mentioned, for my benefit, that we were at the bridge over the canal. They dumped me down clumsily and fumbled with a rope. They tied the rope around my feet and lifted me over the parapet of the bridge and began to lower me, upside down. Decades later, in 1990, when a crowd of us were at the Italian World Cup, we were returning to our digs on a coach and two of my pals were pretending that the coach was a warplane. One was the pilot and the other was the rear gunner. They were ad-libbing as they went along and had the whole bus in stitches laughing. Then the pilot suddenly shouted 'Hey, rear gunner, I think the plane is flying upside-down!' The rear gunner replied, 'I know, Captain. The shit's running down my neck.' The whole bus fell about in heaps. So did I, but I remembered hanging upside-down that night on the bridge at the canal. It was another one of those moments where, as an adult, I should simply have been laughing and joking with the rest of the people on the bus. But instead, I withdrew into myself again. I think today we call such things flashbacks. I do not wish these memories to be part of my life and to keep coming back at me when I least expect them to. But they do and I know I have to accept that.

As I was lowered towards the water, the shit was running down my neck. Having been an ardent fisherman in previous years, I had already studied the canal on the few occasions I had walked along it.

I knew that there were huge boulders at the bridge. I was panicking thinking that if these bloody idiots let me go, assuming that I was just going to drop into the water before they pull me up again, I'd be killed. Then a terrible thought came to my mind, what if that brother's death wasn't accidental after all? What if this lot had deliberately killed him in some macabre ceremony? I was just about to go hysterical again, when they did it. They let go of the rope...I braced myself for the impact of the rocks. It never came. Instead, there was a dull thud as I impacted. There were roars of laughter as they pulled the sack from over my head and untied me. I was lying on one of those rubber gym mats at the bottom of the stairs which led to our dormitory. They had only been dangling me over the banister. They all ran off to collect their next victim from the gymnasium. I went to bed totally drained. I only had enough breath to whisper 'Bastards. This is not right.' I was later to find out that I had got off lightly. Some of the victims had been taken up into the forest on the hill behind the college. They had been dumped, in their shorts, into a bed of nettles.

I slept that night. If a green face had appeared I would have punched its fucking lights out. The dormitory lights were switched on at seven o'clock in the morning, as usual. The priest came in ringing the handbell. I thought about the children's TV programme 'Trumpton'. I whistled the tune as I went to the wash rooms. I think I was trying to convince myself that I wasn't utterly devastated. I thought again of Maggs, Jacqui, Brend, Joe and Nige, my pals from the primary school. I buried the pleasant thoughts in the cold shower. I dried off and plodded my weary way back to the dorm where the priest was delivering a lecture to deaf ears, stating that he knew we had all enjoyed the initiation ceremony on the previous evening but 'make no mistake, you lot are back to work today'. I wanted to punch the arsehole. He kept ringing the bell, even though everyone was up. I've got a theory now about bell ringing in institutions. If you get stuck and don't know what to do, just give the bell a good ring. It drowns out all the questions; the ones which the interns may ask but, worst of all, it drowned out the questions that they should have been asking themselves.

As I got dressed in public, I noticed that every article of clothing I was putting on was labelled with my name. Each sock. When I was ordained years later, my mum and my aunts had made my vestments. My Auntie Mary, who wasn't really an auntie but I'd fight for her to be called my auntie, had commented, upon viewing the vestments, that every stitch was sewed with love. Well, years before ordination, every stitch had already been sewed with love. I thought about every family, all the people who had helped my family to enable me to be at college. They did it out of love for the Church and love for my family. They had a very romantic image of the seminary. They hadn't seen the brochure for this college as I had, but they had a brochure already impregnated into their minds about what the Church was supposed to be like. Did any of them ask themselves whether I was actually happy? No. They trusted that, because I was being looked after by priests; I was obviously doing just dandy. Maybe the priest who had spoken to us in the primary school that day had gone around the doors and spoken to them as well. Maybe they thought that I was going away for tree climbing and canoeing and football. Maybe he had convinced them too.

I headed down the stairs, past the entrance to the old library, feeling really down in the dumps, and made my way to the chapel. We had to go through the usual Gregorian chants. I can understand adult, male, celibates having the desire to gather together upon a morning to chant, in unison, a prayer in a foreign language. I do not have a problem with that. But why drag fifty or sixty youngsters into it? Did none of them ever question why a group of kids had to perform all of this nonsense? In what way was God enhanced by it all? God would have been happier if they had let us all go out and play football, I'm sure. However, the solemn stuff had to be performed because...well, because none of these priests had ever asked themselves why they were doing this. They were meticulous in questioning our behaviour, our motives, our thinking. None of them ever seemed to question dictates handed down from above, though. We were told that 'he who sings, prays twice'. Can you imagine that? You can be a mother in El Salvador and watch a group of soldiers butchering your children, you can fall to your knees begging God to let the slaughter stop, but if you sing it, God will listen more attentively. What a load of tosh. We need to grow up. Call me a reductionist, but I think that the best prayer that we can offer God is to reach out in compassion to one another, or tell him honestly what is in our hearts, as if he didn't already know. That is prayer in its purest form.

Anyway, Mass started that morning. I winced as I saw who the main celebrant was. It was the same guy who had taken me for a walk and described the drowning of the brother to me. We were in for a long haul. He spoke with his best priestly voice – his Mass voice. For some reason, God requires priests at Mass to speak in a different voice from the one with which we order a fish supper, apparently. He stepped forward to deliver the sermon; we all sat back to be delivered to. As he spoke he closed his eyes to give off an air of sanctity. 'You young men should count yourselves lucky. You are safe here, away from the evils of women, safe from the evil of this new thing they call "the Disco." The poor guy went on to describe how discos were the ruination of the world as we know it. They were the work of Satan, where young people danced themselves to a frenzy, then came out and…smashed everyone's windows. What?!! I internally scoffed at the suggestion. Were my mum and dad allowing my brothers and sisters to go to satanic rituals back at home? Why was someone who was so obviously disturbed and cranky let loose on us youngsters? The crazy thing about it was, that particular priest never once laid a hand on any student. He was so filled with the terror of going to Hell for committing a sin that I wouldn't be surprised if he never even had an impure thought.

Looking back, I now realise that the staff at the college were not appointed there for their talents and giftedness at teaching or working with youngsters. They were mostly guys who were there because of ill health, or not being able to cope with life in the Missions, or a number of different reasons. The Superiors of the Order actually used the seminary as a pit-stop for some priests until they decided where to send them next. Put in modern parlance, most of these guys were under-achievers. I believe that the seminary was actually used as a dumping ground by the Superiors. They didn't really care what they were exposing us youngsters to. Their concern was getting a place for the priests which would keep them occupied for a few months or years. It was obvious that some priests were totally unsuited to be working with youngsters. Most of them just didn't want to be there, and it showed. To my knowledge, not one member of staff had had any form of teacher training. Any high academic standard reached by the students was not thanks to expert teaching methods. It was solely down to one thing: the unfair and inordinate amount of time we were ordered to bury our heads in books.

If you ask a lot of Catholics when they come out of Mass, what the priest's sermon was about that day, many will give a wry smile and say, 'Eh, now what was he talking about again?' But one of the sermons given by the priest who hated discos will go with me to the grave. He told us about a priest who had worked in Africa all his days and who was considered to be an absolute saint. The priest had died. I took a deep breath; I knew we were heading for another pious ghost story. He told us that the normal procedure when a priest died was that word was sent round all the houses in the world, of that particular missionary Order, to ask everyone to pray for the dead priest. On this occasion, however, because of the high esteem in which this particular priest was held, word was sent to the houses, not to pray for him, but to pray to him. The idea was that he was considered so holy that he had obviously bounced straight into heaven.

The preacher then went on to tell us that, during a Mass at the Mother house for the deceased priest, the dead man actually put in an appearance. Seemingly, he appeared standing in the Sanctuary, leaning against the golden tabernacle. His face was gaunt, 'white as a sheet' was the expression used, I think. The apparition then addressed the assembled brethren in a grave, tortured tone: 'Send the petition round the houses to pray for me, as I am in great torment.' Well, I can tell you, when the preacher came out with this, the back of my trousers were in great torment. And just in case any of us were intelligent or brave enough to question the validity of his story, he went on to say that, to this day, the imprint of the dead priest's hand was still etched on the golden tabernacle on which he had been leaning. It's comforting to know that he made an impression.

When I think of that preacher today, I pity him. I heard years later that he had gone off to join Marcel Lefevbre's not-so-merry band of Tridentinists. They couldn't, or wouldn't, hack Vatican II and were eventually excommunicated. I find it hurtful that everything possible was done to try and keep this group in the Church. Okay, we should always be hospitable to different points of view. But what angers me is that the Vatican bent over backwards and jumped through hoops to keep this lot in the fold, while, on the left wing of the Church, transgressors are issued excommunications by return of post, Fr Tissa Ballisuriya being one of the latest recipients. Those individuals who have taken a more liberal and radical approach to the Gospel of Jesus Christ, have experienced pressure, not to keep them in the Church, but to get them out of it. I think of a famous South American Bishop's words, 'When I give food to the poor they call me a Saint. When I ask why the poor have no food, they call me a Communist.' Those words were not merely aimed at the politicians and the military; they were aimed very deliberately at certain sections of the Church, or, at least, certain prevalent attitudes within the Church.

That day's preacher is now deceased himself, I've heard. I don't know whether it's true or not. If it is, I hope that, when he died, he didn't meet the God he had preached to us about. If he did, he's a goner, and so are we all for that matter. Maybe he got a pleasant surprise and when he reached the Pearly Gates, God came out to meet him with his John Travolta disco gear on, smashing a couple of windows – before he hugged him and welcomed him in to heaven. I hope so.

After Mass that morning I came down the stairs to the refectory for breakfast, trying my very best not to sin on the way. If that priest who had worked all his life in Africa was in great torment, what chance had I got? I mean, I had rude thoughts all the time. They were always telling us how thoughts were sinful. I must have been a terrible sinner because I practically lived in my thoughts. I took refuge in them; I had to, to escape the reality of life in this place. The world of fantasy was easier to inhabit. But now they attacked the world of thoughts, I couldn't even escape there anymore, without feelings of guilt. They controlled everything now. There was nowhere to go, even internally, without the possibility of offending God.

To this day I'm saddened when people say, 'Oh, I've had bad thoughts, Father.' This usually refers to thoughts of a sexual nature. Maybe I'm mistaken, but I was once told that thoughts travel at the speed of six hundred miles an hour from the left hemisphere of the brain to the right. Would any of these religious zealots mind telling us how we are supposed to stop them? Try as I might, I have failed miserably in my life thus far, to master the art of not thinking. To me, the consequences of repressing things are far more damaging than having a wee think to yourself now and again. I heard recently about a guy who went to confession and said, 'Father, I've had bad thoughts.' The priest asked sombrely, 'And did you entertain them?' The guy replied, 'No, Father, they entertained me.' That's the spirit, fight back, folks, and stop accepting immature nonsense dressed up as Catholicism.

After breakfast, yet another bell would herald the beginning of manual labour. We seemed to do an inordinate amount of mopping floors. The place stank of Dettol. We didn't use the nice, wee homely plastic mop buckets you see in the Flash adverts. These were the big iron efforts, industrial mop buckets, which ground along the stone floors, constantly reminding you that you were in an institution. I'm sure the college must have had shares in a disinfectant company – gallons of the stuff were used every day. A priest would wander round intermittently, sometimes capturing you not working. 'Look at the state of this floor…Do you call that clean…? Start at the beginning of the corridor again.' You had to be careful – one lapse and you were on the following week's pyjama parade. Actually, if the priest was in a bad mood, you could end up on the pyjama parade. I suspected by this time that one blemish, one mistake, would see me face-down on the rector's bed, while he gratified himself on my arse with a leather belt.

As I muse on those days, more than two decades later, I question today's accepted norms in the light of those experiences. Some American states have recently introduced a 'three strikes and you're out' policy. If you are convicted three times of breaking the law, an automatic life sentence will be incurred. We had a similar policy. On our weekly report cards, if you got less than five out of ten for three different subjects, you were automatically put on the following week's pyjama parade where you would receive either four or six strokes of a belt or cane on your arse. I wonder if there is any connection between people who enjoy inflicting pain on children and people who relish locking up the have-nots of America for life. You'll probably find the answer to that one if you look up the word 'power' in any dictionary of psychology.

The bell sounded again. It didn't bring any sense of relief because you simply put the mops away and headed for the classroom. One of the things I missed about secondary school was that you went to different departments for different classes. You at least got a change of scenery every now and again. Even in primary school, you moved to different parts of the building for some subjects. Here, you went to class, sat at your desk and that was it for the day. The teachers came to you, not you to them. The only exception was General Science where we all went to the laboratory. It was also exceptional because the teacher wasn't a priest. He was an ex-military man. You could tell because he would say things like, 'Now place the test tube into the flame, you 'orrible lot!' The guy had simply swapped his uniform for a lab coat.

Classes began at nine o'clock sharp. Lack of punctuality meant a red mark on your weekly report. (Any mark under five was written in red.) Another two red marks on your card inevitably meant an even redder mark on your arse the following Monday evening. The report card listed all your subjects, nine or ten, I think. It also had punctuality, deportment, manners and so on. There was a space beside each for a mark out of ten and a space for the teacher's comments. Under deportment, I remember getting comments like, 'Walked sluggishly along the corridor this week.' Were these guys priests or members of the Gestapo? Was I getting followed around or what? How do you exist reasonably happily when every detail of your life is being noted down and held against you?

It was a few weeks before I got my first taste of the pyjama parade. I had committed the heinous crime of failing to conjugate a Latin verb properly. I hated Latin. It was like Arithmetic, but with words. The Latin teacher would often attempt humour. 'Amabo, amabas, amabat…I'm not really a bat, I'm a human being.' That was highly debatable as far as I was concerned.

The weekly report cards were given out on a Sunday evening. That was when you found out if you were on Monday's pyjama parade or not. All marks of five or above were written in black or blue ink. Any below five were written in red and three red marks meant automatic

62

pyjama parade. 'Three strikes and you're out!' They didn't always tell you to be there, you just made sure that you turned up. On that particular week, I knew that there was a possibility of me getting a red mark for Latin so I made sure that I was above board in all other subjects. When I looked at my report card, sure enough, there was a red '4' for Latin, but all my other subjects were well above five. I was just about to celebrate when I noticed a comment next to my red '4' – 'pyjama parade'. I was gutted. Why was I getting the belt? It was my only mark under five.

From that moment I became very nervous. There was a constant gnawing pain in my stomach. It was like a feeling of perpetually knowing that you had the dentist to go to. *Groundhog Day*, with pain. That night, in my bed, I didn't think about ghosts, I just worried about what was going to happen to me the following evening. The real world was more frightening than the supernatural world for a change. I notice that Amnesty International have criticised all those governments of the world who operate the death penalty. One of the reasons they criticise is because there is a death row. They say that prisoners go through psychological trauma as they await what menaces them. They call it a form of torture. We underwent a similar trauma. Not a moment passed without my stomach churning until the punishment had been carried out.

The dreaded Monday night arrived, after much sweating during the day. I had never been belted before, neither at home nor at school. I changed into my pyjamas in the dormitory along with the other 'marked men', then slowly made my way to the priest's building and the rector's bedroom. There was a steep stairway then a long, dark corridor, then more stairs until you came to his room. I will always remember the smell in the corridor although I find difficulty in describing it. I saw a black and white film where condemned men walked to their execution with their heads bowed low. We did the same. Any thoughts of 'Ach, it's only the belt, it's nothing' disappeared as I looked at the expressions on the faces of some of the older guys. They were frightened. They didn't even attempt to tell me that this was just a harmless lark to be put up with, then forgotten. I once heard that if you're on an aeroplane and you hit turbulence, you should watch the expression on the faces of the air-hostesses. If they look worried, then you can start to get worried. If they are reasonably relaxed, then there's no need to worry. This experience was similar. I looked for facial clues from the more senior students. I wasn't relieved by what I saw. If this was a plane, it was about to crash.

I arrived at the rector's room first and knocked very quietly on the door hoping that he wouldn't hear. Fat chance. The door swung open and, in a very businesslike tone, he told me to come in. The smell of rancid cigar smoke hung in the air. The door shut behind me. I got the same feeling then that I get now on aeroplanes, when the doors shut and you know there is no going back. He began to lecture me that, although the rule was that three red marks warranted the belt, he was bitterly disappointed in me and the rule for me, from now on, would be one red mark; a lot was expected of me and he would not allow my standards to drop. I wished he had applied the same criteria to my pyjama trousers as he did to my standards.

My eyes caught sight of the thick leather belt coiled like a snake on his desk. I wasn't listening to his words any more. I stared at the belt instead. He ordered me to lie down on his bed, face down. It's strange what goes through your head at such moments but I swear I said to myself, 'He just used the imperative of the verb to lie down.' My subconscious was still trying to impress him in order to gain me clemency. I honestly remember standing there that first time, inwardly begging him, pleading with him, not to do this. Something told me that there was no way he would belt me – he was a priest after all. Any such thought was brutally wiped out as the first blow struck home. The pain was intense. He delivered four blows. After the second, I thought that I couldn't possibly endure another. He kept going. I had never felt such pain in my life. One of the blows missed its target and struck the top of my legs. That would come up as a bruise later on.

He ordered me to stand up, which I did. He looked me straight in the eyes for a moment. What was he looking for? (As Billy Connolly says, the lost treasure of Sierra Madre, perhaps?) I was determined to show no signs of emotion but the tears trickling down my face were a dead give-away. His lips slapped together again as he said in a derogatory tone, 'Ach, it's just your pride that's hurt, son.' I thought, 'No, Father, it's my arse that's hurt actually.' When I eventually got out of the room to allow the next victim in, I experienced a sense of rage and injustice that I had never known before. I also felt totally humiliated. I was thinking that, since I went to that place, I've never cried so much, shit myself so much or been so miserable in my life. If you ever meet me, don't tell me that you are in favour of corporal punishment because – remember, violence breeds violence, and I may just smack you on the mouth.

When I had calmed down, I met the other guys in the toilets to compare war wounds. I realise now that the scars on our backsides were as nothing compared to the scars on the inside. I kept feeling, how dare they do this to me. I had arrived at this point of my life without the apparent need to be assaulted, thank you very much. Why was this happening? No student, not a single one, ever got through that college without being caned or belted. We must have been a terrible lot. Or was there some other explanation?

The rector spoke to me later, in much friendlier tones, and reiterated that my standards were to be set higher than the other students in the class. I had great potential and he was going to ensure that I fulfilled that potential. I had the overwhelming urge to scream 'Bollocks!' back at him. As an adult, I began to wonder if there was a sexual motivation behind his attitude. Boys in pyjamas being beaten on his bed. Did he fancy me and realised, because I was good academically, that there would be little prospect of me being in the pyjama parade each week, so he changed the rules to make sure I would be a regular attender?

In May 1999 a detective arrived at my door to interview me in connection with sexual abuse at the junior seminary. Amongst other things, I related the story of these sordid beltings to him and told him that I suspected they were sexually motivated, but I supposed I would never know because that priest is now dead. The detective told me that in all other such cases he had dealt with, there was sexual motivation. He asked, 'Why in your pyjamas? Why in his bedroom? Why on his bed? Why late at night? Why on your backside? Why not on the hands? Why not at lunch time?' He then made a statement which nauseated me. He said, 'I can almost certainly guarantee you that, after you left his room after being belted, that priest masturbated.' Well, I suppose, I did ask. It now makes me sick to think that he inflicted such pain on us, purely to get his rocks off.

I now yearned for a return to my primary school days but I knew there was no going back. A situation of 'us versus them' had now developed between the students and the priests. It had always been there, I suppose, but for the first time, I had joined 'us'. We began to curse some of them behind their backs; we made up less than charitable nicknames for them all; we rejoiced in every small victory we had against them – a flat tyre, a slip on the floor, anything. Any misfortune on their part was applauded by us. It was all we had.

Classes continued with an intensity which was far too severe. We were served a cup of tea at four o'clock. They put out industrial-sized tins of jam and big tubs of margarine on the benches. Dozens of knives delved into the margarine, then straight into the jam. Any surplus left on the knife was simply scraped off on the rim of the tin. By the time we had finished, you weren't sure if the tin had actually started off containing jam or margarine. It was now a mixture of both. Since my days at seminary, I have never touched margarine. It repulses me. If I buy a sandwich or a filled roll from a shop, bite into it and realise it contains margarine, I spit it out and bin the sandwich immediately. Another culinary vestige from those days is that I am a very picky eater. One piece of fat or gristle in meat or stew, and the plate gets shoved away. I just can't eat it. I can remember sitting in the refectory having put a piece of stew in my mouth, then realising to my horror that it was a piece of gristle. I couldn't just spit it out because there were priests watching. I would spend up to a minute trying to prepare my throat, then with one huge effort I would attempt to gulp the thing down. I often sat there gagging. If you ever said that you didn't like anything put in front of you, you always got the 'What about the starving children in Africa?' speech. I heard that speech so many times that I eventually began to think to myself, 'Well, why don't you put this piece of stodge in an envelope and send it to them and see if they'll eat it?'

At half-past four, it was into the study hall for another two and a half hours of mind-numbing, supervised study. Nine in the morning until seven at night, and that was only the academics. My dad wasn't putting in the hours I was putting in. They had worked out that, as well as the homework we had to do for each subject, there had to be a study period for each subject as well. I wanted to ask what I thought was an obvious question – wasn't homework study? The study hall was normally freezing and, as a first year, you had no chance of getting anywhere near a radiator. There was also a big clock on the wall above the priest's desk – as a constant reminder that you had forever to go before suppertime. Out of everything at the college I had to endure, I hated study time the most. I constantly thought of my brothers and sisters at home and wondered what carefree thing they'd be doing while I was stuck behind this desk for two and a half hours.

It wouldn't have been so bad had it not been supervised, but the priests took turns about. They would do half an hour or an hour, then another one would take over. None of them would ever stay for the full duration. Why did they find it necessary to supervise us at every minute of the day? What heinous crimes were we liable to commit if they left us alone for half an hour in the study hall? It was no wonder that in the few minutes when we were left alone, some of us did get up to mischief on occasion. I now look back and think that it wasn't us who needed supervision, it was some of the priests. I met a guy years later who had served a life sentence for murder and was one of the founder members of Barlinnie's Special Unit. (The guy was not Jimmy Boyle, by the way.) He told me about the 'dirty protests' which had led to the setting up of the unit. He had written on his cell wall, using his own excrement, 'Treat us like animals and we'll act like animals.' I felt as if I was in a junior version of the same thing. Give us a break, for God's sake. Let us breathe.

I found various ways of occupying myself during the time. Guys in solitary confinement in prison, do press-ups, I'm led to believe. We weren't allowed that luxury. I perfected the art of sleeping with my eyes open while holding a pen. I must have looked as if I was on drugs. It was easy to sleep then because I could never get any at night. I could also have played for Scotland at firing elastic bands. I could take out a fly at fifty paces. It wasn't long before my lack of veneration for the sacred discipline of study was to land me on the pyjama parade yet again.

There was an old rat-infested dump in the college grounds which for some reason, not readily apparent, was referred to as 'the farm'. Thousands of books had been dumped there over the decades and we used to go down and rake about there in the little free time we got. I purloined a big, old book and brought it back to my desk in the study hall. That evening, when I noticed that the priest invigilator was buried in his own book, I stealthily took my book out. I'd had the brainwave of cutting out a secret compartment in the book. I wasn't intending to hide the crown jewels in it or anything like that, it was for – well, to be honest, I didn't know what I was going to use it for. It was just something to do to escape the utter boredom. I began to cut out squares from the centre of each page. I was getting on just dandy and had just about completed the task when a dark, ominous shadow crept across the desk. I didn't look up, but I knew it was the invigilating priest. I could feel his eyes on me.

In a vain attempt to redeem a desperate situation, I picked up the square I had just cut out of the book and stuck it back on its page with a piece of tape, which I had kept handy for just such an emergency. I looked up at him and made as if I was merely trying to repair the book. The priest didn't utter a word. He sniffed a couple of times then swivelled around in his hushpuppies and headed back towards his desk. I sighed with relief – I had got away with that one by the skin of my teeth. Unfortunately, my unbridled joy was a tad previous.

Upon arrival at his desk, the priest picked up his packet of cigarettes – Rothmans, if I remember correctly – in the same manner as one of those slot machines at seaside arcades which reach down and grab a small teddy bear from the bottom of the machine. He swivelled around a second time and came back to my desk. He lowered the cigarette packet and dropped it into the compartment of my book. It was like a hand in a glove. A perfect fit. I couldn't believe the conclusion which I knew he had just come to. I looked up at him with 'I deny it' written in big letters on my forehead. He wore a very smug look on his face as if he had just unlocked the door into the mind of a master criminal. I knew in that instant that I was in serious trouble. He almost danced out of the study hall with his cigarettes and, of course, my book, so that he could give the rector a personal demonstration of just what a clever wee boy he had been.

I spent the rest of that evening in a futile attempt at convincing the rector that I didn't smoke and that the compartment had not been intended to hide cigarettes. I wish now that the compartment had been the same size as a packet of condoms, then I would have been sent straight home. The questioning continued. 'If you don't smoke, how come the compartment is exactly the same size as a packet of cigarettes?' How could I explain to him that the reason I had got involved in the project in the first place was because his pleasant wee holiday camp was driving me to despair? I was belted there and then, an indication of the gravity of the matter. I was in agony, again, but consoled myself with the thought that at least I had had my punishment – I wouldn't have to wait until the following Monday. I turned to leave his room. As I opened the door he said 'And I'll see you in the pyjama parade next Monday.' The rotten bastard. I had yet another week to sweat it out. I thought that he might mellow as the days went by. No chance. Realistic was not my middle name. I was given six strokes on the arse the following week and a lecture that, even if the compartment had not been for hiding cigarettes, I deserved punishment for damaging books.

I tried my best to put some distance between myself and the belt for the remainder of that term. I didn't want them to have the pleasure of hitting me again. I also didn't want to suffer the indignity of it, or the pain. The days of crying in front of them were over, although there were many times when I wept in my bed at night. I used to hate it when they would say, 'This is going to hurt me more than it will hurt you,' before they belted you. We were to feel sorry for them; them belting us was causing them pain. Excuse me, Father, let's see if we can come to an accommodation here. Eh, you don't belt me, I won't feel any pain and you won't suffer the terrible pangs of having to belt me. I hated the way they attempted to shift the guilt on to us. I think of that every time I hear the Gospel about the Pharisees loading burdens on to people's shoulders and not lifting a finger to remove them. I don't think Jesus was simply talking about physical burdens here, he was talking about emotions, guilt, low self-esteem and so on.

Time passed and we approached the Christmas break. One priest lectured to us on just how fortunate we were, to be going home for Christmas. When he had been a student here, forty years ago, they were lucky to get home at the summer. The lecture sounded like

Monty Python's 'Four Yorkshiremen' sketch: 'We had to eat 'andful of gravel…Luxury! You were lucky…!' He droned on about how we shouldn't complain about life in the college. In his day it was far stricter, he maintained. I could quite believe it. Something had to have happened to make them turn out like that. I noticed a distinct difference between the priests who had attended junior seminary and the ones who had not. The ones who hadn't, seemed to be a bit more balanced, a bit more humane.

I try to work out now what was going on in their heads then. Was there a deep-seated jealousy of our youth? Was it too difficult for them to turn around and admit that what had happened to them all those years ago was wrong as well? Would that mean admitting, honestly, that all those years had been one massive waste of time, lives just poured down the drain? That awful possibility must have been difficult for them to admit. Maybe they were just so miserable in this place as children themselves that they would do to us what was done to them. Every time I hear a priest describing how serenely happy his junior seminary days were, I am suspicious of what lies behind such defence of a system which now stands totally discredited. Unfortunately, attempts to avoid another beating were to come to grief two days before Christmas. The guys were all a bit 'demob' happy and excited about the prospect of getting out for two weeks. I was positively orgasmic. I also had it in my mind that, once I got home, I would try to find some way to tell my parents that I was leaving. One of the guys came up with a plan which sounded as if it might be a good laugh. He actually said 'a wizard wheeze', but I refuse to use English public schoolboy-speak. His plan was simple. A few of us would wait until everyone else was asleep, then we would move their beds around in the dormitory. Recognising the potential for a good laugh, and totally discounting the possibility of landing in trouble again, I went along with it. That was the trouble in that place, anything that was worthwhile carried the risk of a beating. We executed the plan meticulously. At precisely two in the morning, my Woolworth's technotronic timepiece roused me to the tune of Clive Dunn's 'Grandad', or some other inane tune. Not that I was asleep anyway. I crept across the dorm to the bed of one of my accomplices. I could hear Rolf Harris's 'Two Little Boys', so I knew he was awake.

We sneaked to the third guy's bed, woke him up, then set about swapping some of the beds of those who were asleep. Part of the reason I was glad to take part in this was that it meant that I wouldn't be the only student in the dorm who would be awake in the darkness. That comforted me. Anyway, the beds were heavier than I thought. Every now and again I would have to put my end of the bed down – I was in kinks laughing. It was the first time in months I had had a good belly laugh. We retreated to our own beds never giving it a thought that in the morning, our beds would still be in their original positions. It wouldn't take Colombo to work out who the culprits were. I lay in my bed really happy that night, it would be a good laugh in the morning when everyone got up. The staff would look on it as a bit of Christmas fun.

The lights went on, as usual, at seven the next morning. The priest came in and began his normal waking call. 'Up you get, everyone. Come on now, rise and sh…it! What's been going on here?' It was priceless. Some guys were climbing out of their beds and going the wrong way. They were bumping into each other and banging into chairs. You could see the confused 'Who moved the wash rooms?' expressions on their faces. The three of us, of course, confidently walked to the wash rooms with a slight spring in our step. Once inside, we crumpled into a heap. I'm sure they must have been able to hear the howls of laughter in the dormitory.

For the rest of that day, I kept smiling when I thought about the incident. Amongst the students it was now an open secret who the bed movers were. What we didn't know was that one of the prefects had gone to one of the priests and named the three of us as the culprits. The prefect concerned was later to become a priest. The only one out of every student there, with the exception of myself, to attain what the college was actually there for. Unfortunately, in his first year of ordination, he took a massive nervous breakdown and left the priesthood. I would like to hear his story.

That evening, we gathered down in the kitchen at nine o'clock for our usual cup of hot chocolate before we went off to bed. One of the priests chatted away to us quite normally, asking how classes had gone that day, were we looking forward to Christmas, and so on. Then, when we had washed the cups, he quietly turned to me, told me to go to the dorm and change into my pyjamas and report immediately to his room. As I left, I saw him approach the two other guys involved in the bed moving. As I was changing into my pyjamas, I became angry. Had this guy been sitting, chatting away to us as if everything was fine, in the full knowledge that he was about to beat the crap out of us? When the three of us were ready, we went to the priest's room.

The door was open when we got there. I remember stepping off the cold tiles on to the warm carpet in his room. He stood up and began to lecture us in a very serious voice. I had never had the belt from this priest before so I scanned the room to see where it was. There wasn't one. I'd had too many false hopes dashed in the past to think that maybe we were not to be belted. After all, he had ordered us to change into our pyjamas. Although, mind you, the way he was snarling at us, maybe we were just going to get off with a serious warning. I argued out the possibilities in my own mind. Suddenly, he reached round a corner and produced a stick, a bamboo cane. I began to go into shock again. Thank God for the body's defences. He barked on about not tolerating this behaviour and, since the belt hadn't taught us anything, we would be caned. He grabbed my wrist, held my hand up, then drew the cane back. I winced and looked away. The cane struck the ceiling and put him off his strike. He looked a bit irritated, like a golfer who is just about to hit the ball when someone sneezes in the crowd. He dragged me out into the corridor where there was a higher ceiling. Strangely enough, I didn't notice the cold tiles on my feet this time. He began hitting me on the palm of the right hand. After two strokes my hand was numb. The third blow struck a nerve on the side of my thumb. A fierce, sharp pain shot up my arm. He kept whipping the cane into my hand. I was just about to shout out and beg him to stop when he did stop. I turned to walk away when he barked at me again 'Where do you think you're going, my lad?' He roughly grabbed my other wrist and pulled me back towards him. He whipped the cane into that hand six times. I nearly self-combusted. When he had finished he stared at me, as they always did. I refused to cry. No, I must be honest here, I fucking refused to cry. As I crept up the stairs, cradling both hands, I heard the other guys being beaten but I was in too much torment to sympathise. When I pushed open the dormitory door with my elbows, everyone stared at me in silence as I walked over to my bed. All the beds were back in their places everything was neat and tidy – except me. I was a bloody mess. I climbed into my bed. Normally I hated lights out as it consigned me to another night of fending off frightening thoughts. Tonight, I was desperate for lights out so I could cry in private. The priest who had caned us entered the dorm and started shouting about that being a lesson to us. He angrily pushed back the switches to allow darkness to descend. I could hear the other guys who had been caned crying. I turned over and just broke my heart.

I now ask why had he asked us to change into our pyjamas that night. He obviously knew that he was going to cane us on the hands, so why the need to have us strip? I don't believe it was anything sexual, although, knowing what I know now, I wouldn't die of shock if that was the case. So why? Why the pyjamas? Oh, that's it. I understand. You knew that you were going to leave our hands in such agony that we would have been incapable of undressing ourselves that night. In telling us to change into our pyjamas before we were caned, you were sparing us the pain of having to get ready for bed with our hands in agony. How thoughtful, Father.

I was in a very different mood from the previous day when I went to the wash rooms the next morning. My hands were swollen. I didn't brush my teeth, my hands were too sore to hold the toothbrush. I made my way down to the church for morning prayers and Mass but I wasn't interested in any of it, not that I ever was in those days. I was away in another world where nobody could hurt me any more.

End of term eventually arrived. The morning timetable was to be morning prayers, Mass, breakfast then off to the train station to go home. At Mass, when it came to communion, one of the students in the queue to receive the wine from the chalice, drank the whole lot and left none for the rest of us. The next guy after him picked up the chalice looked inside of it and saw that there was none left. He made a funny face and held the chalice upside down and shook it. This was done behind the backs of the priests, obviously. Normally, I would have roared and laughed at such impish irreverence. On this day, I just looked down at the black and blue marks on my hands and soothed them with my thumbs. I think a great goodness in me had been all but killed and had been replaced by something negative. Jesus spoke about the little ones and how nobody should ever harm them because their angels are constantly in the presence of the Father in Heaven. I think I stopped being a 'little one' at that time; I think my angel left the Father's presence. I hope I'm wrong. I suppose some people who read this book will say that I still harbour much anger in me. I accept that criticism. I have tried though, to channel that anger into constructive criticism of a system which must change. Are priests who refuse to speak out, or who lack the moral courage to speak out, any less angry I wonder?

We bundled down the stairs for breakfast – my last breakfast. No way was I coming back after Christmas. I would find some way of telling my mum and dad, without telling them the truth of what was going on, when the time was right. There was still one event of some significance to unfold before we left for the train station. During the previous few weeks, raffle tickets had been on sale for some charity or another. First prize was an industrial-size jar of liquorice allsorts. I couldn't keep my eyes off the jar during breakfast. Some guys had spent a fortune on tickets – those were the landed gentry amongst the student body. Their parents used to send them hampers filled with cookies, sweets and an assortment of things that seemed out of place to me. Was this Eton College or what? I had bought one ticket for the raffle. On that morning, I remember kicking myself for not having bought more.

I sat at the table, daydreaming about what it would be like to win the jar, to take it home and share with my brothers and sisters. I had three brothers and three sisters at home, with whom I used to fight constantly. Now, I was just desperate to see them again. It was at this point that I discovered a new type of spirituality which I now call 'Contract Prayer'. It's where you strike a kind of deal with God. If he does this for you, you promise to do that for him. The only thing is, generally, with that type of prayer, his part of the contract is the only part that is binding – God keeps his side of the bargain, then you conveniently forget about yours. Just as the winning ticket was about to be drawn, I made my pact with God. 'Let me win and I'll come back after Christmas.' I had absolutely no intention of keeping my side of the deal. My name was called out as the winner. The strangest feeling enveloped me. God had done the business. Happy days.

Somewhere in all of that darkness, something, someone, loved me. I was presented with the sweets, which were so heavy I could hardly hold them without straining. I absolutely marvelled at them. As I headed to get my things for the journey home, one guy was obviously delighted for me. As I passed him, I heard him say to his mate, 'Lucky Jock bastard'.

Chapter Six

The word 'magic' is misused a lot in Scotland. But my train journey home was truly magical. Everybody on the train was happy; they too were going home for their holidays. All the other students were heading south for the Midlands and London. I got on the train heading north. I began to remember all the previous Christmas times at home. I remembered one Christmas when I had been serving the altar at the first Mass on Christmas morning. My brothers and sisters all had to go to the second Mass. I was left in the house to watch Tom Sawyer on our black and white telly while my mum cooked the Christmas dinner in the kitchen. It was fairy-tale like. I remembered going up to my Nana and Papa's house to show them all my presents. I remembered my Great-Auntie Mary coming to the door every Christmas morning to hand a 'brown' envelope to my mum and dad. 'Just to help oot,' she would say. I even giggled to myself as I recalled the go-kart I got from Santa one Christmas. Somebody had nicked it by New Year. Story of my life, I suppose. All I knew was that I was going home and that my mum and dad would, as always, make it a fantastic Christmas.

The priest who had so brutally caned us drove us in the college minibus to the train station. He came out with a very ominous statement on the way. 'Now listen, lads. The college is where you all now live. We're your family now. There is no need to be saying anything bad about the college to your mums and dads. We deal with things together, here at the college. Okay?' He wasn't just frightened that we would tell our folks what he had done to us. His words were far more sinister than that. I now believe that they were a direct reference to what one of the other priests had been up to. His words that day are testimony that the staff at that college knew all along what was going on. At least one of the priests was a child sex abuser.

As the train drew into Waverley Station in Edinburgh, it passed alongside Princes Street gardens. Darkness had fallen and the gardens were spectacular. Steven Spielberg eat your heart out. Anything that was stationary had Christmas lights wrapped around it. The train came to a halt, I grabbed my bag and what was left of the jar of sweets – well, it had been a long journey. I jumped down on to the platform and I could see my dad through the crowds in the distance. As soon as he came near, I just broke down and cried. My first words were,

'Dad, I don't want to go back to that place.' He hugged me and told me not to worry about all that for the moment. We were just going to concentrate on having a good Christmas.

As we drove home through Edinburgh, it was dark, but it was a beautiful, warm darkness. This invisible thing which we call love was all around. I felt loved and accepted again. Those feelings had been absent for months. I had been so used to a darkness which was terrifying, it felt moving to rediscover a darkness that was warm and welcoming. Over the next two weeks, I rediscovered a lot of things, like how to be a normal person again, or how to live in an atmosphere which wasn't threatening. Nobody in my family gave jack-shit about my 'deportment'. My three sisters did things which, to this day they don't know, made me howl with laughter. It was nice to be nagged at again; I had missed it. There had been no females in my life for months. I realised that males and females had differences which went much deeper than mere physical make-up. I enjoyed it. I look forward to the days when women will finally be allowed to fully bring their feminine qualities to the Eucharistic table.

Other things made me happy as well. I could keep my eyes open in the dark again without worrying about something awful appearing. I remembered a Christmas Eve years before when my older sister, Bernadette, and I had stood at the bedroom window in the dark, looking out at the snow on the street. We could see the reflections of the fairy lights from our neighbours' Christmas trees in the snow. We still both believed in Santa Claus at that time and neither of us could sleep for the excitement. We stood for ages just staring in wonder at the beauty of the falling snow. I yearned for those days to return.

I also enjoyed the fact that the food actually tasted the way it was supposed to taste. There was a jar of jam on the table instead of a huge tin with smudges of margarine decorating it. It was nice to go to church and drift off during the priest's sermon instead of being given a graphic description of Hell and a detailed list of all the things which would book you a place there. One of the best things was getting a guitar for my Christmas. It was by far and away the best present amongst my brothers and sisters. I knew I had been given it because my mum and dad wanted to show their love for me in the short time I was home; when I was away they couldn't reach out and touch in the same way that they could with my other brothers and sisters. My parents didn't know it, but the guitar was my redemption for the next two years. If someone had stolen it, like they did my go-kart years before, I would have been carried off to the funny farm.

The holidays passed so quickly that the timekeeper should have been brought up on a charge. It was an injustice. Since those days, I've never been able to totally enjoy a holiday. I am always conscious of the seconds ticking away. I had waited for the appropriate moment to tell mum and dad that I wasn't going back. It never came. Dad hadn't told mum that I had been crying when I got off the train. He knew that it would have upset her. My dad was trying to be logical about it all and he didn't want a decision to be made on emotions. He wanted me to give the college a fair go. If he had known what was going on there I would have been home immediately. I've been asked by many people, in their best 'complaining to the BBC' voice; 'Why, oh why, oh why didn't you just tell them what was happening and come home?' They haven't asked that question as often as I've asked it myself. I suspected that it was because I didn't have the guts to do it. I thought of myself as a coward. Years later, as part of the healing process, I was to find out the answer to that one. It would have meant telling my parents what was going on – and I couldn't do that. I had to protect them from information which, I believed, would devastate them.

The train pulled away from the station for the long journey south. Well, it was long to me. When I'm returning from holidays, I always have this thing about remembering what I was doing and what I was feeling on the journey there. I sat and wished I could reverse time. I remembered how exhilarated I had been on arriving in Edinburgh. But it was now all over. Travelling back became almost unbearable. I could feel the tears running down my cheeks again. I raised my hand to my face to hide my state from the other passengers. An older man, sitting opposite leaned over, seeing my distress and asked, 'Can I help you?' My reply was along the lines of, 'Not unless you've got a return ticket to Edinburgh, Mister.' The man was really kind all the way to Lancaster. That sounds as if he suddenly became unkind after Lancaster. He didn't, I just had to get off the train there. Whoever you were, thanks for your concern, friend.

I hoped that I would meet up with other students for the short journey to the station near the college. Ever since the night I got lost on the moors, I hated the thought of having to walk on my own, from the town to the college, along the dark road. Luckily I did meet up with some of the guys. During the walk back, what is now called 'bonding' took place between us. They openly referred to the college as 'Colditz' by now; everyone expressed their sorrow at being back. There was a feeling of us all being in it together. I felt older, somehow, and in my mind I decided that I wasn't going to take any more shit. In fact, I went on to take copious amounts of the stuff. I was a harder person now, but I don't mean that in the sense of being broad-shouldered. I was harder in terms of being more defensive.

The next few months were marked by me sitting in the toilets at every possible opportunity. I hadn't overdosed on laxatives or become a pervert or anything, I was playing my guitar. The toilets became our gathering place. The guys who smoked would go there. I never smoked one cigarette in all that time. If I had, it would have justified the beating I took the previous term and there was no way I was going to allow that to happen. Yes, it's true, I was holding a grudge and I don't deny it. Could anyone blame me?

Recreation was indeed provided for us at the college. They used to build canoes but I stayed clear of that at first. I didn't fancy the launch which invariably took place at the location on the canal where the brother had drowned. I loved the football though. I used to play a lot in the gymnasium. I was good at football and used to enjoy running rings round guys much older than myself. It's a great feeling to nut-meg someone who has been bullying you for weeks, then to turn round and nut-meg him again. There was one part of the football scene I detested. We were never allowed to enter a league. Instead, the priest would just phone the local borstals and arrange 'friendlies'. You can imagine what that was like. The hardest young nutters from around Manchester and Liverpool playing the inhabitants of what they referred to as 'Fairy Castle'. The matches were always anything but 'friendly'. Our team was picked from all six years in the college. Even although I was only in first year, I was always in the team. I was quite proud of that, until we played our first match against a borstal.

There were some bone crunching tackles going in – however, you can't beat skill. By half time we were 2-0 up. During the half-time interval, their club-psycho approached our team with some halved oranges. I was just thinking that this was very nice of him when, as we went to take a piece of orange, he dropped them into the mud. He then addressed us menacingly: 'The next one of you lot who scores is getting his fucking legs broken.' To give added weight to his words, he stomped the oranges into the mud. They won the match 11-2.

As if getting kicked up and down a football pitch wasn't bad enough, we also had to take them on at table tennis and cross-country running on alternate weeks. At least at the football we were all together to provide each other with moral support. At the cross-country running, you were on your own. It was a three-mile route which was lined every so often with guys from the borstal to tell you where to go. They frequently did. I had no concept of them being underprivileged or anything like that, at that age. As far as I was concerned, they were just nutters who gobbed on you or threw things at you as you ran past. Some guys even got beaten up. Needless to say, I did the fastest three miles in the history of things with legs.

Lent was now looming. I was the sacristan, by this stage in my career. That basically meant that my manual labour was to look after the chapel. There were two of us assigned to that particular task. We were told that since the great festival was approaching, we had better get the chapel in shipshape order. The other guy who worked with me was a scream. He was a Geordie, and whatever the reason he had ended up at the college, it was certainly not to become a priest. He was the guy who had turned the chalice upside down and put on a funny face just before Christmas. On Saturday mornings we had to do three hours manual labour. For us, that meant sweeping, mopping, polishing and then shining the church floor. This particular morning, it also meant doing the brass. A thousand Catholic women across the land will tell you, it's a killer.

The two of us set to work. He had brought a record player which was blasting out Status Quo at nine point eight on the Richter scale; he had unplugged the Sanctuary lamp and plugged in the Quo instead. I can't understand to this day why he never got a hammering for his irreverence. Guys could be belted for talking in church and here he was, giving it 'Woodstock'. Priests would come round to check that we were doing our work, but they never once pulled him up. My Geordie mate gave me my first unconsecrated host to eat. It was strange; I expected it to taste different from the 'real' ones, but it didn't. As I say, he openly admitted that he was not becoming a priest. He used to do things which I thought he would go to Hell for. He would take the big consecrated host out of the tabernacle and replace it with an unconsecrated one, just to see if any of the priests would notice the difference on the Sunday when we had Benediction. We all had to go to Benediction every Sunday. On that particular Sunday, the priest on duty held up the monstrance. He spoke about the real presence of Christ. My mate had told his year-mates that it was a 'dud' and they were whispering to each other, contradicting what the priest was saying. 'This is Jesus Christ,' he would say. 'Oh no it isn't,' they would whisper back, as if it was a pantomime. I worried that what the guys were doing was really evil. They were not taking the mickey out of mere temporal powers here, they were laughing at God himself. Now I believe that they were doing no such thing. I envisage God saying, 'Go on, lads, expose that bunch of hypocrites.' When it comes to Judgement Day, I picture Jesus smiling at some of the antics of the students. I hope he uses the same humour when it comes to judging some of them. I suppose I've carried that attitude into priesthood. I see people showing the utmost reverence for 'sacred' things, and yet they give themselves permission to treat human beings appallingly. After six years of Scripture Study, Theology and so on, and ten years of priesthood, I have long since come to the conclusion that the whole point of Jesus coming to the world, was in fact, to inform us that people are what God considers sacred; he's not too worried about the bejewelled tabernacles, which so many people seem to bestow upon him.

Lent was woeful. I never thought it possible to cram so many rosaries, novenas, stations of the cross, benedictions and spiritual talks into one day while, at the same time, keep up the relentless academic timetable. We didn't get out of Latin or Maths so that we could take part in these religious exercises; it was our own free time which was usurped. Rosary was every night at nine o'clock, Lent or no Lent. Most of the time, none of the priests turned up and we would ask one particular student to lead the rosary. It wasn't that he had a beautiful praying voice, it was because he spoke at about ninety miles an hour. The quicker it was over with, the better, as far as we were concerned. I think it would be fair to say that the students totally resented having to perform this 'babbling' every night, especially when the priests didn't even bother their clerical shirts to turn up. Special Lenten services were held during tea breaks. It was totally unfair and all so totally unnecessary. Of what possible use was any of this to God? I think of those days when I hear the prayer at Mass today, 'Lord, we cannot add to your greatness…' We certainly attempted to. Why did God require all this babbling at him by bewildered youngsters? Surely a youngster running through a field playing, is of much more pleasure to our Creator than being told to go into a church and ordered to 'Love God'.

To this day, I will not preach at parents and tell them to make sure that they make their children say the rosary, or this prayer or that prayer. Children are prayers. I cannot understand why some people want to subject their children to something which their children can't understand and do not want to do. I do not have children, but if I did, I would not impose upon their creativity and their freedom of spirit in such a way. They have a natural ability to give glory to God simply by being. The endless repetition and recitation of religious formulae will, in the end, chase most of them from the Church. We must stop imposing our longing for the past on those who 'will inherit the earth' and the future.

As I said, Lent was filled with all sorts of oppressive religious observances which were beyond our years. One of the practices I detested at this time was when we all had to gather in church to learn Gregorian chant. We were each handed a huge, leather-bound book containing page after page of Latin words with square, as opposed to round, musical notes above them. We sat for hours chanting this stuff. We didn't even know what the words meant but we were told that we had to have it learned for Holy Week, the climax of Lent and the Church's year. My question regarding all of that is a very simple one: why?

Lent continued mercilessly. By the time we got to Good Friday and were given a graphic description of the horrors which Jesus must have endured, what the pain must have been like, how terrible he must have felt, I was gradually beginning to feel that what happened to him was all my fault. One of the priests made a great deal about Christ's scourging at the pillar. He described, in picturesque detail, the piercing pain Jesus must have experienced as the blows struck home. 'Eh, excuse me, Father, but you're speaking to the converted.' We all knew only too well what it felt like to be whipped. Can anyone explain to me why it was morally repugnant to whip Jesus, but whipping us was a justifiable necessity? The priest spoke about Jesus being stripped of his garments and how it was all designed to humiliate him. He went on at length about how these evil people were stripping him of his dignity. Again, we all knew just exactly how Jesus felt because every one of us had to strip before we were physically punished. Sit down, Father, and let me give a sermon on humiliation. What they were condemning in the Romans and the Jews, they were actually doing to us themselves. When Jesus says to the Pharisees, 'By your own words, you condemn yourselves,' he was simply exposing an almighty, timeless truth: hypocrites will always eventually put both feet right in it. The Indians call it 'Karma'; the good or bad you have done will eventually sneak up behind you and bite you on the arse. These guys simply did not make the connection between the Gospel they were so zealously preaching, and their behaviour towards us. One Holy Week Gospel did jump out at me, though. When Jesus meets the women of Jerusalem he states, 'Do not weep for me, but weep rather for yourselves.' I got that one alright, I knew what he meant.

On Easter Sunday morning the painful sermonising was then transformed into a story of unbridled joy and happiness. None of us was particularly moved. Our unbridled joy was for the fact that the torture of Lent was now at an end.

I've just noticed that when I've been referring to God, I haven't been using a capital H. It brings back to mind a magazine I read recently on a long-haul flight. The 'letters' page contained the following offering:

Dear Editor,
How come when people are referring to God by using the words 'He, Him or His', they always use a capital H? Yet us mere

mortals only get a small h? I think this is a clear case of discrimination and should be stopped. Yours sincerely,
John Smith

When I turned the page over there was another letter:

Dear Editor,
My house has just been hit by a bolt of lightning, my body has come out in suppurating boils and my back garden has just been infested by a plague of luminous green frogs. Please inform your readers that when referring to God in future, they must always use a capital H.
Yours sincerely,
John Smith

When I read this I roared with laughter. Other passengers just stared at me. When I showed them what I was laughing at, they didn't think it was all that funny. Obviously they hadn't been to junior seminary where, if you didn't give God a capital H, you were for the high jump. To this day, I still find it incredible that some people choose to express their respect for God in such superstitious, childish ways. I picture him looking down from heaven, scratching his head with a puzzled expression, saying, 'Will they ever learn? What I want is mercy...not capital H's! This lot think that I came to earth for reasons of punctuation!'

One of the most warped events had taken place during that Lent. During one lunchtime, Marty, a first-year classmate of mine had come running to me in a hysterical state. He was shouting that he had just encountered Satan. To put you in the picture, Satan was never very far away in that place. As much emphasis was always placed on fear of him as there was on love of God. This neurosis was so powerfully ingrained in us that it was only relatively recently that I was able to finally shed it, after reading the excellent book by Gerry Hughes, *God of Surprises*.

In the book, he tells the story of a couple who take their children to see Uncle George every Sunday. Uncle George has a long beard and a short temper. On this particular Sunday, Uncle George takes the two children away from their parents and descends the stairs of his forbidding mansion and leads them towards the basement. As they descend, the atmosphere gets hotter and they begin to hear unearthly screams. The children are terrified by the time they arrive at a huge door which Uncle George slowly cranks open. The children behold a hellish scene: ugly demons with pitchforks, casting screaming children into furnaces. Uncle George turns to the two petrified youngsters and says, 'That's what will happen to you if you don't come and visit me every Sunday.' On the way home as the children clutch on to their parents, still numb with fear, mum says to them, 'Don't you just love Uncle George with all your heart, with all your soul and with all your mind?' The two children answer, 'We do.' The children are lying of course; they don't love Uncle George at all. They actually despise the old ogre, but they will never admit it. The author goes on to state that, at a very young and tender age, religious schizophrenia has already set in.

Reading that passage was another moment of liberation for me. Another door opened inside me which had been closed for twenty years and I was able to understand more about what had happened to me and who I was. It's sad, but I was nearly thirty before I reached the stage where I could no longer be manipulated or coerced by religious terror tactics. How many other people are out there who have never had that door opened? How many people, as Hughes says, are being 'driven' by God, instead of being 'drawn' to him? How many people don't even know what is going on inside them? I believe it is a huge problem which is crying out to be addressed. Parish renewal programmes only scratched the surface, but, I suppose, it was a start.

Anyway, back at Maplin's holiday camp, I was nervous at what Marty had told me about his meeting with Satan. He told me that he had been listening to a tape through his ear-phones, when suddenly the music had come to an abrupt halt. Suddenly, a horrible guttural voice began to laugh, getting louder and louder. He just whipped off the ear-phones and ran for it. Unwillingly, I said I would go and investigate. Sure enough, when I entered the classroom, there was a tape recorder and ear-phones lying on one of the desks. It was still playing. Nervously, I put the ear-phones to my ears. To this day, I cannot erase the horrible piercing noise which shot through my whole being and sent shudders to my bowels. It was Jimmy Osmond singing, 'I'll be Your Long-haired Lover From Liverpool'. I think an utterance by Satan would have been preferable.

I laughed off the whole incident and told the student that I had heard nothing. He kept insisting that he had heard Satan. I was left with a nagging doubt that, indeed, something must have happened to make him act like that. In the afternoon, instead of tea break, there was to be a voluntary-compulsory special church service to pray for vocations to the priesthood. I say voluntary-compulsory because you didn't actually have to attend this service. However, if you didn't attend, you would pay a price later on, once your absence had been noted. What could be more important than praying for vocations? I went to the service, but I didn't pray for vocations to the priesthood. I wouldn't wish this life upon any child. My prayer was that this place would close, we would all get home and that nobody would ever come here again. Halfway through the prayers, Marty suddenly grabbed my arm. He was white with fear again; his nails were actually digging into my flesh he was so tense. He told me that there was a goat's head, with red eyes, floating in the air and staring at him at the back of the church. I slowly turned my head to look…nothing, bugger all. This was not surprising given my religious inferiority complex. If God never appeared to me, why should the devil? I say this because, when I was a young child, when I looked around me in church at all the serious pious faces, I actually thought that they could see him. I thought he wouldn't appear to me because I had stolen tuppence from my mum's purse.

A distressed Marty was quietly ushered from the church by one of the priests. He later reappeared in the study hall for the beginning of our two and a half hours of boredom. It seemed that even visionary activity did not warrant missing study time. He sat across from me and took out a book to pretend that he was studying. It was Dickens's *A Christmas Carol*. He opened the book at a page with a grotesque picture of a ghost, presumably of Christmas Future. He began to crack up again, crying and moaning that the book had just opened at that page on its own. I was now beginning to crack up myself. The priest with the cane duly arrived on the scene and dragged him out into the corridor. We watched his silhouette being beaten mercilessly to shouts of 'I've had enough of this nonsense, my boy.' Call me a big softie, but I don't think that physical violence is any way to treat a child who was so obviously in the throes of a nervous breakdown. Who put Satan and the ghosts in the poor guy's head in the first place? The youngster was only reaping the grim results of what had been sown for him. As the beating was taking place, I thought about this student's dad, whom I knew very well. If he had been there and witnessed what that priest was doing to his son, he would have flattened him, priest or no priest. One of the tragedies of it all was that none of our parents actually knew what was going on, because we couldn't tell them. Twenty or so years later, I would like to bet that most of those students still haven't told their parents.

When, a few weeks later, Marty's physical health broke down, I was not surprised. He was carted off to hospital for an operation to have his appendix removed. His parents went to the hospital to collect him and take him home. I thought that he had become the latest entry in the never-to-return book. I envied his escape. He had been belted and caned more than any other student at the college. He was almost weekly on the pyjama parade and he was also a victim of the more normal form of bullying, from other students, one in particular.

Recently I found out the true story behind Marty's appendicitis. Two students had gone down with the condition during the previous term. We were told that the cause of one of the ailments was that a peanut had lodged in the student's appendix. Knowing this, Marty decided to start eating peanuts without chewing them in an attempt to give himself the condition, and escape from here. Nothing happened, not even a tummy rumble, so he simply began to feign the illness. He had seen what the other two students had done before they were taken to hospital, so he had simply copied them, holding his side and groaning with pain.

His parents had arrived after the operation was carried out. The surgeon told them that there was absolutely nothing wrong with their son's appendix, but since they had cut him open, they had decided to remove it anyway. No one seemed to wonder wonder why Marty would put himself through that ordeal just to escape life at the seminary

If he thought that the operation would finally be his ticket to get out of the college, he was sadly mistaken. He arrived back at seminary a few weeks later. The beltings and canings resumed for him almost immediately. He had now fallen behind academically so it became even more difficult for him to avoid the weekly pyjama parade. He then put into practice 'plan B' in a last-ditch attempt to escape.

A group of men used to hire the college gymnasium one evening a week. They would hang up their jackets outside the gym in the sure knowledge that, because this was a seminary, their belongings would be safe. Marty stole £2 from one of the jackets, hoping to be caught and expelled. Unfortunately, he was also being bullied by Peter, the Cockney student who had played such a prominent part in my initiation ceremony. He was forced to hand over the money to him to avoid getting beaten up. When the group of men informed the priests that money had been stolen, one priest gathered all the students in the chapel and demanded that the culprit come forward. The bully then handed in the £2 and grassed on Marty. Peter earned a pat on the head, and Marty a caning. They then phoned his parents and asked them to come to the college. Marty felt that, even though he would be labelled a thief and would have desperately disappointed his mum and dad, at least he would be out of this place, at long last. He waited outside one of the priest's offices while his dad was inside being told the terrible truth that his son was a thief. After about half an hour, his dad emerged from the office. He took his son up the corridor then stopped and, turning to him, said, 'It's okay, son, don't worry. They've kindly decided to give you another chance!'

Never mind, there was a feast day coming up. That meant that there were no classes for the day. To celebrate, they replaced the relentless schoolwork with even more relentless religion. Extra prayers were the order of the day, followed by a big Mass. I've never quite grasped the concept of big Masses. Mass is Mass, no? Priests from the order would visit the college for the day, knowing that Mass would be followed by a meal and a good drink. Our reward was to be taken to the pictures in the evening of such occasions. On this particular day, we headed to Lancaster to take in the movie, *Planet of the Apes*. We were herded into the picture house and we all had to sit in the same row. That annoyed me: the institution had come to town. Nobody who saw us thought, 'Oh, there's a big family.' We stuck out like a sore thumb. We were 'schoolies', or boarders, or whatever. When the film finished and the titles were going up, we all got up and shuffled along the row. One of the students stepped out into the aisle and automatically genuflected to the screen. What had this lot done to our heads? It was a tell-tale sign of the amount of time we spent in church, if nothing else.

Before long, another student was to find himself in the back of an ambulance. A group of us were out on the lawn at the back of the college, doing nothing in particular. Doing nothing in particular was frowned upon; idle hands and the devil's work and all that. One of the priests came out and made some comment that we should be doing something to occupy our time. Some guys muttered, 'Piss off and leave us alone. We get little enough time to ourselves.' We were quite happy just sitting on the lawn, chatting, but he decided that we were incapable of occupying ourselves so he went off to find something for us to do. A few minutes later, he returned with a long rope. I giggled as one of the older lads said sarcastically under his breath, 'Oh good, we're going to have a lynching.'

The priest climbed a tree and tied the rope to the top of it. He climbed down then secured the other end of the rope to something at the far end of the lawn. He then held up a smaller rope and said, 'Right, who's first?' I was beginning to get the picture. He wanted us to slide down the rope. One guy, who was to become a lifelong friend of mine, volunteered. He took the small piece of rope and climbed the tree. At the top, he looped the small piece of rope around the long rope, held on to both ends, then he let himself go. I was never very good at science, but common sense told me that rope on rope frays. It did. The small rope disintegrated with the friction and the poor guy crashed to the ground, landing awkwardly on his back. He was rushed to hospital where he was kept in overnight. I think of him every time the yearly figures are released for working days lost through back problems. Sadly, this was not going to be the last time that guy landed in hospital as a result of what that place did to him. He would not be the only one either.

Good times lay ahead however. Two new students were to join the college. They were brothers and they were Scottish. They were not going to be priests though. Their family had just moved from north of the border to the Lake District and they were only at the college for their education. Such students were referred to as 'day boys'. The younger brother, Sam, came into my year and the older one, Willie, went into one of the top years, the same year as Peter the bully. The three of us became good friends immediately thanks to the fact that we were not English.

The friendship was cemented almost immediately when I found myself sitting beside the two of them and Peter, the cockney bully, at the lunch table. Thinking back to what happened that lunch time, I can only conclude that the bully felt threatened by the presence of the other two Scots. I don't know how I had provoked him, but he suddenly started the usual spiel about me being a Jock bastard. He was holding his knife rather threateningly. I felt a new air of confidence with Sam and Willie being present, so I didn't make the usual sheepish apologetic noises. I stood my ground and refused to be intimidated. He held the knife to my throat and started to speak even more threateningly, through gritted teeth. Now, I don't want to give the impression that this was some sort of razor fight outside a sleazy back-street bar in Mexico; it wasn't like that. This was pathetic. He was threatening me with a butter knife. I made a comment about him causing me more damage if he threw the butter at me. I didn't want to lose face. Actually, I don't think I did feel threatened. There was so much iceberg anger in me, ready to turn into Vesuvius rage, that I wouldn't have minded sending some of it in his direction. I didn't get the chance. Sam up-ended the table and left the bully sprawling on the floor, covered in boiled – no, incinerated – cabbage and flat meat. (Flat meat was the collective term for the non-vegetable part of your dinner which wasn't your plate.) He looked totally humiliated and wore an expression exactly like someone who wouldn't be giving me any more problems. We turned to leave the refectory as the other students cheered and rattled their cutlery. That's what they do at boarding schools in England. The only thing missing was the chant of 'Rah! Rah! Rah!' and 'Jolly good show, chaps!'

I felt great. These guys were teaching me that I didn't have to take bullshit from anyone like that bully. I found Sam's antics funny as well. He feared no one. One dinnertime, I was in the toilets, playing my guitar as usual. I had now aspired to the heights of playing

Cockney Rebel's 'Come Up and See Me...' which was quite appropriate since Peter was a Cockney. I was sitting there minding my own business when suddenly the door burst open and someone ran in to say Sam had just thumped Peter out in the quadrangle. Foghorn Leghorn suddenly appeared and shouted, 'That's ma boy!' I couldn't believe it, this young guy had flattened the bully and he didn't even get a belting for his efforts. Half murdering somebody was acceptable. Failing to conjugate a Latin verb wasn't.

There was still the small matter of the football match against the borstal to be resolved. Everybody had been so impressed by Sam that we could only imagine what his older brother Willie was capable of. He was immediately made captain of the team. He was informed about the history of these matches against the borstal and the orange-stomping psycho was pointed out. The pre-match talk from our new captain consisted of, 'You guys just play your normal game. I'll take care of Jaffa.' At the start of the game, the captain made a few changes and placed himself marking their psycho. It wasn't long before our captain was kicking lumps out of the guy. The psycho looked as if he was ready to run for his mum. We gubbed them as we did in every game we played against them from then on. I used to think of the borstal lads the night before any subsequent games. I imagined them saying, 'Oh shit, we're playing the trainee priests tomorrow.'

The effect those two brothers had on the place for me was brilliant. Now a Scottish accent would gain you respect whereas before, it would earn you a kick-in. A whole section of life which had thus far brought me nothing but grief, was now removed. I would never be bullied by other students again. Now all I had to worry about was avoiding the pyjama parade...and the ghosts.

Chapter Seven

We didn't get home for Easter. Instead, one of the priests took some of us camping in the Lake District for three days. We set off in the college minibus, those who wished to go that is, and headed for no particular place. We parked the bus on the side of a hill where other tents were pitched and set up our tents. The priest told us to go and collect firewood or we wouldn't be having a hot breakfast the next morning. That evening we had crisps for supper. I remember picking them out of my sleeping bag for the rest of the night. I fell asleep dreaming of the next morning's fry up.

As usual, the dream eclipsed the reality. Breakfast consisted of an industrial-size tin of baked beans placed on the fire to heat up. I'll never forget sitting there, dipping my margarine-and-grass-covered bread into the beans, while watching the other campers with their gas stoves, frying bacon, eggs and sausages. The odours wafting across the campsite were glorious and to die for. The priest aware of our drooling, commented, 'Don't pay any attention to them, lads. They're not proper campers like us. They'd have been as well staying at home.' Sure. Was a dozen rolls and a few eggs too much to ask? Our twice-a-day diet of baked beans was to have serious repercussions in the tent at night. It was like a hot air balloon, only the gas was methane.

Two tents had been set up. One tent was for the priest and the bigger one for us. When it came to bedtime, the priest told the most senior student that he was to sleep in his tent. I never gave it a second thought then. I do now. Maybe I'm being unfair, maybe the priest was just frightened of the dark. Maybe he asked the student to sleep in his tent in case he woke in the middle of the night and wanted to cane someone. The senior student who slept in the priest's tent that night was committing horrific sexual assaults on junior students. Where did he learn his 'skills'?

That night, one of my friends complained of a sore stomach. He was desperate to go to the toilet but, because there were no toilets, he tried to hold off until morning. Eventually, one of the older students took him out of the tent and reassured him that it was okay to go to the toilet. The young lad shit himself in the dark, at what, he thought, was a discreet distance from the tents. Daybreak was to prove embarrassing for him. He had not relieved himself as far from the tents as he had thought. The priest went ballistic and totally

96

humiliated the student, not just in front of us, but in front of all the campers who were nearby. The former student still remembers that incident, twenty-five years later.

During the summer term, the college held a parents' day. Our folks were invited to the college to find out how well their little cherubs were doing. The priests called this feast day 'Whit'. I used to laugh at that because in Scotland 'Whit' isn't a feast day, it's a question. A Summer Fayre was to be held on the same day to raise money for the college. I was aching to see my mum and dad again. They had written to say that they would be bringing my youngest brother, Fran, the baby of the family. I had missed him especially. I had enjoyed looking after him when mum was in hospital. Totally unbeknown to me, two days before they arrived, he was knocked down by a car and nearly killed. Nobody told me. I was standing in the quadrangle anxiously awaiting their arrival. I recognised the car coming slowly up the driveway. I was delighted. The car stopped, the door opened and out clambered my young brother, covered from head to foot in cuts, scrapes and bruises. It looked much worse than it was because the doctor had covered his wounds in a bright red solution which looked like blood. I just stared at him in horror. He didn't seem perturbed in the least. The thought of what the rector might say to my parents about my conduct over the year just vanished from my mind. I took my brother by the hand and showed him around while my mum and dad met with the rector.

My parents met up with us later on. I had got a gleaming report from the rector. I was a star pupil, top of the class, although once or twice I had merited a 'ticking off'. He didn't tell them that the ticking-offs he had so picturesquely referred to, were, in fact, brutal beltings on the arse and canings. They had omitted to mention, on the colourful brochure, what they had meant by 'discipline'. We didn't dwell on my report. We spent the rest of the day wandering around the fayre. I hardly let go of my brother's hand. I was constantly conscious of their departure time looming. Time was going too fast, I couldn't slow it down. Eventually, we made our way back to the car. They hugged me as my brother climbed awkwardly into the car. I knew my mum was fighting back the tears. She whispered in my ear, 'Never mind, son, it'll soon be the summer holidays.' As they drove away I could see the tears falling down her face. I found out years later that she had broken her heart all the way to Edinburgh. In fact, she constantly broke down all the time I was away. She must have spent hours on end writing letters to me, that being the only form of communication we had. They didn't have a phone so I had to write to tell them to be at my auntie's at a set time if I needed to speak to them or if I just needed to hear loving voices.

I went up the stairs to the toilets, without my guitar. I just sat on the end of the bath and broke down. That awful empty feeling had returned and I could do nothing about it. My mate came in and saw the state I was in. He went out of the toilets and returned a minute later with his mum. She hugged me and did her best to console me. I look back now and wonder, was anything worth that amount of pain? It was like going through a bereavement every couple of weeks, and for what? As an adult, I have never experienced the depth of anguish I felt during those years. What the hell was the point of it all? Did none of those priests ever ask, what the hell was the point of all of this? I don't think so. They were too far gone, too brainwashed by the system. Years later, some of the students went out of their way to contact other students to express sorrow if they had treated them badly. No priest has ever done the same as far as I know. We learned to block out the pain. They obviously learned to block out the inflicting of it. Does none of them, given the years of reflection that have passed, think that damage was perhaps done to youngsters and that maybe there is a moral and pastoral responsibility to contact them and offer them some sort of help?

The ten weeks to the end of term dragged along. We had exams to study for. Passing them was not a problem since the length of time spent studying was beyond all requirements. The only memorable events were a number of expulsions which took place. All the best guys got kicked out. One guy was red-carded for stealing cigarettes from one of the priest's rooms. Another bit the dust for helping him smoke them. Some guys got the heave for no apparent reason, something the seminary would have called 'lack of Christian witness'. These guys were returning to their communities in shame. They had been treated appallingly in the college and were now going home to face the disapproval of the Catholic community. The Catholic community were, and remain to this day, clueless as to what was actually going on. I hope this book informs them.

To the non-religious reader, the disapproval of the Catholic community may not sound the worst torment in the world. But for a youngster, it could be devastating. One expelled student told me years later that he heard people saying in front of him things like, 'What a complete waste of time and money.' The effect on that student was that his already battered and bruised self-esteem took a further body-blow. He grew up believing that he was trash and that he had let everyone down. The way they treated him, he would have been as well walking around in sackcloth and ashes, ringing a bell to warn people of his filthy presence. As soon as that student finished normal secondary school, he left his home town and set up house in the anonymity of a large city where no one would know what a monster he was. When I look back, I know who the real monsters were.

Some other guys just left. To a man, they left full of bitterness. I recall some of them packing their suitcases in the dormitory. They had a peculiar way of packing the case, it was different from the way you would pack if you were going to the Costa del Sol. They threw their clothes in with real disgust on their faces. Sometimes a priest would shuffle past and ask, almost apologetically, 'Can I give you a lift to the train station?' It was the nearest you ever got to an apology. The reply was always a frozen 'No', without the addendum, 'Father'. These guys were leaving the place and they were damaged. It would be years before I found out just how damaged they were – and that I was in the same boat. I received a number of beltings and canings over the next couple of months, for the usual minor misdemeanours. Other guys got it more than me, though. One of the saddest things I saw was a guy who was a fixture on the pyjama parade, opening his weekly report and jumping for joy. He wasn't on the pyjama parade that week. How sick. In the year that this particular boy was in the seminary, there was only one week that he wasn't belted or caned or both. During that one week of respite, the rector passed him in the corridor and sniped, 'You'll be back on the parade next week, sonny, you haven't got it in you to stay away.'

There was one last act of treachery that term which I didn't find out about until the first day of the summer holidays. As you can imagine, I was delirious to get out of the place. Eight weeks of freedom with very little mention of God, well, their God, at least. No Satan, no ghosts, no beltings, no study. Butter instead of margarine. I had eight weeks to enjoy. It wasn't the Christmas holidays, where we only got two weeks; this was the summer, the time-keeper couldn't shorten eight weeks. It was forever.

My delirium was cut short when I got home and my mum handed me a letter from the rector. It stated that, even though we were on our summer holidays, we were students for the priesthood, and so we were to attend Mass every morning. I still have that letter to this day. It still angers me when I read it. Perhaps it will give the reader an idea of the ethos which pervaded the place.

Dear Parents,

It was a very great pleasure to welcome you all once again on Parents' Day. There was a very good attendance. I would like to say a special word of greeting to those who were not able to come…we missed you, but understand perfectly why you were not able to make the journey. This short letter will let you know what was discussed at the meeting.

After Holy Mass at 10 a.m., during which the boys sang really very, very well, there was a coffee break, and the meeting began somewhat later than was planned.

The Rector gave his report first, and in it drew attention to the generally very good results that had been obtained in the 'O' level GCE exams this year. He praised not only the staff, but also the students on their hard work and pointed out that this should be a source of great encouragement to the rest of the school. He went on to say that the general standard of work was quite good, and that the re-introduction of the House system and the awarding of House points for hard work had been a positive incentive, which had had very good results. The one complaint that had to be made was on the question of the very poor standard of speech as regards both pronunciation (irrespective of local accents) and the standard of English used. A member of staff also stressed that the poor quality of English was also evident in the students' written work.

The Father Spiritual Director then gave his report. He said that he was very happy to report that there was a much better atmosphere in the school; that matters of serious complaint from the previous year (smoking and vandalism) had very greatly diminished and that the integration of seminarians and day-boys was very good indeed. He raised one matter, which was discussed for the rest of the meeting – and this was the question of 'seminarians on holiday.' Two major points were brought up: one was that of students working during the holidays, and the second was that of leisure time. In both cases the point at issue was the preserving of the ideal of the priesthood, and the developing and fostering of one's vocation. The first difficulty that was seen by Rev. Father Director was that some boys were taking on holiday jobs which prevented them from going regularly to Mass. He stressed that it was during the holidays that a boy really showed his sense of vocation by his willingness to get up in the morning to go to Church, thereby developing his love of the Mass, which is the only firm basis for a true vocation. A difficulty that one parent saw was that boys wanted to work to help out their parents, especially over pocket-money and clothes, and that it was impossible to get a job that would allow them to go to Mass first. While appreciating the difficulties and the motives, Father Director maintained that it was a matter of getting one's priorities right, and with this the parents agreed.

The second point that was raised was the unsuitability of some of the jobs that had been taken on by students. Even if the first difficulty was overcome (getting to Mass) yet there were jobs which were not at all suitable for a boy who intended to give his life to Almighty God in the Priesthood and the Religious Life. Parents had nothing to say about this, except to agree with what Father Director had said. There was another problem connected with this, namely the use of the wages earned. It was pointed out that for a boy to be allowed to use the money earned as he wished, was not fitting for a boy who, in a couple of years, would be making a vow of Poverty in the Order. It was also added that many schools did not favour the idea of holiday jobs at all, because the 'feel' of having plenty of money in his pocket often lured boys (and girls) away from their schools, where they would normally be taking 'O' and 'A' levels.

The next matter to be raised was the delicate one of the use of leisure time. Many students want to keep the same friends that they had before they came to the seminary, and this involved sometimes doing the same things that they were doing. To take girls out, to go dancing, to go to discotheques etc...was, it was felt, to be putting oneself quite deliberately into an occasion where one's ideals of going on to the priesthood could very easily be tarnished and eventually destroyed altogether. Yet it was felt by parents that boys should not go on to the priesthood 'blindly', without knowing 'the other side' of life. The Rector agreed entirely, but pointed out that there was a big difference between realising that there was another side to life, and actually experiencing it. One does not become a priest, he said, because, having tasted, as it were, both, one preferred the priesthood to the other. A boy should realise fully what he is sacrificing for Almighty God, and, in faith and love, make the sacrifice if he really feels that this is the life to which he has been called. It was clear that the only thing that was worrying parents was that they were afraid of the boys becoming priests 'in the dark' and having grave misgivings afterwards. I think it is fair to say that at the end of the discussion all were agreed on the serious dangers of losing one's vocation by acting in any way which could so easily lead to a lowering of one's ideals.

God bless you all,

On behalf of the staff.

P.S. I have just been down to see Father Director to go over this report before printing it, and he asked me to remind you of the point made about the type of films that a seminarian should not see, and likewise the discretion that should be had as regards television programmes.

What? Students for the priesthood? I had just turned thirteen the previous week. If you take woodwork in first year at secondary school, it hardly makes you a trainee carpenter, does it? I couldn't believe it. They wouldn't even let us alone when we were hundreds of miles away. The going to Mass every day of the holidays wasn't a problem for the first few weeks because the church was just down the road. But then the local priest went off on his summer holidays and there was no Mass. This meant that I had to get a bus to go to the next town to attend Mass every day. Half my holidays were taken up travelling to and from Mass. I totally resented this intrusion; it just wasn't fair. Had I not done enough praying over the last year? Had I actually enjoyed going to Mass, it wouldn't have been so bad. But by this stage I hated it. To me, it was just some old guy droning on about things which I didn't understand. My mum told me, years later, that she wished she hadn't allowed me to go; this was my time, it was precious time and it was just so unfair to have it stolen from me like that. This is probably getting to the heart of why I am publishing this book. What kind of power is at work which is strong enough to override a mother's natural instincts? My parents wanted me to enjoy my holidays but they felt duty bound to follow the dictates of the rector, because he was a priest. The Church is riddled with that type of attitude. It is a cancer, in my opinion. Any priest worth his salt rejects such unquestioning adulation and power.

The above letter is worth reading over and over again just to see what kind of warped minds we were subject to: the almost paranoid hatred and fear of women, for starters. How did the mothers feel at that meeting when women were described as dangerous? They must have sat there and thought that they were a bunch of sluts, who had seduced their own husbands from the purity of the priesthood. They were effectively telling our parents that repressed homosexuals make the best priests. Holiday jobs, if you were fortunate enough to get one, what you got paid, what you did with the money – how the hell was that any of their bloody business? What we watched and didn't watch on television? It also makes me sick to read the way they pulled the wool over our parents' eyes. 'House points' had been a great incentive, they said; for 'house points', read getting the belt or the cane. In two and a half years of being top of the class in almost every subject, in almost every exam, I was given a grand total of one house point. Turkey gets more each year in the Eurovision Song Contest, for God's sake.

During my 'supervised from afar' summer holiday, I was now finding out just how high a pedestal I had been placed upon. People would give me gifts and ask me to pray for them. This wasn't faith; this was superstition, although I didn't realise it then. I'll never forget one of my mates telling me what happened to him. He was upstairs in a double-decker bus. Two ladies, who were on their way to the bingo, were sitting near him. One of them recognised him and wrestled a fiver from her handbag. She leaned over to him and pushed the fiver into his hand asking, 'And how are you getting on at the college now, son?' He answered honestly, 'I'm not...I've left.' She snatched the fiver back quicker than a viper striking its prey, and fumbled it back into her bag. My mate said the two women then began to shake their heads and talk about what a disgrace he was. They agreed that it was 'a right shame' for his parents.

I wasn't at the stage of being humiliated like my mate; I was still a student for the priesthood. People were nice to me because of that. I much preferred those people who were kind to me because of who I was, and not what I was. It's strange, but the people who were genuinely kind all those years ago, are still my good friends; they supported me through thick and thin and never made any moral judgement of me. They just accepted me, rejoicing with me when I did something right and turning a forgiving, blind eye when I botched it up. The ones who only saw a 'student priest' have long since rejected me; some of them have actually gone out of their way to let me know just exactly what they think of me. Their problem.

The trouble with pedestals is that, once you're on one, it becomes comfortable; I began to act the part. If there was a 'special' Mass on, I would be asked to read at it. I suppose I was seen as a role model for the other kids. I began to realise that I couldn't just say and do anything any more. Sometimes I would say or do something and I would hear people saying, 'And he's supposed to be a priest as well.' I then had to work out what it was that I had done wrong. I still get that to this day. Some people would rob you of your humanity, if you allowed them. Is it beyond the realms of possibility to have a priesthood where you can simply be yourself? A human priest, with everyday faults and failings? Surely the Gospel would be preached much more honestly and movingly from such a person.

At that stage of my life I became at least two people. The public me, who struggled to keep up to other people's false expectations, and the private me, drowning in a sea of confusion. That was my mindset when I returned for my second year at the college. Because of my mental state, I found the music of David Bowie attractive. (Sorry, David, if that sounds a bit like a back-handed compliment.) I immersed myself in it. It gave me solace. Yet again, the black robes were to interfere in one of the few things I enjoyed, one of the few places to escape to. My favourite Bowie album at the time was 'Aladdin Sane'; 'A lad insane' was what Bowie was referring to. Why were so many of us attracted to such music? One of the priests discovered that in the track 'Time', the lyrics mentioned the word 'wanking'. He confiscated the album. I never saw it again. At least at the primary school you got your confiscated sweets back at the end of term. After I got out of the college, it was one of the first albums I bought. Nowadays when I listen to Bowie, I can almost taste and smell the college again. Incidents which I had long since buried, come back to me. People say that language is limited, and it's true. Music and art can convey so much more. I feel frustrated at times that I can never share totally what I felt at that place and what I feel now. Sometimes when I listen to Bowie, I experience the most profound emotions which are impossible to elucidate; they don't translate into language. Its like being in a prison with a population of one – me. No one else will ever fully know or fully understand.

Chapter Eight

I can't remember how I got back to college for the start of that second year. It's a complete blank. Asking to leave was now an impossibility for a variety of reasons. I believed I would be letting everyone down if I left. One of the positive things was that my mum had sent a letter to the rector asking if I could get away for a long weekend because my auntie was making her final profession as a nun, in France. A few days before we were due to leave, the rector still hadn't said anything to me about it and I began to wonder if the letter had arrived or not. I faced the possibility of another letdown. Then, out of the blue, he came into the study hall one evening and told me to see him in his room after supper. It was the first time I had walked up those steep stairs without the prospect of being belted.

The rector spoke to me that night as if I was asking for a seat at God's right hand instead of a few days off. I actually felt that he thought I had been underhand in getting my mum to write and ask for permission. It was as if he felt cheated somehow. His freedom to refuse my request had somehow been compromised because it was actually my mum who was asking, not me. He made clear the gravity of the request and the seriousness with which he had viewed it. He had eventually decided that I could go, but with one condition: I was not to travel up to Edinburgh on the Thursday evening, as my mum had asked, because that would mean missing one study time. Instead, I was to leave on the Friday morning and travel straight to London where my family could meet up with me, before flying to France. I wanted to spit in his face. Why couldn't he just let me go home and travel with my family? Neither I nor they had ever been to London before. They would be arriving at one station, I at another. What if we didn't find each other? What if there was a delay? As I descended the stairs, I felt as though I had just been belted. He had just destroyed the whole weekend, as far as I was concerned. I spent a while brooding. Wouldn't it be a good thing for a 'trainee priest' to attend the final profession of a nun? What was his worry about my study time? I was top of my year group in every single subject; I could have taken a bloody month off and still passed the exams with my eyes closed. I came to the conclusion that the rector was a shit. That was the only explanation. He was just a shit. My mum and dad had only wanted me to go to the nun's final profession because that's what they thought the college staff would expect. Isn't it absolutely, ludicrously crazy? Everybody in this mad Church of ours is trying to do what they think is the right thing, according to what they think other people expect. For once, why can't we just all start doing what we think is the right thing and sod everybody else? It simply frustrates me today to think of that small-minded man causing such pain in our lives. He had gone to junior seminary as an eleven-year-old; senior seminary at eighteen; ordained when he was twenty-four; and now, years later, we were victims of his screwed-up life. My frustration is not so much that we were victims then – it's that we still are, now. A lot of this behaviour was the 'acting out' of the unresolved problems of an eleven year old; and the tragedy was – is – that he had been given so much power over ordinary people's lives. The rector's reason for not allowing me to travel to Edinburgh was not, as he told me, that I would miss study; that was an excuse. I believe that I was being dictated to by a 'child with power', who was angry that I was trying to get out of school before him. So he stopped it, as best he could.

The day came for my departure for France. Some of the guys were envious of me getting away but they were also glad for me. I made my own way to the train station as the guys headed for classes. I wasn't offered a lift – well, I wasn't leaving, was I? I was now entering new territory. The landscape was totally alien to me. I had never been further south than the college in my life before – well, apart from the time they had taken us down the road to see *Planet of the Apes*. I was worried that I wouldn't find my family in London. I needn't have bothered. When I stepped off the train, my mum, granny, cousin and uncle were all waiting for me. It was fantastic to see them all and…we were going to another country. The college instantly became a distant memory.

When we arrived at Heathrow we checked in our luggage. My granny (whom we called Nana, to distinguish her from my other granny, if that makes sense), had baked a two-tier cake to celebrate my aunt's final profession. She carried the smaller top cake while I carried the bulkier base cake. They were both in plastic containers with handles. As we were passing through customs, one of the officers stopped us. He took the lid off the cake my Nana was carrying and then produced a knitting needle. He made as if to push the needle through the cake. My Nana, one of the finest Catholics and Christians I have ever known, grabbed his hand and said, 'Stick that needle into my cake and I'll stick it up yer erse.' She was referring to the needle, not the cake. I creased myself laughing. The officer got the message and backed off.

We had to get a wee happy-bus out to our plane. There was a huge Air France jumbo jet parked on the tarmac. I began to get really excited – until the bus drove past it and stopped at a tiny propeller plane around the back of the jet. As the doors shut and we taxied out to the runway, I promised God that I would be good from now on. I asked for a window seat, but as soon as the seat-belt signs were switched off, I thought better of it and swapped with my uncle; I didn't fancy this flying lark. We soon landed in a town called Dinard and made our way to our hotel for the night. I laughed at the funny round pillows on the bed.

It was a strange and wonderful land. I loved the cafe bars where, as a thirteen-year-old, I could order myself a beer and nobody gave a damn. What a difference from having every move monitored and judged. I decided there and then that I would leave college one day and come and get a job in France. Twenty years on, I still love France and I still hate the Lake District. That's a shame; it wasn't really the Lakes' fault.

I loved my Nana dearly and it was on occasions such as this that she surpassed herself. She took charge in one of the cafes and ordered – in her best French – 'Deux tasses de thé…' The guy interrupted her, 'Aye, two cups o' tea, Mrs.' She continued, 'Et deux tasses de café.' The guy was rolling about laughing. He said, 'Mrs, Ah come fi Scotland. Jist speak in English.' Later in a restaurant, when we had just finished our meal, the waiter came over and asked, in broken English, 'Did everyone enjoy their meal?' She replied, 'Aye, son, but the meat was gey chough.' I folded. The phrase is an old saying in Scots for 'a bit tough'. How was this poor wee French guy supposed to know what she was talking about? My Nana just about split my sides many times over that weekend. She only died two years ago. My mum and dad will never forget the day she died because her death was not the only catastrophic news they received that day.

The final profession went well. The nuns were so kind and

hospitable. This is how religion should be, I thought. I was wrong about that as well. After the church service, when my aunt finally became a nun, all the new nuns were told which part of the world they were heading to. My aunt, who is one of the most beautiful human beings you could ever meet, had always dreamed of going to work in China. She wanted to work with the poorest of the poor. All the new nuns had been asked to give a first and second choice of destination. As the names were called out, it became clear that none of the sisters were being sent to the place that they actually wanted to go to. My aunt's name was read out, she was to stay in France and work in a plush home for the elderly. It was exactly what she didn't want. She wanted to pick up broken human beings from the gutter and love them. I could see that she was bitterly disappointed. She smiled and made little of it. She would go where God was sending her. I don't think God was sending her anywhere; the Mother General was though. Maybe that's just reality-induced cynicism on my part.

There's a technique used in religion sometimes, which was designed, supposedly, to teach you humility. Your superior would ask you what you would like to do, then when you told them they would tell you to do the exact opposite. This would be done for your own good, of course. Because you have taken a promise of obedience, you are required to conform to the Superior's wishes. Twenty years later my aunt was to leave that Order of nuns and go off to work in an orphanage in Bolivia, where she is now blissfully happy, doing what she always wanted to do in the first place – help the poorest of the poor. As an adult, she had lived under a regime which was just as oppressive as the regime I was living under as a child. Why wouldn't they let her do what she wanted to do twenty years ago? It tells me that in their eyes, obedience is of higher value than compassion. I think they are wrong.

I can understand why the military demand obedience from the junior ranks; in a situation of war, they need to know that everyone is doing what they are supposed to be doing. There is no time for questions. I disagree with the whole set-up, but I can understand it. I cannot, however, comprehend the over-emphasis on obedience within the Church – an institution which is supposed to be seeking the truth. If all dissenting voices are quashed and only certain voices are heard, then what we arrive at is anything but the truth, no matter how much those voices claim to have a monopoly on it. Today, I have a framed text on my wall which reads:

It is often better to live under a cruel robber baron than to live under an omnipotent, moral busybody. The robber baron's cruelty sometimes has to sleep; his cupidity is sometimes satiated. However, the person who oppresses you for your own good, will do it without end, for he does so with the approval of his own conscience.

I wish my auntie had read that twenty years ago. She would have left for Bolivia then.

As usual, the trip came to an end too quickly for my liking. My family took me to my train station in London before making their way to their station. As the train pulled away, that awful feeling of dread returned. It hadn't really impacted on me when I returned to college in the summer, because I knew, or at least hoped, that I was going to France. Now, it bit into me with a vengeance. I was crying before the train had even reached the end of the platform. There was nothing to look forward to now. I felt a huge void. I had nothing to sustain me.

Five hours later, I was walking down the drive to the college, thinking of what stage of the journey home my family would be at. I put on my college head again and stored the magical trip to France in my heart, to be brought out when I was in my bed that night. It was just after half-past four, so study time had just begun. I felt sorry for the guys, as I pictured them stuck behind their desks. I entered the college through one of the side doors and went up to the dormitory. My main priority was to make myself scarce so as not to get captured for study time. I had hardly formulated the thought, and remember – thoughts travel at six hundred miles an hour, when the dormitory door was flung open and the rector came in. 'Right, Mr Gilhooley. You know damn well that study time started ten minutes ago. Get yourself down there.' I tried to remonstrate with him and explain that I was only just in the door. 'Now!' he bellowed. He knew what time my train was due to arrive and had actually come searching for me.

He had reluctantly let me go to France and had felt humiliated that he had had to let me go. Now, I was back in his clutches and I was going to pay the price. I plodded off to the study hall. I actually thought about walking straight past the study hall door and going to one of the priests' rooms to tell him that I was leaving. I think that process is called 'growing up'. I regret today that I did not follow my instincts. Friends who know me well have said to me, 'Your years at college, the pain that you suffered, have given you many good points and strengths.' Yes, they certainly have. I still wish though, that I had been man enough to face up to the priests at that point in time. I regret not having told the rector on that day that I wasn't taking this any more. I was so close to actually doing it.

I decided that I would need to think about making such a momentous decision. After all, what would the consequences be? I entered the study hall and sat at my old wooden desk, nodding to my mates, with a frown on my face. I sat down and pulled out a book to stare at for two and a quarter hours. I noticed a pencil I had put in the corner of my desk before I had left for France. I knew when I had put it there that when I next saw it, I'd be on a downer. I'd be back.

As I sat there, I tried to figure out whether I should leave or not. I didn't get much thinking time. The door suddenly opened and in walked the rector with an armful of homework which he dumped on my desk. 'There. Get on with it. You've got a lot of catching up to do, my lad.' I felt sick. All I had to do was stand up and walk out, but I didn't. On the previous evening I had been in a French café, sipping lager. Now I was trying to translate what Pliny had said to some guy hundreds of years ago. I truly hated the rector by now. I had gone through all the phases of being hurt by him, then healed, then hurt again. I was past the stage of making excuses for him. I stopped thinking 'Maybe he's not so bad after all.' Now I didn't allow myself to fall into that trap. I got off the emotional seesaw. Negative feelings towards him ran so deep that, years later, when I met a group of my college mates in a pub in Glasgow, one of them said, 'Oh by the way, did you hear that the rector died?' My response was, 'Did he?…Whose round is it?' I was told that he had been moved to Rome after the college had closed. A priest from his Order had told one of us enthusiastically that he had done some wonderful work there and had received some Vatican award or other. Were we supposed to be impressed by that? I'm sorry, but I just couldn't join in the congratulatory backslapping. He may well have achieved magnificent heights during his Vatican desk job, but my memory is of being belted on the arse by him on too many occasions. Instead of congratulating him, did none of his brother priests ever consider trying to help him see through the shallowness of it all? Did none of them ever attempt to tell him that he had never even thought about who he was? Did he himself never read the quote, 'The unexamined life is a life not worth living'? The night that I was told of his death, as well as experiencing anger at the very mention of his name, I also experienced a profound sadness at the senseless waste of it all. He was just as much a victim of the system as I was – probably more so. He never woke up and smelled the coffee. He never became conscious. He, along with many of his brother priests, never once in sixty-odd years uttered the word 'why?' It is a human tragedy of massive proportions, because people like him have so much power in the Church.

Chapter Nine

Thus far I have made little mention of something which has to be said. I'm sure I will suffer the ire of some of the self-appointed defenders of the faith for saying it, but I will not remain silent any more. From the day I arrived at the college, there was a priest whom we called Bertie Bligh who used to frequent the place but who seemed to have no particular role. He never taught any classes, he didn't provide spiritual direction or anything like that. He was just there. Most of the time, only one or two priests would say the main Mass for the students, up the stairs in the main chapel. The other priests would be downstairs in the crypt at their individual small chapels. A junior student was allocated to serve Mass at each crypt chapel. I served Mass for a number of them and I didn't mind it. I couldn't understand why they felt the need to say Mass on their own though, when they could have been up the stairs in the main chapel joining in with everybody else. Who wants to go to a party with only you there? There are still priests today who refuse to concelebrate Mass. There is no 'body' in the Church to try to reconcile old and new attitudes, or at least none that seems to be effective. Most seminary systems achieved the goal of totally brainwashing their inmates. If a priest was taught one way at seminary, he was not readily going to adapt to another way later on in life. That would mean admitting to himself that what he had been doing thus far in his life was wrong or mistaken. It takes a brave man to take that step. However, it takes a foolish one not to.

A rota was up on the notice-board indicating which student was serving which Mass down in the crypt. I was down to serve the whole week at Bligh's Mass. He was one of the more friendly priests so I wasn't unduly worried. However, one fourth-year student had pointed him out to me in the refectory and warned me ominously, 'You see that guy over there, never be alone in the same room with him.' I didn't have a clue what the student was talking about. I confided in one of my mates, who then informed me that a prefect had given him the same warning. We were both at a loss to understand what they were alluding to.

On the Monday morning, as the other students made their way to the upstairs chapel, I went down to the first small chapel in the crypt. I heard a couple of students sniggering at me. The fact that I was serving Mass for this priest seemed to be a cause for laughter among some of them. Mass was strange. The priest went through the ritual on his own, it was as if I wasn't there. I still ask myself what was the point of it all. He did everything perfectly, bowing and genuflecting at the right moments. He looked as if there was something incredible going on. He seemed consumed by it all. Later on, as a priest myself, I gave a sermon ridiculing the old Sacramentary (which we still happened to be using in that particular church). In between the lines of black print, which were the words the priest was to say, there was small red print. This contained ludicrous instructions to the priest as to what he was to do with his fingers, hands and arms while uttering the words in black print. 'Priest joins thumb and index finger on each hand then says the following…' The red print was almost farcical. I asked my people to think about it; if the priest didn't join his thumb and index finger at the approved moment, was the Mass invalid? The reason I poured such scorn on such trivial nonsense was because of what followed that morning in the crypt.

This priest followed the small print to the dot. He elevated the host with pinkies extended, he bowed with much reverence and put on the face of a saint. At the consecration, he actually looked as if saying the words was causing him physical pain. I stood and watched in utter amazement. Tragically and pathetically, it was all one, big, sad act. At the end of Mass, I put the various things away. He took off his vestments, then turned to me and firmly grabbed my arm. I had a dish of water in my hands which he took off me and placed clumsily on the altar. Some of the water spilled out on to the altar cloth and began to spread through the fabric. I noticed it because it would be my job to clean it up. He then put his arms around me and began to ask how I was getting on, and was I happy at the college. I mumbled that I was happy (Huh!). He pulled me towards himself and began to hug me, rubbing his face against mine. It was sore on my face, like sandpaper. I knew in that instant that this was not right. This was not just affection; this was something different and it frightened me. The hugs became kisses. The smell of his breath was unpleasant and I tried to turn my head away. His hands began to wander. I stood there, pinned against the wall with my arms folded defensively while I stared down at the ground. His hugging and kissing became more intense.

He pulled me towards himself very tightly. I could feel something hard pressing against my stomach. I protested, 'I don't like that, Father,' but it didn't seem to register with him at all. He was whispering to me what a great lad I was. I was totally uncomfortable with all of this but I didn't know what to do. He kept kissing me on one side of my face then when I tried to turn away, he started kissing me on the other cheek. Each time he moved from one side to the other, the smell of his panting breath hit me. I looked at the door to see if it was shut. It was. I wanted it to be open so that I could run away, but I was also relieved that it was shut so that no one would inadvertently see what 'I' was doing. In that moment, I had begun to take on the guilt. I didn't want anyone to see what 'I' was doing. I was nearly thirty years old before I was able to accept that I had actually done nothing. He did it, not me.

The kissing continued, getting closer to my mouth. The awful realisation hit me that he was about to kiss me on the lips. He didn't. He stepped back and unfolded my arms and tried to put them around him. He was trying to get me to respond sexually towards him. My arms just stuck out behind him in mid-air. He lowered his hands and gripped my buttocks and pulled me towards him again. I felt something hard against my stomach again. By this time, I had a fair idea that it wasn't a prayer book. I was utterly lost. What the fuck do you do in a situation like that?

Is that swear word a sin, by the way? Will God cast me into the burning fire for using it? All the priests of Scotland…go on, read this chapter to your people on Sunday, then preach on it. Tell the people about how offended God is by bad language. Tell them that you are so upset that it is a priest who used it. Then have the guts to tell the folk the truth. Tell them that many priests constantly use such language in private. Let's stop the lie. For once, let's take the risk of telling the folk the uncomfortable truth and stop pandering to religious snobs. Explain the rest of this chapter to them. Tell them that you are only human, that you always knew these things were going on but didn't have the courage to say it. They'll understand and they will love you for being honest. They will tell you that it's okay. They will hug you and be delighted that you took the risk of being brutally honest with them for once. The Gestapo department of the

Church will slag you, but that's okay. They're the ones who don't want these things to be known in case someone points the finger at them. It's that lot and their unquestioning obedience who provided the abundance of abusers. It is they who want the cover-up. Why should you be tarred with their brush? Come on guys, isn't it about time that we, as the leaders of our good and great people, stopped arsing about, explaining to the people about the evils of bad language and the heinous crimes of contraception? 'No, you can't get your child baptised, Miss, you're not married, I haven't seen you at Mass for a while and in any case, you have to go on a two-month baptism course.' How dare we, as the clergy, treat our people like that? We do not deserve their loyalty, and yet they remain loyal. Imagine what the Church could be if we priests actually risked telling them who we are and stopped being frightened by what the middle-class minority might say. Why are we so terrified of offending their sensibilities?

It is a subject dealt with in the excellent film, *Mass Appeal*. Jack Lemmon is a well-respected parish priest who has settled into a very comfortable lifestyle. An outspoken and troublesome curate is appointed to his parish. Jack Lemmon tries to draw the curate into his comfort zone. He attempts to teach the young man how to be a 'nice' priest. In fact, the opposite happens. The young man's sincerity and his refusal to compromise the Gospel have an impact upon Jack Lemmon. He begins to become conscious. He realises that he has been living his life frightened of saying or doing anything which ran the risk of offending certain sections of his parish. One evening at Mass, in an emotional outburst, he confronts his people, 'I can't do this any more. I never loved you enough to take the risk of losing your love.' From that moment, he begins to preach the Gospel honestly again. It is a conversion which will lead him into direct confrontation with Church authorities and with those who would prefer to see religion remain at the level of harmless, uncritical prayer-saying. The film was very close to the bone and reflected a truth which I had seen time and time again in the Church – except that, for the most part, in real life, the priest would not have been converted. It was no surprise when I found out that one of the advisers in the making of the film was indeed a Catholic priest.

Sorry, I went off on an important tangent there.

Suddenly the sound of voices broke the awful silence of the helplessness I felt. The students were running down the stairs from the main chapel to the refectory. The priest stood back so I bolted out of the door and ran into the refectory as well. I was totally confused at what had just happened. I couldn't make any sense of it. I didn't know whether to be happy that this priest obviously really liked me or to be angry that he had touched me in a way which I knew was wrong. I've tried to recall my exact emotions at that moment, but I can't. As we all sat down at the benches, the abuser priest walked out of the crypt and into the refectory. I watched him like a hawk. He stopped at a couple of tables and chatted away to various students, slapping them on the back and joking with them. It seemed strange that one minute he was acting so weirdly with me, and now he was acting like everyone's favourite uncle. He went from one table to another but, for some strange reason, he missed out my table. He disappeared out the door and went off to the priests' refectory to have his breakfast. They had butter.

I thought about what had happened all day – during classes, at study time and in my bed that night. I didn't tell anyone. Was I supposed to pay attention in class that day? If I was, I didn't. That happened during my first few weeks at the college in 1974. I didn't tell anyone about it until nearly twenty years later. Consider everything I've written so far: the beltings and canings, the ghosts, the initiation ceremony, the bullying and Satan. All of that came after the sexual abuse. I don't know if you can understand; I still can't. One minute somebody wanted to kiss you and fondle you, the next minute somebody wanted to belt or cane the bloody life out of you. I truly did not comprehend what was going on. As I lay in my bed that night, I worried about the next morning's Mass in the crypt. I was to serve Bligh's Mass until the end of the week. What if he did it again?

He did. The next morning as soon as he finished Mass, I picked up a few dishes and left the small chapel as quickly as I could. I didn't go back in to finish tidying up until he left. I thought I had worked out a way round the problem. He worked out a way round my solution. The next day, because he knew I would be out of the door as soon as he had finished the final blessing, he turned to me before he did the blessing. He started the same carry on again, this time during Mass. The fact that it was during Mass was very significant to me. All this bowing and genuflecting, all this display of piety…it was all a whited sepulchre. This priest was sexually abusing boys during what is absolutely sacred to every single Catholic – the Mass. That event has had a profound effect on my life. I have been extremely suspicious of overt shows of personal sanctity ever since. I know what sometimes lies behind it. I've found that true holiness doesn't need to put on such displays. Those who feel it necessary to show how holy they are, are to be watched closely. But taking on such people and confronting them has cost me dear. If you refuse to kowtow to such people and won't join in their spiritual insincerity, you will very quickly find out just how 'unholy' they can be in terms of what they can do behind your back. If someone publicly acts very piously and you don't, it's relatively easy for that person to discredit you in front of the Church. They know that a beautifully robed, prayerful priest with the voice of an angel, is going to be believed before another priest, who happens to wear jeans and a T-shirt and who sometimes goes to the pub. Easy target. Jesus' sevenfold indictment of the Pharisees has been very effectively hoovered from the Sanctuary. Thankfully, there are still some people out there who wish to switch the hoover to 'blow'.

I still can't work out exactly what I was feeling then. I know it was a negative feeling but I can't describe it in any more depth than that. I think I felt as if I had done something wrong. I must have felt that because I didn't tell anyone what was going on. I was frightened that I would be ridiculed. I was ridiculed anyway. Some of the older students made comments about me being this week's 'bum boy'. At primary school, a 'bum boy' was the teacher's pet. Here, it had a very different connotation – a more literal one. For the rest of the week, he did the same thing. He kissed me, hugged me, fondled my buttocks and my genitals. I wouldn't let him put his hands down my trousers; in fact, I tried constantly to fend off all his advances. He never overtly asked me to do anything to him, but he constantly tried to move my hands to respond to him. I think it became clear to him that I just wouldn't do it and by the time we got to the last Mass of the week, he just said Mass and pissed off, leaving me alone. I felt relieved, but I also felt rejected in that somehow I had angered or disappointed him. A former student later told me that he was not even a very good abuser. By 'good' he meant accomplished or expert. He seemed to just grab anyone, whenever he got the chance. 'Good' abusers can go to extraordinary lengths to lay the trap, to groom, he told me. Good or bad, he was certainly sad.

As a twelve-year-old, I had it firmly lodged inside my head that all priests were good. That knowledge overrode the reality of what I was experiencing. I was trying inwardly to work out how what this man had done to me was good. I was trying to comprehend how this was explainable, comprehensible. Was this type of thing what we were all supposed to be doing? And if so, why had my parents or teachers never told me? I want to put something on record here. I have since read, watched and heard about abuse cases involving Catholic priests, where the young victims were forced to perform oral sex, masturbation or they were buggered. I never experienced any of that from this priest. I honestly believe that it could very well have led to such things. But I now know that these things did happen to other students. I wanted to say that 'In his favour, he did not do that to me...' How can I seriously say anything like, 'In his favour...', or 'To be fair...', when he did it to other youngsters? In trying to reflect upon what happened, I always told myself that somehow I had got off lightly. I didn't. What he did to me, coupled with all the other things which were going on in the college, damaged me profoundly. To this day, I still bear the legacy of what he did. I did not get off lightly; none of us did.

When I hear men, today, talk about how they were abused at 'normal' boarding schools, I realise that what we went through had an added dimension of wickedness. This was not a deviant teacher, pervert social worker or a suspicious-looking man in a grey mac. This was a priest. What he had done to us meant that everything our parents had taught us about Christ and the Church was a lie. Only our parents didn't know it yet. There were no counsellors there to tell us that it wasn't a lie, that most priests are decent human beings. We were left with the feeling that we had discovered an awful secret, one which we could never divulge to our parents. When I speak about our teenage years having been stolen from us, that is not the whole story. One former student recently said something very profound to me. 'They stole the Church from me...and I want it back.' The sinful thing is that when any of the abused admit it, pressure is exerted to make them feel that it is not their Church. They're made to feel treacherous and disloyal. I can't think of a more loyal statement: 'I want the Church back.' I realise now that I have felt that too, although maybe not as consciously or as acutely as my friend. It has probably underpinned every sermon and every viewpoint I have given about the Church since I was ordained ten years ago. (I also realise that in stating that, I leave myself totally open to the criticism that I should never have been ordained in the first place. We'll just wait and see who is first to come out with that one.) Because of the negative experiences of the Church during those years, I have a very clear idea in my mind of what the Church should and could be like. If this book brings even a few people further towards that realisation, then it will have accomplished something of what I set out to achieve in writing it.

After that week, I never had to serve the altar for that priest again. As I say, I think I got off lightly compared to some of the others, in terms of what he did to them. I do not know if he was able to influence the rota so that he could have altar servers whom he could abuse more easily. All I know is that, in the following months, I was never asked to serve his Mass again. It seems too much of a coincidence. It is yet another question I will never find the answer to. I do know that, later on that year, it was announced that students no longer were required to serve the altar for crypt Masses. I believe now that this decision was taken because they all knew what was going on. One former student told me that he had served Mass in the crypt for one priest, and knew that the abuser priest was due to use that chapel for Mass immediately afterwards. The first priest told him that he didn't have to tidy up after Mass that morning, he would do it himself. He told him, 'Now, get yourself out of here, quickly!' Sadly, I have to admit that, yes, the other priests, without a shadow of a doubt, knew what was going on. Today, they seem to be very reticent about admitting it. I find it tragic for the Church and for that missionary Order, who have many good men working for them (and some nutcases), that it is going to take a police investigation and the publication of this book, to eventually make them hold their hands up and say, 'Yes, we knew and we are sorry.' Unfortunately, apologies given under such circumstances ring hollow. If they really were sorry they would have brought this matter to light themselves. Their attitude to this day is that, at all costs, the Church must be protected…and to hell with the victims.

One student in particular often used to go out for a drive with Bligh. We would see them leaving the car park on Saturday lunch times. We all knew what was going on. The priest would never take a group of us out

123

for a drive, only ever one student at a time. We had a college minibus, which another priest used to pile a crowd of us into, to take us out for the afternoon. This priest never did that. He only ever took one passenger. He was systematically abusing almost every junior student. He never once invited me to go with him on his 'away days'. He realised that, if he was going to get any gratification out of me, he was going to have to work at it. There were easier targets. I do not mean that as an insult to the kids he seriously abused. We were all kids – none of us wanted to co-operate. He simply picked on the most vulnerable and exploited their vulnerabilities.

I found out, years later, that one student hadn't been sexually abused. He was no oil painting and carried quite a bit of weight – no stranger to a fish supper and a single steak pie. When we were beginning to broach the subject of our abuse at the college for the first time, whispering to each other in pubs, in case anyone heard us, he pulled me up abruptly. He said, 'Remember how you lot always used to take the piss out of me for being overweight?' I actually couldn't remember, but I agreed with him anyway. 'Well,' he continued, 'I was never abused. No one ever touched me.' 'Well thank God for that,' I responded. 'Aye,' he said, 'There's a lot to be said for being a wee fat ugly bastard after all!' I creased myself. The ultimate rejection – 'even paedophiles hate me'.

Anyway, the priest with a penchant for slim guys would go to any lengths to carry out his abuse. I found out, in adulthood, that he had offered to go and pick up one of the students at home to bring him back to the college for the start of term, a journey of not inconsiderable length, as John Major might say. As I have said, I know now that child abusers will go to any lengths to groom their victims. This was living proof of that theory. He fondled the student in the car for the duration of the journey back to the college.

Occasionally, some of us were given permission to camp overnight in the college grounds. The first time I had gone, in the summer term of my first year, I hadn't slept a wink. We had set up the tent at the far end of the football field, next to the dreaded canal. During the night I heard the sound of heavy breathing outside the tent, and I spent the rest of the night lying awake listening to the sound of my heart thumping. In the morning the boy brave enough to go out and investigate found a cow grazing outside.

The last time I ever went, the last time any of us ever did, I suggested we choose a different site, well away from the canal. We agreed on a campsite at the other side of the college, a place quaintly known as the 'rosary garden'. The tent was erected, and soon night fell. There was the usual banter between us – some boys'-talk and a few giggles. As things quietened down, one of the guys suddenly sat bolt upright and whispered with a hint of terror, 'Someone's out there.' We all immediately went quiet. Nobody volunteered to go out and look around. The silence continued for quite a while. Then we heard it. Someone or something was moving around outside, near the tent. I froze. Who or what was out there?

Suddenly, a very quiet but serious voice from outside the tent pierced the darkness. 'I heard what you were talking about and you boys should consider yourselves an absolute disgrace. I will be reporting your conduct to the spiritual director in the morning.' We all recognised the voice. It was Bertie Bligh. We believed, deep down, that he couldn't tell on us for using bad language. Surely what he had done to us meant that he was in no position to grass on anyone. We didn't actually verbalise this to each other, because none of us was prepared to admit to another what he had done to us. But we all knew that he couldn't tell the spiritual director anything.

Wrong again. He complained to the priest concerned that he had overheard the campers using bad language. We were called into the priest's office and each of us were given four of the cane on the hand. We were told that camping was now at an end and that we had abused a privilege which had kindly been granted us. No questions were asked as to why a priest had been creeping around a field at midnight. What was he doing? Was he out for a midnight stroll? Just a wee breath of fresh air after watching 'Match of the Day' on the telly, perhaps? Or was he out there looking for another victim?

Today, I could not put a figure on how many youngsters that man must have abused. He was doing it for at least three years at the college before he was caught. On that day, I was sitting in the wash rooms, playing the guitar, when one of the students ran in and shouted excitedly that the police were here. We ran downstairs into the quadrangle and, sure enough, a police car was parked there. Two policemen were standing there with one of the second-year students, looking dishevelled and crying. I thought at first that he must have been caught shoplifting in the local town, or fighting or something like that. The rector appeared on the scene and took the policemen and the student to his room. We all went back to the dormitory to speculate on what was going on. The student concerned was one of our best friends and we couldn't believe that he would have done anything wrong. Suddenly, the doors at the far end of the dormitory swung open and in walked the student. He was dragging his suitcase behind him. He unceremoniously flung it on his bed and began to fill it with his belongings in that 'not going to the Costa del Sol' manner. He was still crying. We asked what had happened and he shouted at the top of his voice that 'that bastard' had put his hands down his trousers. The student had cracked up and was found on the railway line in a distressed state, trying to walk home to Blackburn.

The student's parents arrived shortly afterwards and were ushered into the rector's room. When they came out, they were crying. Eventually, the police left and so did the parents, with their son. He never came back. The priest mysteriously disappeared. I found out later that he had simply been moved to Africa, where he could continue to operate freely. God only knows how many youngsters he damaged in his time. Everything was hushed up by the police, the priest's religious superiors and the college staff. College life continued as if nothing had happened.

I've been asked the question, 'Why didn't you just leave?' It's a very difficult one to answer. I think I might very well have been able to get out of there if there had been no sexual abuse right at the outset. I believe that, because of the abuse, I had to protect my parents from knowledge which I knew would devastate them. My main consideration, even above all the hellish things that were happening to me, was not to let them find out that I had been doing 'dirty things' with a Catholic priest. I did ask to get out, but my parents always put it down to homesickness. I never pushed the subject of leaving too far because it could have jeopardised my secret. I couldn't tell them. I couldn't do that to them.

Chapter Ten

During the rest of that summer term, there was a sense of relief that the abuser priest was gone, but nobody said much about it. I think everyone was too frightened to say anything about him in case someone pointed the finger at them and said, 'Weren't you with him too?' I thought that, since one of the priests had been exposed in this way, maybe our minor transgressions might be overlooked from now on. Wrong, yet again.

A group of us went up to the local town on a Saturday afternoon. We did this most Saturdays, but this one was to be different. During the previous week, one of the students had been showing off a new flick-knife he had got from somewhere. We saw the same flick-knives in a shop window. We normally spent our money, if we had any, on sweets. On this Saturday, we bought flick-knives. We left the town immediately and made our way to a cliff which overlooked the sea. We played around with knives cutting sticks and so on. We eventually returned to the college for evening prayer. We hid the knives up our sleeves. It became common knowledge amongst the students that some of us had these knives.

I was no longer spending my lunch breaks playing the guitar in the toilets. I would disappear into the forest on the hill, with the guys who smoked, and just spend time blethering away. Or I would simply sit in an empty classroom on my own just wanting to come home. Wanting to come home was a pastime, just like playing the guitar. During one lunchtime, I took out my flick-knife, rolled up my sleeve and began cutting the back of my arm. I would slice away until I drew blood, then I would move on to a fresh piece of arm. One of my mates suddenly entered the room. I tried to hide what I was doing but I was too slow. He seemed fascinated as he looked at my arm, then he slowly rolled up his sleeve. He had been doing the same as me. His arm was red raw. He then told me that one of the other students had been doing the same. The three of us continued this self-mutilation for a number of days. Then, during one class, the rector walked in, unannounced. He ordered everyone to stand, take off their jackets and roll their sleeves up. He slowly walked around the class, inspecting the arms, front and back, of each student. I began to panic and toyed with the idea of saying that I had merely borrowed a knife to cut my arm and that I didn't actually own a knife. I realised that it would be a futile exercise. The three of us were immediately ordered to his room.

He demanded that we hand over our knives and sent us away to bring them to him. We were not being offered an amnesty to hand over our weapons; we knew we would be belted anyway. We chucked our knives into the canal and made up stories that we had just cut ourselves with bits of glass and so on. He did belt us, anyway, and told us to be on the following week's pyjama parade. I had totally forgotten about this incident until I heard about Princess Diana's story where she admitted that she was so full of self-hatred that she mutilated herself. Had we been doing the same thing?

During one lunch break, near the end of term, my depression was interrupted by a crowd of students running excitedly behind the classrooms. I followed to see what was going on. There were about twenty guys gathered in a circle, pushing two students towards each other, goading them into fighting each other. The two students were obviously unwilling to fight; they were only pushing each other back and forward like we used to do at primary school. The crowd jeered at them and demanded action. One of the would-be fighters suddenly drew back his arm and let fly with a right hook. He connected with the other guy's jaw. There was a dull thud as he fell to his knees and burst out crying. The crowd roared their approval. That should have been the end of it, but it wasn't. The guy who had thrown the punch stood where he was and rejected the opportunity to walk away as victor. I could almost hear his mind, 'Should I go further or not?' Suddenly he shot forward, drew back his right leg and booted the poor guy full in the face. There was a loud crack as the guy's nose disintegrated. There was an explosion of blood. The crowd immediately ran in all directions, knowing that this had gone totally over the score and that anyone who had been involved, even as an onlooker, would be belted or caned. The victim was dispatched for treatment. The guy who had kicked him was sent home.

That moment has always remained on the surface of my thoughts, not hidden in the depths, like many other memories. I still cringe to think of how cruel we could be to each other. One memory of a particular Sunday stands out. Sundays at the college were very empty days, probably because every other day was so packed full. The priests would be out saying Mass in local parishes or visiting family or friends. They were certainly scarce on the ground in the college. It gave us a bit of a breathing space. I enjoyed going to Sunday lunch when there were no priests there. Meals were something to write home about – to complain, that is. On numerous occasions I found a dead worm in a boiled potato. The spuds were peeled in an industrial machine. The machine didn't seem to exhibit much care and concern about how peeled the spuds were when they were emptied into a huge pot for boiling. The bad ones were never discarded until they landed on your plate. You discarded them, along with your whole plate, as you tried not to vomit.

This particular Sunday, about ten of us turned up to see what tasty titbits were available from the snack-pot symposium. The usual: flat meat, boiled potatoes and even boileder cabbage. Pudding was a square thing covered in lumpy custard. There was a student there who was constantly picked on because he wasn't very big in size, but he was enormous in terms of body odour. The bully, Peter, who had long since left me alone, picked on him. He asked the young guy if he wanted another potato. Unfortunately, he answered in the affirmative. The bully just squashed a potato on to the top of his head and rubbed it into his hair. Trying to save face, the poor guy made the fatal error of saying, 'Aw, look what you've done. Now I'll have to take a bath.' The same thought hit everyone at that precise moment. He was immediately dispatched to the washrooms where a cold bath was hastily prepared. We filled it with exotic perfumes such as Daz, Omo and Vim. The poor guy was still laughing thinking that we wouldn't throw him in. Bzzzzzz! Wrong! We dropped him. He suddenly stopped feigning laughter and went absolutely berserk with rage. This lad had come from a normal Catholic primary school, like my own, where bad language was a rarity. We – yes, myself included – had reduced him to screaming 'You fucking bastards' at us. He ran out of the washroom, crying his eyes out, just about taking the door off its hinges. He was soaking wet from head to foot, but I saw the tears. I recognised what he was feeling.

That night, when I lay in bed, I couldn't get the incident out of my mind; I felt guilty. What we did was wrong. The bullied had become the bullies. I tried to justify it by telling myself that the guy did need a bath. That didn't work. I hated what we had done. A year later I was to have a run in with the same guy. He hit me over the head with a brush…a sweeping brush, that is – not a hairbrush. Any time I argued with him after that, I made sure we stayed well away from the broom cupboard. Deep down, I always felt sorry for that guy and what he went through at the college. Then I met his mother and came to the conclusion that he was probably better off where he was.

Looking at it from this distance, there was no way he was leading a happier existence there than he would have done at home. I don't think he was being sexually abused, there were 'nicer' boys. He was also extremely good academically so the pyjama parade would not have been too frequent an occurrence for him. However, he was bullied more than any of us and for that the students, including myself, have to accept responsibility. I know that at least one student has contacted him and apologised. I hope to do the same some day.

Many years later, when I saw the film *Lord of the Flies*, I wondered if a similar scenario had happened to us. *Lord of the Flies* portrayed a group of children tragically descending into anarchy when there were no adult role models to influence them. For all the structural discipline we were subject to on the surface, I think we were all dysfunctional at a deeper level. There were no adult role models. Most of these priests had been at junior seminary themselves and had simply never grown up.

Later on, on the day of the big fight, as I daydreamed in class, I remembered the fight I had witnessed at secondary school. I remembered thinking that I would avoid such stuff if I went to this nice place called the junior seminary. There were probably more fights in this place than there were at the school I should have gone to. We were a collection of angry young men. At least if there was fighting or belting or bullying at a normal secondary school, there was some respite. You could go home every day to a family where you could escape it all. Here, it was twenty-four hours a day, a fact I was reminded of when a fourth-year student belted me one in the face at two o'clock in the morning and yelled, 'If you don't stop that fucking snoring, I'll kick your fucking head in, you little Jock bastard.' I lay there sobbing as quietly as I could in the darkness. I don't think I could have taken much more but I was incapable of taking the steps to get out of there. However, that decision was about to be made for me – for all of us.

We split up for the summer holidays, with the usual expulsions and others saying that they would not be back after the holidays. As we waited on the minibus to take us to the train station, one fifth-year guy appeared with his cases. He was wearing a pair of Chelsea bags and a pair of platform shoes which would have given Elton John vertigo. He had been kicked out and this was his way of making a statement to them. I once saw a colour cartoon of a huge eagle swooping down to kill a defenceless little mouse. The mouse was standing on a fence post, sticking the fingers up at the eagle. The caption underneath read, 'The last great act of defiance.' Something similar was going on here. Such clothes were absolutely forbidden in the college. This guy was simply sticking the fingers up at the staff before he left. The sad thing about this particular expulsion was that this was the student who had warned us not to be alone in the room with Bertie Bligh. He was a decent guy who was well liked by all the students. He was, however, deemed unsuitable material for priesthood and had been told to go. No doubt, when they saw his outrageous attire, the priests probably all congratulated themselves that they were right to kick him out.

I recall very little of those summer weeks. All too soon we were back at college. I was in third year by then, so I didn't feel as threatened as I had before. I had also been top of my year group for the first two years, but my academic form was about to begin to slide. Half-way through that first term, one of the priests made a strange announcement. We were all to go and see him individually at a given time. As usual the first student in to see him came out and told us what was going on. I couldn't believe the news. The college was closing and it was closing at Christmas. I was going home at last. Nobody could say that I was a disgrace, because I was not leaving, the place was closing. It wasn't my fault. I could quietly slip back home and get back to my life again.

I bounced down the stairs to the priest's office when my time came. I listened as he told me that, because there were now very few students, the college could not maintain itself financially. I just wonder why there are very few students, I thought. He confirmed that the college would, therefore, be closing at Christmas. The student hadn't been lying after all. It was true. I was delirious. As with most things, there was a bitterly disappointing addendum for me. He explained that all the other students would be going home. Those who wished to stay to sit their national exams would be allowed to do so. However, I and two other Scottish students, who did not have national exams imminent, would be carrying on our studies at a Scottish junior seminary. He had spoken to the rector of that college, who had agreed to take the three of us in, even though the college was run by a different missionary Order. He then went on to say what lucky lads we were. I told him immediately that I would not be going to any new college, I was going home. He argued, 'How can you make a decision so quickly? You haven't even thought about it. I told him again directly, 'Father, I am not going to another seminary, I am going home.' He told me that I was being too hasty and that he would speak to me the following week when I would have had time to think about it. I told him the same thing the following week – I was going home. He sighed and acted as if I was a total disappointment to him. I was getting a guilt trip laid on me again. He eventually promised that he would write to my parents to let them know that I was coming home at Christmas. I had finally done it, I had escaped. This would be the best Christmas of my life.

By this time, because there were so few students, we no longer slept in the dormitory. We had been moved to a room full of cubicles which had formerly been inhabited by the senior students. It was good to own your own private cubicle, but this arrangement also had its drawbacks. At night, you didn't know who was wandering around outside the cubicles. One of the priests would often stand in the darkness, just listening to us. He had often done this in the main dormitory, standing behind a partition so that we wouldn't be able to see his outline. In this new cubicled dorm, you would often bump into him if you went to the toilets. I was annoyed at this particular priest because he kept hounding me about going to the new junior seminary, so I talked about him behind his back or so I thought. I called him for everything. Two and a half years of bitterness began to spew out. His voice stopped me abruptly: 'If that's the way you feel, Gilhooley, I'm glad you're getting out of here. See me in the morning.'

It was to be my last caning.

The priest had arranged to take the two Scottish guys up to Scotland to see the new seminary on the last day of term. He told me to go with them. I could at least have the decency to look at the place, he told me. We could then go home for Christmas after one overnight stay in the new place. When we got there, I paid very little attention to the seminary although I did notice that it seemed far more liberal than the place we had been in. As I lay in my bed that night, I heard the students coming in from the school Christmas disco. I couldn't believe that they were allowed to go to such things. Still, who cared? I was going home in the morning and I wouldn't be back.

Thus that particular two and a half year nightmare came to an end. It had left its mark on all of us. I don't know the exact number of youngsters who actually passed through that place in those two and a half years, but it would be somewhere in the region of sixty or seventy. Before that, the college had been open as a junior seminary for many decades. During those decades, it had been far more populated than it was in my time. In adulthood, I only found out the story of what happened to about six or seven of those students when they grew up – let's say ten per cent of them. Their stories were tragic. I am now left wondering what befell the other ninety per cent, of whom I know nothing. If what happened to the guys I know about, also happened to those guys, then a crime has taken place on a massive scale, and it is time that the Church faced up to this honestly and humbly. The cover-ups stop here.

Chapter Eleven

During that Christmas, I felt as if the world had been taken off my shoulders. I made a point of meeting up with my year-mates from home to find out what the secondary school was like because I would be going there after the Christmas holidays. I was looking forward to it. As the new term approached, an almighty bombshell was dropped. A letter had indeed arrived from the priest at the old college, but it didn't say that I had decided to leave. It stated that arrangements had been made for me to start at the new Scottish college after Christmas. To this day, I do not know the contents of that letter, but it had been intimated to my parents that if I showed any reluctance to go to the new seminary, they were not to worry, it was only nerves at having to start at a new place. I was an excellent prospect for the priesthood, blah, blah, blah, and I should be encouraged to go. That meant a crying match in the house again. My dad argued that I should at least give it a bash and we came to an agreement that I would go for one month. If, after that time, I still wanted to come home, I would come home. That seemed disappointing to me but I had done two and a half years in the other place. One month wasn't going to kill me. I'd go and sit out the month, then I'd be home. But I was upset that the priests had taken something very important from me. They had stolen the chance for me to return home without a cloud of shame hanging over me. If I had come home when the other placed had closed, none of the pillars of the community could blame me. Now, if I was to leave the second seminary at the end of the month, it would be back down to, 'Oh, did you hear, Jessie, he's left the priesthood...tut...tut.'

The new college was totally different from the other one. It was like stepping out of the Dark Ages. We attended a normal secondary school on the outskirts of Glasgow during the day only returning to the college at night. We were known in the school as 'the college boys'. Most of the guys at the college were very friendly. It was relatively simple to adjust from one seminary institution to another, especially when the second one seemed much freer. Adjusting to the secondary school was a different matter. I was a damaged young man, I just didn't know it at the time. Things were about to happen which I just couldn't understand or explain.

The school had about two thousand pupils. It was like being

plucked out of a pond, then dropped into the ocean. About to take place was the first incident which would set alarm bells ringing. It happened in my Chemistry class. There was an English guy in that class who was constantly picked on for that simple reason – he was English. I had suffered enough being a Jock in England, but it didn't guarantee him any sympathy from me. I think, now, that he saw me as a newcomer to the school and that, consequently, I was lower down the food chain than him. He tried to divert the focus of the piss-taking from himself on to me. I walked into my first class aware that I had to stand up for myself or I'd be buried. The English guy made a derogatory comment about me. I don't know what set me off, maybe his accent and everything I had left behind me, or the fact that everyone in the class was sniggering at me. Anyway, there were syringes full of liquid sitting on each bench. I just picked one up and squirted it in his face. The class went silent in disbelief, then all hell broke loose. The guy began to scream as he clutched his eyes. The classroom door burst open and the teacher ran in demanding to know what was wrong. One of the girls shouted out, 'Sir, it's that new guy, he's a mad bastard, he's just squirted acid in John's face.' The teacher raced over, grabbed the pupil and unceremoniously stuck his head into the sink where he bathed his face. When it became clear that the guy was going to be okay, it also became abundantly clear that I was not going to be okay. The teacher hustled me to the front of the classroom, then belted me four times in front of the class.

What possessed me to do such a thing? The truth is that I did not know that the syringes contained acid. I genuinely thought I was squirting water at the guy. In the previous establishment, we didn't do Biology, Chemistry and Physics as such. We did General Science. Any experiments involving acid were carried out as demonstrations by the teacher. I didn't know that the lab technicians had set out the experiments for the class that day and that the syringes contained acid. This was all totally new to me. Anyone who deliberately squirts acid in another person's face deserves a lot more than four of the belt, as far as I'm concerned. I had been belted, for the first time in my life, with justification. How was it, then, that I still felt hard done by? Maybe I had been attacking my past, I don't know. I was made to stand outside the class. An indication of the gravity of what I had done hit home when my offence was reported to the headmaster. He, in turn, reported the incident to the rector of the college. I would get it again when I got back to the college that night. I began to fear that this life was going to be no different from the past – double rows for everything you did wrong.

As I stood in the corridor, I pictured the headmaster on the phone to the rector. 'Excuse me, Father, just to inform you that one of your trainee priests, yes, the one you said was an excellent prospect when we agreed to accept him at this school, well, he threw acid at another pupil today.' I looked at the square tiles on the corridor floor and disappeared into myself again.

When I got back to the college that evening, I waited for the call up to the rector's room. A message was passed to me by one of the other priests that I was to go upstairs at eight o'clock. I asked one of the students if I had to go in my pyjamas. He asked me what I was talking about. I told him to forget I had even asked. I knocked on the rector's door, then he knocked me for six. He told me to come in and 'grab' a seat. How was I getting on? Did I enjoy the Christmas holidays? Was the food at the college okay? I thought, 'Is this guy for real, or what?' I just didn't know how to respond to him. Maybe this is a ploy to lull me into a false sense of security; he'll wait until I trust him, then he'll get the belt out. I remembered the priest who had sat chatting away to us that evening before he had so brutally caned us. After about ten minutes of trivial banter, he then spoke very softly, 'They tell me you had a bit of bother at school today. Do you want to talk about it?' Beam me up, Scotty! I couldn't handle this. I tried as best I could to explain what had happened, but I didn't know what 'really' happened, so how could I tell him?

Teenagers are not brilliant at giving a good account of themselves – especially damaged ones. I should have said, 'Well, Father, it's like this. I've had a shit of a time in England for two and a half years. An English guy picked on me at school today. My life flashed before me. I should have punched his specky lights out, but I'm not a violent person, so instead, I squirted what I thought was water at him. That's what happened.' I should have said that, but I didn't. What I actually said was, 'A guy was getting on my nerves so I squirted acid at him.'

To this day, I think that the priest knew that we were scarred. He knew the kind of tyranny we had just escaped from and he was going to try to help us. He said that if I ever wanted to talk, his door was always open. He told me not to let what had happened at school that day worry me. He poked fun gently at me for what I had done: 'Heh, you're not going to try and blind everyone who disagrees with you, are you? I like seeing.' This was so new to me; someone had actually treated me with a modicum – no, a skip-load – of compassion. I still believe that it was attitudes such as his that kept any semblance of priesthood, Church or a loving God, alive within me. I knew that this was what the priesthood was supposed to be like. That night as I lay in my bed, I didn't think of ghosts, or of what had happened at school. I was trying to figure out why the rector hadn't belted me.

I was beginning to find out that this college was a very different animal from the previous one. It was much more humane. We were encouraged to play as full a role as possible in our school life. I joined my year football team and athletics squad. Those two years of battering through the countryside trying to escape a 'do-in' from the inhabitants of the borstal had trimmed me down into a fairly decent long-distance runner. We were also encouraged to go to the school discos. Mixing with girls was seen as a positive thing, something which would bring balance and normality. These priests didn't see it as a 'threat to our mortal souls', like the previous lot. This was all completely alien to me. So far in my life, anyone who had expressed any notions of wanting to be a priest was plucked out of reality and hidden as far away as possible from it.

I began to enjoy school and college life. I began to admire the priests who were trying to cultivate as normal a life as possible for us. We were attending a normal Catholic secondary school. I listen to people waxing eloquent about the importance of Catholic schools and how good they are. Fine. If they were that good, why were young prospective priests taken from them to be placed in all-male junior seminaries? Surely the best place for a possible candidate for the priesthood was at home with his own family, attending a normal Catholic school? I admired this seminary for giving its backing to the Catholic education system by sending us to that school. What was good enough for normal Catholic kids was good enough for supposed trainee priests. Most junior seminaries of the time did not share that attitude to Catholic schools. Why? Because normal schools had things called 'girls' in them.

I now believe that the Church's attitude towards women is not just misplaced, it is an evil. I'm not just talking about the old chestnut of the refusal to ordain women. (Not only that, but now the refusal even to allow discussion on the subject.) The refusal to allow women's ordination is only the tip of a very distorted iceberg. There is, without a doubt, a fear of women in the upper echelons of the Church – possibly a fear of sex. For all the official teachings on the beauty of sex and sexuality, the high standing of the married state and so on, the Church is still extremely uncomfortable with anything to do with sex. Women are still seen, first and foremost in terms of their sexuality. On one of the feast days for Our Lady, the opening prayer at Mass reads, 'Oh, Jesus, born of purest love...', that is, a love which did not involve sex. The statement goes against every modern outpouring of the Church as regards marriage and sexuality and the beauty of it all. During the Mass I say every day, Mary is always referred to using the epithet 'Virgin'. She is never referred to as anything else. Some of the most radical words you will find anywhere in the Bible are attributed to Mary. In the Magnificat, the Evangelist has her stating that Kings are going to be thrown down from their thrones. The rich are going to be stripped of their riches and those who have plenty are going to be left with nothing. Instead, the poor are going to be raised up by God, those who are starving are going to have good things to eat. Those who weep now, are going to laugh and be happy. Is any of this bellowed from the roof-tops of the Churches? No; only Mary's virginity and the fact that she said 'yes' to God, in very difficult circumstances. That is what is proclaimed and, according to Scripture, it is dubious. It is almost certain that Jesus had brothers and sisters. The insistence on Mary's virginity has more to do with present insecurity than it has to do with historical fact. What does it matter? What Jesus said and did is what is important, surely. Would we accept that only white people can be priests and not black people? Are only some people made in the image and likeness of God? Recently there has been a movement in the Church to label Mary as 'Co-Redeemer'. Would you believe it? If these mad Mariolatrists ever pull that one off, the Church would be as well folding on the spot.

Anyway, coming from an all-male environment and an abusive situation I found, girls a very difficult problem. I said before that it had been great to go home at the holidays and to enjoy the female influences in the house. The girls made me laugh and brought an added dimension to life. However, by the time I landed in this secondary school, I had not developed any normal boy-girl relations the way everyone else had. A counsellor was later to invite me to realise that my psychological, emotional and sexual development had been stunted by the experience of the previous junior seminary. My outlook as a teenager, and even later as an adult was very often that of a twelve-year old. Girls were still for kicking, not kissing. I was painfully and pathetically shy. If a girl spoke to me, I would become totally uneasy and embarrassed. These young Glaswegian ladies were on it in a second. They could reduce me to a sad, red-faced little wimp in the twinkling of an eye. I hated myself for it. I agonised over why I couldn't just be like the rest of the guys. I couldn't understand what was causing me to take a red face all the time. If I only knew, I could remedy the situation. I had a deep-seated belief that something was wrong with me. I wasn't normal.

One particular girl called Jaffa made my life a misery. Looking back now, I can laugh at it. At the time, I could have murdered her. She wasn't blessed with the greatest of looks. In fact, she was a plug. Maybe her behaviour was a compensation for her looks. She had a tremendous, but very raucous, sense of humour. She had tattoos, I remember that. She could smell weakness at fifty paces. One day in the dinner queue, in front of all the other girls, and in front of my mates, she groped me. I tried to be nonchalant about it, 'I'll give you half an hour to stop that...' and so on. It didn't work. The girls were in kinks as I could feel my face go red. My mouth was doing its level best to get me out of the situation and divert attention elsewhere. But no. It was awful. My pals started to roar with laughter as well. I was over the moon when she got expelled for setting the school on fire.

There were some magnificent laughs to be had in this place. I was often in tears, but this time they were tears of laughter. I really thought I had put the past behind me, then things began to happen which proved that, sadly, life just isn't that simple.

In the tradition of the Church, all potential priests had to learn

Latin. Even though Mass was now rarely said in Latin, we were told that it was such an important language to have under our belt. They would always say, 'Even doctors write their prescriptions in Latin.' I would hardly say that this justified subjecting us to five years of Virgil and Pliny. Anyway, I've never seen a doctor's prescription which was legible in the first place. It could have been in Japanese for all it mattered to me. I had taken two and a half years of Latin so far, so when it came to deciding what subjects I should take at the new school, the rector at the college felt that I should continue with the subject. I didn't. I wanted to ditch it. It held too many bad memories for me. It also struck me that, since I was training for the missionary priesthood, woodwork or metalwork would probably be subjects that would come in handy in my future life, long before the ability to regurgitate Latin verbs. Anyway, Latin it was to be.

My teacher was okay, at first, but he began to find my constant Church-Latin pronunciations irritating, especially when he was trying to impart Classical Latin to us. It was like trying to learn the language all over again. His irritation turned to a basic dislike of me. I got the impression that he just didn't like the college boys. Our relationship was at the stage where we just tolerated each other. Then things just blew up.

One day, I was in the gymnasium changing rooms when the PE teacher came in and told me not to get changed but to go up and see the headmaster. He wanted me to do something. I wandered along the corridor and headed out across the quadrangle in the direction of his office. As I entered the quadrangle from one door, who else but my Latin teacher came out of the door diagonally opposite, and began to walk towards me. I looked at the ground, then at the sky. Should I say hello or just walk past? As we passed, it looked as if we were just going to ignore each other. Suddenly, in his teacher's voice he grunted officially, 'Morning'. It was more like a reproach than a greeting. I toyed with the idea of answering him in Latin but thought the better of it. 'Morning', I reciprocated. I thought I deserved at least nine out of ten for effort, but I had gravely miscalculated. He turned and roared at me, 'You boy, come here immediately. When you address me, you address me as Sir.' My heart sank, please God, not again. I seemed to be a magnet for fascists. I said nothing but just stared at him. He barked again, 'Did you hear me? I said call me Sir.'

The Latin teacher suddenly decided to drop the disrespect rap and plumped for a much more serious charge, 'Wait a minute. What class should you be in at the moment?' I informed him that I should be in PE at the moment. I chose not to inform him that I had permission to be out of class and that I was in fact on my way to see the headmaster. He frog-marched me up to the headmaster's office. He met the deputy head and informed him that I was dogging classes. I let him hang himself. It was bloody magnificent. The deputy head asked me why I was out of class. I answered, 'I have an appointment with the headmaster – for which I am now late.' The Latin teacher just about collapsed. 'Why didn't you tell me?' he shouted. 'You didn't ask, SIR!'

The deputy head looked bemused. Secretly, I think he was highly delighted that this teacher had just made a king-sized plonker of himself. I was then told that the headmaster would be waiting for me so I had better 'Run along'. I disobeyed the deputy's instructions and walked along to the headmaster's office. He told me that there was a special Mass coming up and he wanted me to do one of the readings. No problem. In seconds, I was out of his office and heading back down the stairs again. As I reached the bottom of the stairs, the Latin teacher suddenly emerged from the shadows. He ordered me to go to his room immediately. I wanted to stand up to him and say that I was due in the PE department, but I lacked the courage to do so. I went to his room. He walked in and went straight to his desk. He opened his drawer and withdrew a belt. Then began the lecture, 'I am sick of you defying my authority and not addressing me as Sir.' We were back onto the first charge, now that the 'dogging class' rap had been flung out of court. He ordered me to put my hands out. I do not have the language to elucidate what happened inside of me at that moment. Maybe I just grew up. I was raging. No chance was I going to take the belt from this creep. It wasn't a conscious decision which I argued out in my mind. It was just, 'No bloody way are you, or them or any friggin body going to assault me ever again.' I told him that I was not taking the belt; I had done nothing to deserve it. My heart was pumping so fast I could feel it in my ears. I would have fought him rather than take the belt. I walked out of the class angry as hell, but proud. My anger at the situation overcame any fears of the consequences of what I had just done. He screamed at me to get back there. I'm not well built but, take it from me, John Wayne never made a better exit.

The rest of the day was strange. I had done something which I should have done years before, but I was still upset. I thought that life here would be different but it was turning out to be just the same as the last place. I returned to the college on the school bus that evening saying very little. I heard my mates discussing my refusal to take the belt. They were saying that I was in big trouble. I began to worry what the rector would say.

I was called up to his room after supper, during which I ate next to nothing. Rows should be given before teatime so that at least you can have a feed later. God only knows how the guys on death row manage steak and onions and pecan pie an hour before they're executed. I mentally prepared myself for the meeting as I went up the stairs. That seemed to be the story of my life. If anyone ever asks me what I did as a teenager, I think I'd reply, 'Eh, I walked up the stairs to rectors' rooms.' I knew the rector had found out what had happened, but I didn't know how. Had the Latin teacher phoned him? Had the headmaster? I was invited to take a seat again. He told me that he had received a letter, from my teacher, which one of the first-year students had been asked to deliver to him. The letter pointed out the gravity of my offence in my failure to respect his authority. He also said that I had refused proper punishment. He had asked the rector to order me to go to him first thing in the morning to receive the belt.

I interrupted the rector mid-speech: 'Father, before you go on any further, I have to tell you that no matter whether you get an order from the Pope, I will not take the belt from that man.' I couldn't believe the words which were tripping off my tongue, but to this day, I'm glad I said them. The rector listened as I explained my version of what had happened that day. There was a long pause as he pondered what to do. Then he said quietly, 'Bend over the seat.' What? I was shattered; the rector was going to belt me. I bent over, reluctantly, and studied the needlework on yet another cushion to divert my attention away from the impending blows. I waited for the first one to hit home. It was weird, it hardly hurt at all. He struck me four times. It

144

was like being stoned with popcorn. When I stood up, I saw him putting his slipper back on. I was confused. He went to his desk and began to write a note. He put the note in an envelope and sealed it. He came round to the front of his desk again and handed the note to me. He then said words that I will never forget him for: 'I have given you your punishment. I now expressly forbid you to take the belt from that teacher at school tomorrow.' I stood there bewildered. He spoke again: 'Do you understand? If you come back from school tomorrow and I find out that you have allowed that teacher to belt you, I will be extremely angry with you.' That night, I pondered over the immensity of what had happened. The rector was backing me against the teacher. Somebody at last was showing support. I now trusted him. That was a momentous step for me because I had grown to trust no one.

At registration class the next morning, I asked to be excused, and went to the Latin class. The Latin teacher had a group of first years with him. I knocked and went in. As I approached his desk, he leaned back in his chair and took the belt from his desk drawer: 'Ah, you've come to receive your punishment I presume.' I tossed the letter from the rector on to his desk and said coldly, 'You presume wrong.' I deliberately left out the word, 'Sir'. I turned and left the classroom as he tried to wrestle the envelope open. He shouted at me to come back immediately. His shouts became muffled as I closed the door. I do not know what the letter from the rector said, but the teacher never crossed my path again. To this day, I don't get Christmas cards from him.

Life at the seminary was okay now. The rector struck me as a very wise and good man. He gave me a lot of encouragement. When there were downers, I just reminded myself of what the previous place was like. We played five-a-side football or volleyball in the evening after our one and a quarter hours study. What a difference. There was no supervision at study time and it was only half as long as it had been in the previous prison. I sometimes thought that the guys who emerged from this seminary would be thick, but happy. The previous place would only produce dysfunctional Bamber Gascoignes.

The only evening we didn't play sports was a Thursday: 'Top of the Pops' was on. On one such evening we all ran along the corridor, from the refectory to the TV room, to get the best seats. The programme started, 'Now then, now then, now then, how's about that then, guys and gals…' Okay. I'm not very good at impersonations, but that was Jimmy Saville. Anyway, on one such night the music started and we all began to stamp our feet to the beat. Suddenly, there was a deafening crash. We turned round to see that the electric radiator had fallen over and had shattered into fragments. Just at that moment, one of the priests came in. He ordered one of the students to go and get the rector immediately. The rector promptly arrived and ordered us all out of the TV room. He added that he and the other priest would stay there until whoever had broken the radiator came back and admitted what he had done. He tried to put pressure on us by saying that the TV room would not be opened again until the culprit was caught. The trouble was, no one had vandalised the radiator. It had fallen over on its own.

The reaction of the priests might seem over the top. But, in truth, there was a context to their reaction to this minor incident. During the previous week, a couple of students had stolen drink from the staff common room. They had been caught and kicked out of the seminary. The drink smuggling had been accompanied by an unrelated confrontation between some students and a gang from the local town. The college was well supported by many people from the town but, being in Scotland, there was an element that was anti-Catholic. Some of the local youths had tried to arrange a fight with us. The problem was, some of the guys in the college came from places like Duntocher in Clydebank and the Gorbals in Glasgow. They were really decent guys, but they weren't going to take any shit from a few local bigots. A fight had been arranged. A crowd of us got tooled up. We took the poles out of every sweeping brush we could find and headed towards a disused car park on the outskirts of the village. I was nervous as we walked down the drive. One of the guys had gone to the farm shed to get his weapon. Everyone laughed in a bravado type of way when he uncovered it. It was an axe. The peer group pressure was immense to go along with this. Anyone who tried to pull out would have been scorned mercilessly. I expected us to get to the venue, find a crazy group of maniacs and for us to run for it. The opposite happened. They caught one glimpse of us and they scattered. They had expected a group of rosary bead-wielding pansies. They got a fright.

We jeered at them as they ran and then turned to head back to the college. Someone shouted that they could hear a car coming down the college driveway. We all dived into the trees. One of the priests drove past at some rate of knots. We returned to the college by the scenic route, staying off the road. Everyone tried to return the poles to their respective brushes but it was too late. We had been caught by a quirk of fate. The priest who had whizzed past us in the car had been making a cup of tea. He had knocked over the sugar bowl and had gone to find a brush to sweep up the mess. Not one brush in the college had a pole. He had suspected that something was wrong, asked a few questions, then forced the truth out of one of the first years. He had dived into the car and driven towards the battle scene to try to avert a catastrophe. Nobody was there when he arrived, but we were all captured anyway. They didn't attempt to find out exactly who was involved – there were too many. But the rector called the student body together and delivered a scathing speech. He was raging that the college's good name could be jeopardised in such a fashion. An indication of his anger was his reaction when he saw one student, who is now a priest, doodling on a piece of paper while he was speaking. He grabbed the piece of paper and yelled at the unfortunate student, 'Son, if I kick your arse out of this place now, do you think you'll get a job?' The student shrugged his shoulders. The rector bellowed, 'Aye, you'll get a job alright, son…Shovelling shite!'

Given this climate in the college, maybe you can understand why the rector reacted the way he did over the broken radiator. I think that he thought that the college was falling apart at the seams and he was at a loss as to what to do about it. We gathered in our common room and talked about how we would handle the situation. I volunteered to go back to the TV room and explain to the two priests that the radiator had simply fallen over. I really trusted the rector. I felt that if I just told him the truth he would accept it. Unsurprisingly, the other students agreed that this would be a good idea. I set off for the TV room. As I opened the door, the other priest scoffed to the rector, 'Huh, here's Gilhooley. This had better be good.' I entered the room and explained that we had all been stamping our feet to the music on

'Top of the Pops'. The radiator had simply toppled over and smashed. Nobody had done it deliberately. Nobody was near it when it fell over. The rector sat pensively as the other priest shouted mockingly, 'Ah get out of here, ya great galoot! Do you take us for eejits?' I deemed it safer not to answer that one. He snapped at me to get out. I then returned to tell the guys that the priests hadn't believed me. My mates were frustrated because 'The Things We Do For Love', by 10 CC, was at number one that week and we all wanted to hear it. We didn't get to see the end of the programme. It didn't really bother me. I had lived in a world which didn't make any sense for long enough. This was quite normal to me.

Maybe the reason that the priests had been on edge was that parents' day was coming up. As in the previous seminary, the parents had the opportunity to speak to the rector on their own but, before that, everyone gathered in the library where he was to give an address to parents and students alike. He was still in a passionate mood when he stood to speak. He told the parents exactly what had taken place over the previous weeks. The stealing from the staffroom, the confrontation between some students and a local gang, the broken radiator. Unlike the previous rector, he outlined for the parents the steps he had taken. He had expelled some students. Again, whether I agreed with his actions or not, I found myself respecting this guy. At least he was being honest with our parents and telling them the truth, whether they found it palatable or not. He was up-front about everything. Well, nearly everything.

Suddenly, in front of a few hundred people, he turned and pointed to me: 'Steve Gilhooley, stand up.' I think I sat there for a minute, not comprehending what was going on. He gestured to me reassuringly, 'Stand up.' My face stung as I slowly got to my feet. He continued, 'In all of this trouble, this is the only student who has come through it with flying colours. He was the only one who had the courage to come forward and offer an explanation as to how the radiator was broken.' He stated that, the more he had thought about it, the more he believed my explanation as to how it was broken. He went on to remind everyone that I wasn't studying for this college's missionary Order, I belonged to another Order. As I stood there, I felt awful. I knew, and so did all the other students, that I had been at the confrontation down in the village. The complimentary speech from the rector was totally undeserved. When our parents went home, I felt so bad that I went to see the priest in charge of our year group. I admitted that I had been in the gang who had stolen the broomsticks. He burst out laughing and said, 'Didn't you think the rector knew that?'

It was strange to hear something nice said about me. The lowly state of my self-esteem didn't readily take to it. I just didn't see myself as a good person. I couldn't understand why then, but I know now. My badness had been reinforced so often that it was now a part of me. I condemned myself more acutely than anyone else. While the rector's affirmation did a lot for my self-esteem, other incidents undid any good it may have done for me. My manual labour in the new college happened to be the same as it was in the old place. I was the assistant sacristan again; I looked after everything to do with the chapel: polishing floors, cleaning brass, getting things ready for Mass and putting things away afterwards

The rule in this seminary was that only the priests drank the consecrated wine at Mass. There were no crypts. The priests all said Mass together. I put out everything correctly for Mass. The priests did everything correctly during Mass. They unvested in the sacristy afterwards. They all headed off to get on with the day's business. I hung up the vestments, did this, did that. I thought that I was finished, then I noticed that one of the chalices still had wine in it – consecrated wine. I pondered for a moment as to whether I should drink the wine or not. I decided against it. Only the priests drank the wine. Maybe one of the priests had deliberately left it as a test to see what I would do. I decided that the best idea would be to pour the wine down a sink in the back sacristy. I knew that the pipe from that sink went through the wall into the garden and not into the sewerage. As Catholics, you just don't pour sacred things down the toilet or into a trash can.

I carefully lifted the chalice through to the back sacristy. I turned on the cold water and rinsed the sink out so that the precious blood would not come into contact with anything defiling. I gently poured the wine into the swirling, cold water in the sink. I watched the dark red colour become diluted to a light red, then a pink. It was a spiritual titration. When the water was completely clear I turned on the water tap to full and swished it round the sink with my hand. When I was perfectly satisfied that everything was pure and clean, I turned off the tap and began to dry my hands with the neatly folded towel which lay to the side of the sink. I turned to walk out of the small room and suddenly jumped back in fright. A priest stood in the doorway. He screamed at me, 'Just what the hell do you think you're playing at?' He then began a tirade of abuse, accusing me of sacrilege. 'Imagine pouring the precious blood down a sink! What kind of a person are you?' I was the most blasphemous, evil, disrespectful, ungrateful low-life whom God had ever made the mistake of breathing life into. He slammed the door shut in my face and stomped off in a rage. I just leaned back against the sink, totally wiped out yet again. All the positive experiences I had had at this new seminary were crushed in that instant. I was a piece of shit once more. All the horrible feelings returned again. That priest never spoke to me for the remainder of my time at the college. If I passed him in the corridor, he made a show of turning his head away from me. It was actually worse than being belted or caned. His daily looks of disgust at me were constant reminders of just what I was. Even if I did something praiseworthy, if I received a compliment from the rector, he could give me a look which said, 'You may have fooled that lot, but you don't fool me, son. I know who you are. I know what you are.'

Chapter Twelve

As if I wasn't in a confused enough state, something was about to happen which almost drove me over the edge. It was just a normal day. We returned from school and made for the refectory to enjoy the tea, toast and jam. The food was prepared by nuns so it wasn't like feeding time at the zoo. There was some care and love put into it all. I finished off my last diagonally cut slice of toast and headed to the dorm to change into my jeans and a sweatshirt. I was soon at my desk in the senior students' study hall, actually enjoying doing my homework. After the two and a half hours of slave labour we had endured every night at the previous college, this hour and a quarter was actually a delight. The priests trusted us to get on with the study and didn't feel the need to invigilate us. Never once during my time at that college did I feel the need to fire elastic bands at flies or find something to help me endure study time. It was all okay.

At a quarter to six, I put the finishing touches to an English-to-Latin translation. It was in the pluperfect tense so I wasn't confident that I had got it right. Then I made my way to the church for evening prayer. Considering the amount of time we spent praying, it's strange that I can really only recall one prayer which we seemed to say all the time. We finished off the Office (the term used for the official prayers of the Church), and read that bit about 'Satan prowling around like a roaring lion, looking for someone to devour'. That's the one I remember. I tried not to allow it to worry me and wandered along to the warmth of the refectory for supper. The rector sat at my table that night. We chatted away about football. He was passionate about the game. At the end of the meal he said the prayer of thanks, then almost nonchalantly turned to me and asked me to come to his room at eight o'clock that night. I never gave it a second thought. I trusted him by now and was used to having pleasant experiences in his room, as opposed to being violated. I wondered if he was going to congratulate me on getting the highest mark in the year for English. At two minutes to eight, I bounced up the stairs and knocked on his door. When I went in, he was behind his desk. He told me to grab a seat while he finished off whatever it was he was doing. I sat there and occupied myself by looking at the framed photographs on his wall. I was totally at home and perfectly at ease. Eventually, he rose from behind the desk and sat down on an armchair opposite me. He asked me to stand and come over to him. I knew immediately by the tone of his voice, and by his strange request, that something was not right. I walked towards him tentatively, but in my head I was saying, 'Please, God, don't let this be what I think it's going to be.' He sat forward in the chair and put his hand on my hips, pulling me towards him. My zip was in front of him, no more than a foot from his face. In a very matter-of-fact voice he told me to undo my belt and to lower my trousers and pants. I could not believe what he had just said. To this day, I swear that my concern at that moment was not the humiliation of being abused again. My biggest fear was that this guy, whom I now loved and trusted implicitly, would turn out to be just like the others. I didn't want this guy to let himself down. I lowered my trousers and pants and stood totally exposed in front of him. He stared for a while, then grabbed my penis and testicles in his hand. I begged God not to give me an erection. He told me to move my head to the right and cough. I did. He then ordered me to move my head to the left and cough. He eventually withdrew his hand, but stared at my genitals for a while longer. I bent down to pull up my trousers, without being instructed to do so. My face was burning with embarrassment. He muttered something about having to make sure that my testicles had dropped. He was actually trying to pretend that this was a medical procedure. I left his room feeling utterly devastated. I went to the dormitory and lay on the top of my bed. The shock of what had just happened eventually evolved into tears. I'm now left with the belief that, while I was weeping that night, he was masturbating. Why couldn't he get his kicks out of 'Top of the Pops' like the rest of us? I think that with the exception of the priest who came to talk to us at primary school, this incident had the direst consequences on my life. I was shattered. I don't think I have ever really trusted another human being in my life since then.

When I came to write all this stuff down, the previous paragraph was not included. The rector's nephew became a friend of mine in later life at senior seminary. While we were there I did not tell him what had happened. I didn't want to embarrass my friend or hurt his family. My brother and brother-in-law urged me to include what had happened in the book. I decided that they were right. How can I be selective about the truth and retain any integrity? I'm devastated that the priest did what he did. But he did it and I will live with it for the rest of my life. I apologise for the pain and suffering this knowledge will cause his family, but that is what happened. I'm so sorry, but it happened. I try to look back on the incident with compassion. He was a decent bloke who was kind to me in so many ways. I could never remember him with hatred. Maybe what happened was simply 'the thorn' in his side

I was now a screwed up mess again. I trusted no one. In fact, I mistrusted everyone. A bizarre event was now to put the finishing touches to junior seminary for me. It all started in a very humorous way. A group of us were standing around a warm radiator in the college corridor, trying desperately not to break it. We were waiting to venture out into the cold to go for the school bus. Suddenly, the door at the far end of the corridor burst open and a student came bouncing (he was tubby) along to us, waving a piece of paper in the air. He was shouting, 'I've won. I've won.' The piece of paper was headed with the logo of a national newspaper. It informed him that he was the winner of a competition and that he was the lucky recipient of a variety of gifts. These gifts were presently winging their way to him in the post. Most of us remained decidedly unmoved by his good fortune and headed off to the bus. 'Lucky bastard' was whispered, I admit. He told everyone at school later that day – well, all day actually.

When we arrived back at the college that evening, we were met at the front door by the rector. He ordered everyone into the study hall. As he followed us in, a hush descended on the room. Something serious had happened. He informed us that £200 had gone missing from his room a few days before. He had thought, at first, that he had possibly just misplaced the money. But, this morning, another priest had gone to him and told him that a large sum of money was missing from his room too. One of us was a thief. I don't know if it was just my low self-esteem, but I thought that everyone thought that it was me. The truth was, everybody thought that everybody else thought it was them. Everyone acted very strangely that evening. Nobody took out any money in case the finger of suspicion was pointed at them. You didn't know if the person you were talking to was the culprit, or worse, if they thought it was you. The morale of the seminary was at an all-time low.

To make matters worse, word spread around the secondary school that one of the college boys was a tea-leaf (thief). We had to endure a lot of name-calling and mickey-taking. This went on for days. You would walk into a class and someone would shout, 'Quick, everyone, hide your money.' Then one morning, I was sitting in my French class when a memo came round that I was to report to the deputy head's office and that my teacher was to escort me, presumably so that I couldn't offload any of the swag on the way there. Apart from feeling gutted that I had been accused, I knew that all my classmates would be thinking that I was the thief. I was actually beginning to think that maybe I was the thief. Maybe I had been sleepwalking again. Worse was to follow. I entered the office to find a senior teacher and one of the priests from the college. Seemingly, another couple of hundred quid had gone missing that morning so they thought that the culprit would have the money on him at school. They went through my pockets and found the princely sum of twenty three pence and a broken pencil. As if that wasn't humiliating enough, I was ordered to drop my trousers and my underpants. The outrage I felt years before when I was belted for the first time and the disappointment at the rector having 'medically inspected' me, flooded back. I felt that I had been stripped of so much during my teenage years, now this lot were going to complete the task the others had started. Whatever dignity I had left was now gone as they rummaged through my underwear, lifted my shirt and looked at my backside. The priest looked at me as if he had really known all along that I wasn't the culprit and motioned that I could go back to class now. I shuffled, embarrassed, out into the corridor where I tried to fix the belt on my trousers. I couldn't look anybody in the eye on the way back to class. I was shattered. I was struggling to tuck my shirt in. My heart was in just as bad a mess. Where was all this going to end? Shit! All I did was go to primary school on a day in May 1974 and now look at me. As I went into the class, some of the girls giggled as if they actually knew what had just happened. Someone whispered to me, 'What did they want?' 'They wanted a look at my arse!' I spat. The teacher told me to shut up.

I found out later that all the college boys had been put through the same ordeal that day. There was a lot of anger. We were wearying of the black cloud hanging over us and of the slagging we were taking, not to mention the humiliating strip-search. If we had caught the thief at that time, he would have been hospitalised. That evening, when we got in from school, the rector demanded that we all gather in the college chapel. He said that more money had gone missing. I looked at the floor and shook my head; I couldn't endure much more of this. The rector went on, 'The good news is, we know who the thief is.' We all looked around at each other. Surely, they were bluffing? The rector said that they were giving the thief one last chance to own up. If he didn't, the police would be called and the name of the suspect would be given to them. I then understood the choice of venue, the chapel, as opposed to the study hall. It was to pressurise the thief into owning up, this was the house of God. There was a dreadful silence. Suddenly, a very soft voice from behind me whispered, 'It was me, Father.' To this day, I can never play Cluedo without thinking of that moment. Everyone in the church turned round and stared in disbelief. The guy who had stolen the money was the type of goody-two-shoes that you would never have suspected of being capable of carrying out such a thing. He also happened to be the same guy who had won all the prizes from the national newspaper.

Not for the first time in my life, I watched a pathetic little figure packing his suitcase and waiting for his parents to arrive and take him away. He came into our study hall to collect his belongings from there. I thought someone was going to stand up and punch him one, but nobody did. We all just sat quietly and said nothing. The sense of relief amongst us was almost tangible. I didn't care that another student had been heaved; I was just glad that it was all over. Now I wonder why the student did what he did. I think he just wanted out of the college but couldn't say it. He brought his departure about in another way.

The rector invited the two top years up to his room that night. He gave us all a tin of beer each, amazingly enough. He then told us the whole sad story. He said that they had suspected the eventual culprit from day one. The student had been in charge of the college office. It had been there that he had written his fake prize-winning letter. When expensive toys began to appear for him by post (one of them was a cross-bow and bolts! What was his intention?), they knew it was him. The thought struck me, if they had known from day one who the thief was, why did we all have to endure the humiliating strip-search at the school? That question still hasn't been answered. He was eventually caught when the priests had asked the school teachers which of the college boys had access to a locker. It turned out that, because he was also the school librarian, the culprit was the only one of us who did indeed have a locker. They had burst it open and found hundreds of pounds. I asked why they hadn't nailed the guy there and then. The rector said that if they had just bust him, nothing could have been salvaged from the situation. There was nothing redeemable about it. However, by giving the guy the opportunity to own up, he can at least say, 'I had the courage to own up.' I would have been impressed at the rector's wisdom, but I still felt the humiliation of his 'medical exploration' on me. The thief had merely stolen money; I realised now that people could steal more important things from you.

The college was left in a state of turmoil after this. I think that's what lay behind the rector's offer of a tin of beer. The guy who had stolen the money was considered the most pious person in the place and that includes the priests. If such a saint was capable of such a breach of trust, where did that leave the rest of us? The last five years of my life had seemed to be filled with a succession of people on pedestals coming crashing down to the floor. I suppose because of that, I have carried a suspicion of overt piety into adulthood. As I said earlier, those who make a show of their personal sanctity are to be kept at arm's length. I will also not get involved in clericalism of any sort. I found out to my cost on so many occasions what lay behind it.

I had managed to progress through the second college without the beltings which so etched the first college in my memory. But there was one incidence of violence which has to be recorded. I feel that I want to apologise for writing this, but it happened – and the priest concerned has to own it. I've written about my past and struggled with it. He has to do the same and come to terms with events of which I know he won't be proud. When the crowd of us went to our beds at night, we didn't switch off, like the lights. We waited until the priest went away, then we chatted. Sometimes our conversations went on deep into the night. Sometimes we would gather in one guy's cubicle and blether away for ages.

On one such night, a few of us congregated in one guy's cubicle and sat talking about, I can't remember what. A couple of the students opened the fire exit door at the end of the dorm and were enjoying a fly smoke on the emergency exit stairs. I was at the opposite end of the dorm from where my bed was, when suddenly someone gave the warning that he could hear footsteps coming up the stairs. We all scattered and tried to get back to our cubicles. I had the full length of the dorm to run. As I got to my cubicle I could hear the footsteps approaching the dormitory door. In one motion, I dived into bed while trying to close my curtain which guarded the entrance to my cubicle. I lay there, attempting to muffle my out-of-breath panting, when I heard the dorm door open. Too late. A big hand appeared at the end of the curtain and pulled it half open. It was one of the priests. He ordered me out of my bed and told me to stand at the front of my cubicle. Shit! I slowly climbed out of bed and stood at the entrance to the cubicle. The half open curtain covered the left hand side of my body as I stood there. I could only see him with one eye, my other eye was behind the curtain. He began shouting at me. It was the usual stuff which I had heard a hundred times before. What the bloody hell did I think I was playing at…blah…blah…bloody blah…I wasn't listening again. The harsh words just bounced off my invisible protective shield. Unfortunately, it didn't protect me from a punch in the jaw. If I had seen it coming, I could have steadied myself to take the impact, but the curtain blinded me from the blow being thrown. There was a thud as his fist connected with my jaw. The blow knocked me off balance. I fell backwards and hit my head off the corner of the cubicle shelves. I got back on my feet again and stood in front of him, staring at the floor. There was a pause as he realised he had gone over the score. He smiled an embarrassed smile and muttered something about not meaning to have hit me so hard. It never seemed to cross his mind that he shouldn't have struck me at all. He told me to get into my bed. I closed the curtain and climbed into bed. I nursed the lump on my head and realised that it was bleeding. I reached for a towel and put it over my pillow so as not to stain it. When it was clear that he had gone, a couple of the guys shouted down the dorm, 'What the fuck happened, Steve?' They had heard the noise of my head connecting with the shelves. I didn't answer. For the millionth time in five years I just lay there crying silently. It was that moment which finally made me decide that junior seminaries and myself were parting company. I realised that night, for the first time, that I did not have to put up with this any more. I was getting out and I didn't give a shit any more what anybody thought. All those people who would say, 'Oh, he 'left' the seminary…He isn't going to be a priest…Oh the scandal of it…' They were talking about my bloody life in the same way they would talk about the latest scandal on 'Coronation Street' or 'Crossroads'.

I must admit that this college had been far kinder to me than the other place. Even though some of the events which befell me were painful, during those times I reminded myself what the other place had been like. I do have some happy memories from there, namely the many uproarious laughs I enjoyed at the secondary school. But I was now at the stage where I felt I could stand up for myself. Common sense would have dictated that I stay on at school for my sixth year and attain more qualifications. If I had stayed, I could have topped up my qualifications and waltzed into a university of my choice. If there was any moment in that last five years when the priests, teachers or my parents should have moved hell and earth to make me stay on, it was then. But I wasn't interested. 'Shovelling shite' would do me just fine. That was all I was good for.

Exam time at the school was looming. I had various Highers to sit, and also one O-grade. At the beginning of the year I was told that my timetable wasn't full enough so I had to choose an O-grade crash course. I had to choose a subject where the class times for that subject didn't interfere with my Higher subjects. The only one which fitted that criterion was Spanish. I was okay at languages so I eventually had to take it. I had treated it throughout the year as what it was, a subject I was forced to take to fill up my timetable. If I had a lot of homework, Spanish was the subject I would leave until last.

Little did I know it, but it was my Spanish exam that was to be the catalyst for my departure from the college. Maybe it was something to do with the volatile Latino temperament. The rule at the college for the senior students was that, once you had taken your last exam at the school, you were free to go home for the summer holidays. All my exams were over with after the first two weeks, except Spanish. There was a two-week gap between my last Higher and this exam which I had only taken on as a Mickey Mouse subject. My year-mates had all finished their exams and had gone off for the mother of all summer holidays. I was ordered to come back to the college three days before this stupid O-grade. I resented it deeply. I was the only senior student in the college for that week.

The younger college students thought that this was brilliant; they took every opportunity to slag me. Why not? Had we not done the same with the prefects at the first college? The night before I was due to sit the exam, I was lying in bed listening to some of the younger guys taking the piss out of me in their own coded language. I was frustrated at having to still be there and I cracked. I got out of bed to go and confront the little buggers when suddenly, something weird happened. It was like a deja vu experience. I realised that I had come the full circle. These young guys were only doing to me what we had done to our prefects years before. I then made the most momentous decision of my life. Still in my pyjamas, I headed out of the dormitory along the corridor to the rector's room. This was going to be the last pyjama parade of my young life.

The rector looked startled to see me. He didn't get the chance to even ask me what I was doing. I informed him in a very businesslike manner that I was going into school in the morning to sit my Spanish exam, then I would be taking the train home and I would not be back. I was finished. There was a protracted silence, then he offered me a tin of beer. I declined. I turned to leave the room. He asked me to come back and sit down and reconsider my decision. I just shook my head. I think he knew that that was it. He wished me good luck, dismissively. There was a touch of anger and I think, regret, in his tone. I always thought that when I finally got out I would be happy as Larry. I wasn't. My memory is that I was just profoundly sad. I didn't hop, skip and jump back to my bed; I just plodded back, climbed in and wanted sleep to take over me as quickly as possible. I didn't cry that night although I felt I needed to. I just lay there shrouded in sadness. Life just didn't make any sense any more.

The next morning at the breakfast table, the rector came over to my place and put an envelope in front of my cornflakes. He said nothing, turned and walked away. I thought it might be a letter wishing me well. On the bus going to school for my exam, I opened it. It was just my medical card, nothing else. I felt flat. I was to find out later that the rector had written to my parents a very short and sweet letter informing them of my decision. He expressed his disappointment. My parents told me they detected hurt and anger in his letter. On the bus journey, I remembered how I had watched so many guys before me leaving seminary in bitterness, anger, sometimes even rage. In all that time, I never saw one guy going home at peace, balanced and happy. I was now on that long list of guys.

One of my regrets about the manner of my departure was the good friends I had left behind. I didn't even say goodbye to my closest friend at the college, probably an indication as to my frame of mind at the time. I didn't know it, but during that same summer, he had been kicked out. We were not to meet again for years.

There were now two distinct groups of people who were absent from my life: my mates from the first junior seminary, who had long since disappeared into the ether, and my mates from the second junior seminary in Scotland. I had walked out on them and did not feel the need to keep up with them at that time. Teenagers really don't have any idea, at the time, that the people with whom they grew up are important. It is these people who give us a sense of who we are, where we've been and who we have become. Out of my peer group at the second seminary, quite a few of us became priests. Recently, one of them, who had been working in Africa, came home for a break. He decided to contact our year group and hold a reunion in a pub in Glasgow. Something very poignant happened that evening. Five of us met up. Myself, the priest who was home from Africa, a priest who, like me, had left the seminary and eventually was ordained for his own diocese, and two other guys who had not become priests. I knew that they all knew that I was in the middle of writing a book because it had hit the Press by this time. I decided that I wasn't going to mention abuse at all, mainly because I felt that the real abuse had taken place at the first seminary and none of them had been there. However, as the pints flowed, the tongues loosened. The subject of abuse came up. One of them said, 'There wasn't any abuse at our seminary though, was there?' There was a silence. The diocesan priest suddenly stated in a very cold voice, 'The rector was a fucking

161

pervert.' The missionary priest ridiculed him and told him he was talking crap. From being of a very gentle disposition, the diocesan priest suddenly exploded in anger, 'Listen you, don't you tell me I'm talking crap. When I was off school with the flu, that man came in to my cubicle, pulled the covers back and fondled my balls!' The missionary priest tried to argue back that this was normal and that it had happened to us all. It didn't mean that the priest was a pervert. One of the other guys cut in, 'It certainly never happened to me.' The evening finished on a sour note. When the diocesan priest went home, the missionary priest called him for everything. He was so angry, I thought he was going to choke.

At the senior seminary where I studied for the priesthood, the rector's nephew was one of the students. He told me that the rector was dying of cancer. He went to visit him and told him that I was now training for the priesthood again in the diocesan senior seminary. The rector expressed delight at that and told his nephew that he had always liked me and thought that one day I would make a good priest. I was relieved that, in some small way, we had made our peace, even though it was at a distance. He also told him, concerning his impending death, that he had been with so many dying people as a priest and had helped them to die as best he could. He would now face this moment himself without fear or panic; he would follow the advice he had given to so many others. I would have expected nothing less from him. I could now add courage and bravery to his long list of qualities. The one fault he had exposed in himself no longer mattered to me. He died a few days later.

On my last day at school, I made my way to the Spanish exam hall, upstairs, in the library. The exam paper lay face-down on my desk. I just wanted to get on with it and get it over with. I remember feeling irritated that we had to wait until dead-on-time before we were allowed to start. Were they frightened that if they let us start early, one of us might run down the road to the Protestant school and tell them what the answer to the first question was? As the last minuscule micro-second, confirmed by Greenwich and verified by three stop-watches, ticked away, the invigilator invited us to turn over our exam papers and begin. The first part was a translation from Spanish to English. I could make sense of most of the first sentence, but one word, which I now realise was 'cheese', had me stumped. 'Pedro sat down at the table and ate his...case? His keys?' I just didn't know and I didn't care. I must have missed the class where Miguel and Maria had visited the cheese factory. I wondered for a moment if I would get away with just putting 'Tapas', then it suddenly happened. Five years of pain just surfaced in that instant. I just said 'Bollocks' and shoved the desk away from me. I stood up and walked towards the exit door. The invigilator shrieked, 'Where do you think you are going? Get back here immediately, boy.' I kept walking. Most of the pupils looked up from their exam papers. One swotty guy kept writing. He obviously knew the Spanish word for cheese. I walked out of the door and down the stairs. It seemed to take an age to get from there to the school gates where freedom beckoned. I had to get outside the gates, only then would it be all over and I would be safe. I stepped outside then leaned against the wall and just broke down and cried my heart out. I knew that the tears had been on their way for some time now.

I think of that moment every Holy Week when I read about how St Peter had wept bitterly when he betrayed Jesus three times. It was that type of crying that I was experiencing; it was heartfelt weeping. I had gone to primary school on a normal day as a happy-go-lucky kid, five years before. Now I was leaning against a secondary school wall, wailing. What the hell had happened? Someone asked me why I described my crying as like St Peter's. They made the point that his tears were to do with betrayal. Did I feel that I was betraying everyone, letting everyone down? Looking back, although I didn't realise it then, it was me, my fellow students, our parents and every decent Catholic who loved and trusted the Church, it was us who had been betrayed. I also honestly believe that the priests who had treated us so awfully, especially at the first junior seminary, had also been betrayed. They had gone to junior seminary years before me and they had had their minds and lives warped by the system. They never stood a chance; and for most of them, it is now too late.

I had heard about the life-story of St Francis of Assisi, how he had stripped himself naked in the town square and how he had gone off to start a new life with absolutely no possessions. I thought that I was doing the same, in a sense. I actually believed that I could just walk away and leave the past behind me. In actual fact, I didn't leave any of the past behind me; I just buried it. There was no stripping of memories. There was only the painful process of acknowledging them, and that was not to happen for years to come.

Chapter Thirteen

Within a few weeks of leaving the seminary, exam results arrived. I passed all of them except, of course, Spanish. A technician's job came up at Blood Transfusion. Common sense, and my dad, advised me not to take the job – I wasn't technically minded after all. I took the job. I absolutely loved it at first. My bosses were all very fair. If there was an argument between two members of staff, they carefully listened to both sides of the argument before giving their decision. They didn't just automatically side with the employee who happened to be furthest up the hierarchical ladder. There was a real sense of justice, honesty and common sense. There were unions which would represent you if you had a grievance. It made a refreshing change to what I had previously experienced.

I worked hard, but also enjoyed a laugh along the way. My immediate boss was Harry, the man with the gruff exterior and the heart of corn. He ran the laboratory on one simple rule: get the work done, then you can do what you want – within reason of course. Those first few months were carefree and eminently enjoyable. The best thing about work was the social life. That sounds a bit like saying that the best thing about work was not working, but you know what I mean. I loved the nights out with my colleagues. I loved them too much, possibly. I discovered lager in a big way.

Looking back, there were already a few danger signals on the horizon, other than the beer. I was still prone to becoming excruciatingly embarrassed from time to time. If the focus of attention fell on me, I tried to shift it on to someone else. I was always ready with a smart remark but, every now and again, I would get caught out and would feel my face going red. I still hated myself when that happened. Again I felt myself thinking, why couldn't I just be normal like everyone else? Why was I taking red faces so constantly? Another pointer to my inner turmoil was my fear of intimacy. If anyone got too close, I used humour to keep them at arm's length. The prospect of sex terrified me. I heard guys talking openly about women they had slept with. I again felt that I was abnormal, I had no sexual stories to tell, except for one – and I wasn't telling that one.

After a few years, the depressions began to start. The amount of energy I was expending trying to keep up my defences was beginning to take its toll. Everything for me was a laugh and a joke on the exterior. Inside, I felt that I was drowning. Harry would come up with weekends away to see Manchester United and of course, the magnificent World Cup trip to Spain. All that was happening was that I was searching for anything to help me avoid having to face what was buried deep within me.

I eventually decided that I had to make a change. I walked into Harry's office and informed him that I was leaving. I also told the head boss. When they asked what I was going to do with myself, I told them that I was going to be a priest. Harry still laughs to this day when he remembers that moment. I didn't exactly behave like priest material. I applied for the senior diocesan seminary and was accepted.

How I could even contemplate returning to a seminary after my previous encounters with them? I've struggled with that question. I had met various priests since I had started work and they all struck me as very admirable people. Maybe the diocesan priesthood was different from the missionary priesthood. One thing was for sure, I had taken on board the guilt of letting everyone down. If I became a priest, maybe, I thought, in my own screwed-up way, I would be respected again. Another certain factor in my decision was that the Pope had just made a very impressive visit to Scotland. I had shaken his hand and was moved by the occasion. The negative experiences of the Church had been buried deep and in its place there was something far more positive – on the surface. It's strange to think now, that I stood and applauded and cheered during the Papal visit. I was cheering a structure which had mistreated me; and now, I wanted to return to it.

On a deeper level, the question of why I went back has hung over me like a shroud for many years. It was a part of my life which I couldn't understand and I wasn't happy about that. The following reflection, written by my Uncle Tommy, helped me to shed some light on what may have been going on.

'We learn to deal with freedom as we develop as a child. Before we walk, our parents allow us to take risks as we learn to crawl up the stairs. They gradually allow us to take greater risks like taking steps on our own for the first time. In many ways, we are introduced to freedom. This involves risks for both parent and child. As we develop into adolescence, the parents take even more risks like allowing the fourteen-year-old to go to that first disco and allowing them to stay out late. In such steps, the youngster is introduced to freedom and hopefully learns the risks and responsibilities which go with it.

Consider a child moving into adolescence, who moves to a boarding school where the regime is very strict and authoritarian. The child's whole life is ordered by severe restrictions. After five years, the young person is faced with freedom when he walks out. In most similar situations faced by people whose freedom has been restricted, the normal reaction would be to gorge themselves in those areas where they had been deprived. The long-term prisoner may want cash, drink, a good time, sex. The young person leaving junior seminary would probably act in a similar fashion. However, due to what happened in the past, the young person's sexuality has been checked, his development frozen. Faced with the normal urges and needs of a young adult, he is unable to satisfy these needs. This leads to stress and anxiety or, given time, neurosis or worse. Once the facade of trying to appear normal becomes too much, he becomes depressed but doesn't know why. Would it not be natural, as one method of survival, to retreat to the environment which, because of its severe restrictions, could be a secure haven for this individual? Sexuality and its overt expression are forbidden in such a place.

This reflection helped me. Whether it is an accurate assessment of what happened to me, I suppose I'll never know. It certainly helped me to peel back the layers and look into myself. Whatever the real reason for my return to seminary, I honestly believe that it was a decision that saved my life. I was to find some sort of healing.

I received a letter from the seminary in Melrose, inviting me to a psychological screening weekend which was to take place before the first term started. If they had called it a 'come and see' weekend, I don't think I would have gone. The place seemed very friendly; there was a warmth about it which I perceived immediately. When I considered my arrival at the junior seminary and how shocked I was by it, this was the opposite. I liked the look and feel of this place. The other guys seemed just ordinary decent blokes. The screening consisted of hundreds of multiple choice questions which you had to answer, supposedly, as honestly as you could. A few of them were memorable. One question asked:

When you go into a new church for the first time, what is the first thing you notice?
A. The stained glass windows.
B. The wooden benches.
C. God's holy presence.

I remember thinking that anyone who answered 'C' would have to be watched carefully. We were assured that we needn't be afraid of the screening since it had no bearing on our acceptance into the seminary. We were told that we had to give an answer to each question – even if all the choices given were abhorrent to us, we had to choose the answer which we thought was nearest the truth. That became difficult when we got questions like:

I want to be a priest because:
A. I like dressing up in black.
B. I hate women.

I turned over the page to look for answer 'C' but there wasn't one. Those were our choices. You were either a deviant dresser or a misogynist. Help ma boab. I refused to put a tick in either box and just wrote underneath, 'None of the above'. I always wondered if any of the other guys answered that question.

I arrived at the senior seminary with a suitcase full of misconceptions as to what this place was all about. I had turned into an actor who was going to play the part of a pious little saint. I remember not even taking my fishing rod with me because I didn't want to give the priests the impression that I was here for a holiday. It took all of one day to knock that nonsense out of me. The new first years were to meet in the coffee lounge, an old room with an open fire and high ceiling. We were a mixed age group. Some guys had just left secondary school, others were in their thirties, forties or fifties. We all hushed as one of the priests entered the room and sat down to address us. His opening gambit was, 'Well, I suppose you'll all be a bit shagged out after your long journey here.' My jaw locked in the mouth open position. Did I hear him properly? I couldn't believe it! Imagine a Catholic priest using language like that! I was shocked and scandalised – like the true hypocrite I was.

I was to find out later that this college had gone through something of a revolution in the previous few years. A group of courageous priests had brought in changes in response to the Vatican II Council, and had revamped the senior seminary system. Someone described the college as 'trying to take you apart piece by piece, then building you up again with more solid thinking and more credible view points'. You just didn't get away with uncritically regurgitating the party line because that's what you had been taught by your granny; you had to justify any particular stance you took and 'Because the Pope says so' was not considered an acceptable intellectual argument.

I settled in well and really enjoyed college life. I soon realised that you didn't have to be a 'stuck-up sticky-beak' to be a priest...well, not in this place at any rate. I met some tremendous human beings who were trying to teach me that it was okay just to be me, warts and all. Unfortunately, the pious image I had projected in the first few days was to have unwelcome consequences for me. Each Wednesday afternoon we did a couple of hours manual labour. When it came to making up the various work squads, I was put on the library squad. I must have come across as a 'library type' person. I don't know if it was my previous experience with the library at junior seminary, but I didn't want to work in this one. I hated it, especially since all my mates were on the farm squad. After the first week, I decided that I would have to get out of the library and get on the farm squad. Again, I didn't see things in terms of commitment and responsibility at that stage; I didn't like the library, therefore I wanted out. It was as simple as that. Moral developmental psychologist, Lawrence Kohlberg, would have put me at stage two in his theory, I think. The punishment and reward stage.

Anyway, one of the priests came into the library, pushing a trolley which was overflowing with books. He wheeled them over to me and instructed me to place them all back on the shelves in their correct places. This was not a problem. I put all the blue books on one shelf, all the green ones on the next shelf, the red ones on the next and so on. When I had completed the task, I stood back to admire my work. The shelves looked magnificent. I stuck my head out into the aisle and shouted, 'Finished!' The chief librarian came over to inspect my handiwork. He said, 'What have you done?' I told him that I thought the books looked nicer when they were grouped in their colours. He shook his head and muttered something under his breath. He trotted out of the room and returned five minutes later to tell me that he had had a quiet word with the rector and that they had both agreed that my talents would be far better used on the farm. Happy days – a free transfer.

I skipped out of the library and headed towards the farm. My mates were in a field, picking potatoes. I shouted over to them, 'I've been promoted.' I told them what had happened and they all laughed at my ingenuity. One of the guys then handed me a bucket and began to give me a job description. It seemed quite easy. The priest would drive past in a tractor unearthing the said root vegetable. We were to pluck them from the earth, then chuck them in the bucket. Given that the potatoes were all the same colour, the task would be relatively uncomplicated – even for me. I began my new job with gusto. I had managed to get my bucket half filled when suddenly, there was a loud 'thwack!' The guy next to me was holding his head. Someone at the top end of the field had lobbed a potato at us. Retaliation was swift and brutal. We waited until the priest had driven past us in his wee tractor then, when he wasn't looking, we returned fire. Before long, potatoes filled the afternoon sky. I tried to lob one at a guy at the top of the field, but I didn't manage to get the thing airborne. It clouted one of my mates on the back of the head. I think the Americans would call it 'friendly potato'. The tractor engine was switched off abruptly and the priest roared at us to stop fighting and get on with the work. He started up the engine again and drove on.

My mate, Chris, next to me picked up a spud, but instead of placing it in his bucket, he launched it in the direction of the priest in the tractor. Now, if any of you play football, you will recognise this.

You know when you shoot at goal, at the very moment when you connect with the ball, you just know that it's going in the back of the net; or at golf, when you connect with the ball, you know immediately if you've hit a cracker or not. This was the same sort of feeling; I just knew this spud was going to be a home run. Whacko! It bounced off the tractor bonnet. The priest switched off the engine for a second time. I was totally shocked when he called out my mate's name and mine and told us to get over to him, pronto. I couldn't believe it. How did he know who it was? This guy was psychic. A sound, verbal ear-bashing was delivered to us both. Later on, I asked the priest how he had known that we were the culprits. (I wasn't the culprit but for some reason, I always seem to want to share the blame.) He said that it was easy. When the spud had connected with the tractor, everybody in the field had looked up to find out what had caused the noise. My mate and I were the only two who kept our heads down and carried on working. It was a dead give-away.

In many other seminaries, that incident would have been enough to earn you a red card, or as we said in our place, 'a ticket up the drive'. Not here though. Here was a Church where it wasn't a sin to have a laugh now and again. These priests had departed from the notion that the only men worthy of ordination were prim and proper cardboard cut-outs. Many other senior seminaries were filled with students who had been plucked from the Catholic middle class. This place wasn't like that. The inhabitants here were ex-plumbers, joiners, sparks and the like. This place was taking in the same type of people that Jesus himself had urged to 'Follow me.' Unlike other seminaries I've experienced, it was attempting to produce men who weren't interested in 'being greeted obsequiously in the market place and taking the front seats in the Synagogue'. The priests here weren't opting for safety; they were taking a risk and giving some scope for that thing we call 'The Holy Spirit'. I loved it.

The seminary had a very open and relaxed ethos. Very few rules were imposed from above. Decisions were very often arrived at through common consensus. There would be a monthly house meeting where the students and priests discussed issues concerning the running of the house and voted on them, if need be. Sometimes the priests would openly disagree with one another in front of the students, in a very charitable way. Certain things which had been features of other seminaries for years, had been dumped on the scrap heap here. Addressing the priests as 'Father' was out. We were all on first name terms, students and priests alike. Another welcome change was that the bell was no longer used to regulate the daily timetable. Seminaries were traditionally ruled by the bell. The bell told you when to get out of bed, when to go to church, when to go to lectures, meals, everything. You had to use your initiative for matters like going to the toilet, but everything else was heralded by a bell. The rule in this seminary had been changed. There was a recognition that the twentieth century was, indeed, well and truly upon us and that we were all equipped with watches. If something was beginning at half-past nine, it was your responsibility to get your butt there on time. This, again, was a refreshing development. Clerical garb too, was a thing of the past. It was only worn by the priests when they went to celebrate a Mass outside the college.

One other change to the normal seminary routine was noteworthy. Most priests are familiar with the Latin phrase Magnum Silentium; it means 'the Great Silence'. A bell would sound at nine or ten o'clock at night, depending on which particular seminary you were in, and there was to be complete silence until the bell was rung again the following morning. In this seminary, Magnum Silentium had been kicked out on its arsium. Like so many things in the Church, the original idea was basically very good; we need time to be still, to be quiet, to reflect on our lives, to pray. But, as usual, omnipotent, moral busybodies had taken the theory and turned it into something it was never meant to be. In many seminaries, it had become a stick with which to beat the unfortunate inhabitants of the place. The silence became oppressive – a discipline rather than an invitation to be with God. In our seminary, the Great Silence was replaced by the much less threatening Quiet Time. It was two hours in the afternoon when we were asked to respect those who wished to study or pray…or sleep. Effectively, all it meant was no snooker or five-a-side football. I could cope with that.

Life at this seminary was not without its periods of silence. We would have three retreats every year, each lasting anywhere between three days and a week. There were also numerous days of recollection, which were run along the same lines as retreats. A retreat was basically spiritual time-out. We would pray, read and reflect. There was always some input from an invited priest or nun. They would generally give a talk in the morning and in the evening. They would also make themselves available if any of the students wanted to go and have a chat with them. At first, I enjoyed the retreats. They reminded me of the sponsored silences at primary school. However, I grew to detest them. Again, I began to think of myself as somehow abnormal; most of the other guys seemed to enjoy them.

Since then, I read a book where the author claims that the whole history of Western spirituality has been geared towards the introvert – people who are energised by silence. What about the rest of us who are merely irritated by it? Ever since I read that book, I believed that my discomfort with retreats was because I was an extrovert. Silence can drain the extrovert, who is energised by activity and commotion. Maybe that was partly true for me. However, now I know the real reason I didn't like retreats: they were geared towards personal reflection. They were an invitation for you to go into your life, to discover who you were. You were encouraged to peel away the layers, the masks, and go on a journey of self-discovery. Now I realise what my discomfort was – I couldn't go into my past. I was emotionally unable to dredge up the pain of the past. I couldn't peel back the layers; I was too terrified of what I might find. This was not a conscious decision on my part – I simply didn't have the key to unlock the door to my inner self. An inbuilt mechanism was blocking any chance of me acknowledging and owning what had happened to me.

I was however beginning to change radically as a person. The lectures were expanding my mind and making me ask questions which, up to that point, I hadn't even imagined. Also, living with a group of people who were, for the most part, genuinely trying to live the Gospel, influenced me greatly. I began to develop an awareness of issues which I had never deemed to be part of the remit of Christianity. I learned about the Church in other parts of the world. I heard the term 'justice' for the first time and found out how so many people in our world struggle for it. I realised that incidents such as the sinking of the General Belgrano were not, in fact, the unfortunate by-products of a necessary war; such incidents were wicked atrocities. We didn't just look at what events had taken place in history, we asked why they had taken place and what the consequences were. For the first time, I really listened to sermons at Mass. The priests had to prepare them well because they couldn't just ramble on about nonsense to this congregation; they wouldn't get away with it.

While we worked and learned we were also allowed a good laugh along the way. One of the funniest events at senior seminary happened during my first couple of years there. Two of us had been out in the local town one afternoon. I went into a shop to buy cigarettes. As I waited in the queue, my mate nudged me and pointed to a shelf containing videos. I couldn't believe my eyes. On the front cover of one of the videos was a lady, naked from the waist up – not that you could see her waist; she had the most enormous breasts I had ever seen. My mate quipped that if she had been on the Titanic, it would never have sunk. They weren't natural; they must have been photographically enhanced or something. On what little space there was left on the cover of the video, the title *Two Hot Pies* was written. I just collapsed in a heap, laughing. I couldn't even buy my cigarettes; I had to leave the shop.

When we got back to the seminary, the rector, Jimmy, was just leaving to go and say Mass at a local hospital. He was a great guy. He asked us if we wanted anything in the town. We all said no. Suddenly, a microcosm of an idea crept into my mind. I shouted after him just as he was going out of the door, 'Would you pick up a video for us?' He seemed slightly irritated by my request. 'What's it called?' he sighed. My mate and I replied together, *Two Hot Pies*. The rector started shouting that he would never remember the name of it. Little did he know then…he would never forget the name of it. I quickly found a pen and wrote the name down on a scrap of paper. He stuffed it into the pocket of his black clerical shirt, fixed his collar and headed off to say Mass. We then told everyone what we had done.

Approximately an hour and a half later, I was sitting on my windowsill, looking down towards the car park. I suddenly heard a car engine roaring; it was someone coming up the drive at some speed. The car screeched to a halt in the middle of the car park and Jimmy jumped out, leaving the door open, and shouted up at me 'Gilhooley!

You're dead meat! I'm going to bloody murder you!' With that, he ran towards the stairs that led to my corridor. I nonchalantly flicked my cigarette out the window into orbit and made my way to the landing at the top of the stairs. As I heard the footsteps rushing up the stairs, I unravelled the fire hose. When Jimmy came round the last bend, I pointed the hose at him and told him to stand back. Out of puff, he shouted, 'You wouldn't dare – ' Splosh! He got it full blast! When he was suitably drenched, I dropped the hose – and ran for it. I thought he would give up the chase and get me later on in his office. He didn't; he wanted to give me a kick-in right then.

When he eventually caught me, he was too tired to hit. His punches were just pretend; I knew he had enjoyed the laugh. Instead of demanding an explanation, he started to tell me what happened. He had gone into the shop and joined the back of the queue. The woman at the counter saw him and, much to the annoyance of the other customers, she served him first because he was a priest. He said that he was just in to pick up a video for the lads. She asked the title. '*Two Hot Pies*.' came the reply. Everyone in the shop started to giggle. The assistant said, 'I don't think you'll be wanting that video, Father.' The rector then went into his pocket and produced the scrap of paper and said, 'No, it's definitely *Two Hot Pies*, Look, it's written there.' By this time, some customers were bent over the counter screaming. The assistant pointed to the video. The rector said he was absolutely horrified. He slunk out of the shop to howls of laughter. To my knowledge, he never went back to that shop again. Jimmy had a sense of humour and saw the funny side of it all.

Come summer time, I was forced to begin to take things seriously. My report for the year, affectionately called the 'scroot' (scrutinium), was very negative. I was a good prospect – blah, blah, blah, I had heard all that before – but I needed to apply myself more to college life. I was also called 'crude and bolshie'. I was irritated that the priest who had called me crude and bolshie was the very same priest who had told us on the first day that we would probably all be 'shagged out'. I argued that this was totally hypocritical. When I look back now, I was living in cloud cuckoo land. If I had been the rector, I would probably have kicked me out. I needed a good boot up the arse for the way I was behaving but, at the time, I just didn't see it.

News reached us that summer term that a decision had been made that the college was to close. We were all to move, to an ex-convent school in the centre of Edinburgh, after the summer. The rector asked for volunteers to work over the summer, to move the contents of the college up to Edinburgh. A group of us volunteered to work, for a modest fee of course. The main work involved dismantling my beloved library, then rebuilding it in Edinburgh. I must admit, as we began the demolition work, my heart sank. I had become very attached to this place – the college, that is, not the library. I know this to be the case for many priests in Edinburgh. There was something special about this seminary. For me, there was a feeling that we were closing more than a building here. Still, nostalgia and sentimentality wouldn't get the books up to Edinburgh. We rolled up the sleeves and got stuck in.

I spent the first few weeks of that summer at the college, taking things apart. After a while, I moved to Edinburgh and began to help with the rebuilding process at the new college. One afternoon, someone came into the new, half-built library and told me that there was a phone call for me. It was the housekeeper from the old college at Melrose. She was very upset and asked if I could get back there as quickly as possible. I asked her what on earth was wrong. She told me that Jimmy had been carted off to hospital and that someone would need to come back to direct operations from there.

I returned immediately to the college to find out what had happened. Jimmy had some sort of heart problem. I told the housekeeper to tell him that I would take care of things and that he didn't need to worry about the rest of the move to Edinburgh. I didn't see him for the remainder of the summer holidays. We eventually finished the removal of the library. The new term began at the new college. Some things were complete and ready for the new term, other things, like our rooms, weren't.

The first year at the new place was difficult but enjoyable. I don't think anyone realised how much work the change of venues would take. Moving locations was the easy bit. I still hadn't settled down; I don't mean settled down to the new college, I mean settled down to life in general. I still persisted in having a carry-on at every opportunity. I was a manic 'don't take anything seriously' type of person, except when I retired to my own room at night and was faced only with myself. The last thing I said at night, before I went to sleep, wasn't my prayers; I kidded myself on about something or other. I reassured myself that everything was okay. It wasn't.

Something happened that year which was to set me on my road to semi-recovery. We were at the stage of doing a course on sexual morality. As part of the course, a sex psychologist was invited to lecture us. He spoke about many things, including sexual deviancy – of all types, but the part which caught my attention was the section on paedophiles. He stated quite categorically that children who had been abused, if they did not get treatment or therapy, would grow to an adulthood where they themselves would become abusers of children. The lecturer didn't know it, but his words were devastating to me. (A detective who worked in sex crimes, later told me that the abused automatically becoming abusers was a nonsense. Very often, those who have been abused become totally protective towards children and will not trust any adult who goes near them.)

I remember taking a red face when the lecturer spoke those words. I had become expert at hiding my red faces and insecurities. I hid this one as well. But for the first time, things which I had kept deep within me began to surface with some venom. I sat in that class and got angry. I had been abused and had had my teenage years robbed from me. Now this guy was telling me that I would become a child-abuser myself. I envisaged myself spending the second half of my life banged up in prison. It was the first real conscious recognition in all those years that I had been abused. I did not have any sexual orientation towards children but I was thinking that maybe it just happens. Maybe a switch just clicks and you end up doing something wicked to a child. The positive thing about that lecture for me was that it brought the unpalatable truth of my past to the surface for the first time. The lecturer was stating that child abuse has an effect in adulthood. I was now 'thinking' about what had happened to me, consciously. I had never done that before.

There was another reason that I found myself thinking about events at junior seminary very often that year. Each student had been given a pastoral placement for the year. It could range from being a simple parish placement to a more specialised area such as a hospital, a hospice or a school, for example. That year, my placement had been Saughton Prison.

The Home Office had granted special permission for a student priest to join the inter-denominational pastoral team at the prison. The staff at the college seemed to think that I would be the natural choice. The Catholic prison chaplain phoned to arrange for us to meet in the prison car park on the Sunday morning. We would then both go in for Mass. Before he hung up the phone he asked, 'You play the guitar, don't you? Right, bring the guitar with you and you can play some hymns for the lads.' I thought, 'Oh God, no. This guy thinks I'm Johnny Cash.'

I was really nervous as his car pulled into the car park. He stepped out and said, 'I thought you were going to bring your guitar?' I lied that it had completely slipped my mind. He smiled knowingly and quipped, 'I thought you might forget, that's why I brought one along for you myself.' He then produced a guitar from the boot of his car. My heart sank. I envisaged me sitting singing 'Kumbaya My Lord' while all these hardened criminals growled at me. As we walked along the corridor to the sound of keys jingling and gates opening and closing, I pictured hundreds of unshaved men with half of their teeth missing and all their tattoos spelt wrongly. In fact, I couldn't have been more wrong. I very quickly realised that these men were, for the most part, very ordinary people who had themselves been victims – of poverty, of their own stupidity, of drugs, alcohol and so on. That is not to say that there were no truly evil people in prison. I met some men who gave out an aura of real evil. I felt very uncomfortable in their presence.

In the months that lay ahead, I would go into the prison on a Sunday morning, then again on a Wednesday afternoon. Most times, I was accompanied by the priest. On one of the few occasions that I went off to see a prisoner on my own, two guards grabbed me in the corridor and slung me in a cell. They thought I was an escapee. When the priest eventually liberated me, he was pissing himself laughing. He thought it was brilliant. There were other days when we would be walking through the halls and a con would shout down from the landing, 'Stevie, what are you in for?' – I knew some of the prisoners from my childhood. The priest tried his best to keep a straight face, but I think he found it hilarious. I think he thought that I blended in really well.

The place was certainly no holiday camp. During one visit, we had to deal with a guy who had been smashed around the head with a metal pole. His head looked like a butcher's shop window. Those who attacked him had also emptied an urn of boiling water over his genitals. He showed us; nothing was recognisable from his waist down. His crime? He happened to have the same name as a paedophile; it was a case of mistaken identity. Nobody seemed to be all that upset though, except the prisoner – and me.

Our remit also involved ministering to child-sex offenders. They were the most hated people in prison. I often saw other inmates hissing at these offenders and making a sign of cutting their throat or slashing them. I did not hate them or even feel anger at them. My main emotion towards them was one of pity. I didn't think of what they had done in the past, nor what they might do in the future. I just saw them as they were at that moment; they were a pathetic, frightened group of people. I don't know if my anger was so deep-seated that I wasn't even aware of it. I do know that I didn't like the threats or the violence or the hate mail they received. I wanted no part of that carry-on. I realise now why my experiences at the junior seminary surfaced so often at that time; I was being confronted with sex offenders twice a week for most of that year.

During all this time, I said nothing to my spiritual director, Pat, about what was going on in my head. I believe he knew that something was wrong, but he couldn't unlock the door for me. He must have had enormous patience over those three years as he watched me dancing around the main issue, suppressing the truth. The bouts of depression returned but I did not connect them at all with junior seminary. Again, it was that awful depression that gives you a constant knot in the stomach and you don't know what is causing it or you would do something to make it stop. I decided that I wasn't going to be a priest and that I was going to leave. Basically, I was just running away again.

One evening in my fourth year, I was sitting at my desk, unable to muster up any enthusiasm to work, when I just made the decision, there and then – I was leaving. I walked along the corridor intending to knock on the spiritual director's door…but paused for a moment, trying to consider the gravity of what I was about to do. I turned round and went back to my room. Five minutes later, I did the same again, I went to his door. When I returned to the room the second time, I decided that the problem was just that I was thinking about it too much. I told myself to blank out my mind and just go and do it. So, this time, I walked along the corridor more speedily, went straight up to the door and knocked. There, it was done. Then, the strangest thing occurred; when Pat opened the door, he didn't say anything; he just looked at me. I moved my lips to say, 'Pat, I'm leaving' but those were not the words that came out. 'Pat, I was abused at the junior seminary…' I couldn't believe it. For the first time since it happened, I had told it to another human being. I think in many ways I was also acknowledging it to myself for the very first time.

He invited me in. Pat was a very gentle listener. I began to tell him the story from the beginning, but I kept breaking down. I think I felt ashamed and guilty. What I told him was very disjointed but I did the best I could to dredge up what had happened. In some ways, I think Pat seemed relieved. He said that I had been like a jigsaw with a vital piece missing. Now that we had found the missing piece, the rest of the jigsaw made sense. I can't remember everything that was said but I know that we finished up by praying, and Pat doing a kind of healing service where he anointed me. He said that I was very tense and shaky, so he poured a dram for us both. Eventually, the shaking eased off and the knot in my stomach disappeared. From that day to this, I have never again experienced those depressions which seemed to have so marked that period of my life.

Before I left his room, Pat said that we would work on this for spiritual direction for the rest of the year. He promised that he'd help me and told me not to worry – things were going to be okay. He also added that it might be an idea to put Jimmy, the rector, in the picture. As I went back to my room, I experienced an incredible sense of relief and liberation – I was free. In reality, I wasn't free, but it was a first step, a mighty step, along the road.

It was several weeks later, after Mass one Sunday morning, that I went to see Jimmy. As I began to speak, the smile on his face disappeared. Like Pat, he felt that I had just given him the answer to a riddle. He said he had been trying to suss me out and could never quite understand what made me tick. Now he understood me more. He actually apologised to me for what had happened. I told him that it wasn't his fault but he replied that we were all responsible for such things – all of us. He promised me his support and said that he wanted me to come and have a blether with him every few weeks. He said that the Church had done me a serious wrong and he, as a member of that Church, wanted to help in the healing process.

For the next few weeks, many things began to slot into place. Pat had once told me that some of the students were frightened of me because of my barbed sense of humour; with just one comment or jibe I could demolish or humiliate someone, in a crowded room, and have everyone laugh at him. That type of thing began to stop. I found myself using humour for humour's sake and not as a cover for my own insecurities; the constant red faces became a thing of the past; I joined the rest of the human race and, from then on, only took a red face when I did something stupid, as normal people do; I noticed that I could give and receive a hug without putting up my arms defensively; I became more confident in my own intuition and views. Many things changed for me. Then an utter catastrophe happened.

Jimmy came up to my room at the morning coffee break. I had asked him for a loan because, well, because I was skint, that's why. Jimmy came bouncing into the room and grabbed me by the cheek. 'Here,' he joked, 'And don't spend it all in the one pub.' He spied, on my wall, a framed photograph of myself surrounded by a group of Africans. I had recently spent three months in Africa visiting some priests. I looked like the only bottle of milk in a crate. He pointed to it and started poking fun at me, 'I hope you behaved yourself when you were over there. Well – did you?' I told him jokingly to shut up and get out because I had a lecture to go to. He looked at his watch and declared that he had better get a move on as well. He was going off to say Mass at a secondary school in the city. As he opened the door to walk out, I called on him. He turned around. I held up the envelope with the money and winked at him, 'Thanks, Jimmy.' He smiled and ran up the stairs to get changed to go to the school. Jimmy dropped dead as he was changing. 'Thanks, Jimmy' were the last words he heard on this earth. It was somehow appropriate because so many people owed a debt of gratitude to him.

Totally unaware of what had happened, I went off to my next lecture. Five minutes into that lecture, Pat arrived. He said that an ambulance was here and that something was seriously wrong with Jimmy. The lecturer tried to continue, then realised that we were all in shock. He dismissed the class. Some guys went to the church, others to their rooms. I went down to the car park where the ambulance was waiting. They carried Jimmy out on a stretcher. They worked on him in the car park. They thumped at his heart with the defibrillator. Jimmy's arms flew in the air, then fell back down to each side of the stretcher, motionless. One of the students shouted out, 'Come on, Jimmy, fucking fight.' They lifted him into the ambulance. One of the priests went with them. They drove off. It was the last time I ever saw Jimmy.

We walked back up the stairs and gathered in one of the students' rooms. None of us could even contemplate that Jimmy wouldn't pull through. We went back downstairs for lunch, although nobody could eat. The phone rang. One of the priests ran to take the call. There was a hush when he returned. We waited for the magic words, 'It's okay, lads, Jimmy is going to be fine.' Those words never came. The priest stated that Jimmy had died. He was forty-one years old.

The priest began a prayer for the dead, 'Out of the depths I cry to you, Oh Lord...' I didn't want to pray. I stood outside the refectory, just numb. Pat came out and asked me if I knew where Jimmy's mum lived. I did know, because she lived in the parish which covered Saughton Prison, where I had worked. We jumped in the car and headed out to tell her the grim news. When we got there, I couldn't remember which house it was. I knew that it was one of two. Pat said he would go to one house, I would go to the other. As I opened the gate, Jimmy's mum looked out of the window. She smiled and began to wave. I could see her mouthing the words, 'Hello, Steve, come in, come in.' I turned and shouted to Pat, 'It's this house, here, Pat.' I looked back at the old lady again. Her smile stopped when she saw Pat. I saw her mouthing, 'My God, what's wrong?' She disappeared from the window and opened the front door. She asked out loud, 'Don't tell me Jimmy is sick again?' Pat put his arms round her and whispered softly, 'I'm so sorry, Bella. Jimmy has just died.' She collapsed into his arms sobbing, 'No, no. Not my bairn Jimmy.' I got the phone number for Jimmy's brother's work. I asked him to come to his mum's as soon as possible. He asked if his mum was ill. I replied that she wasn't but could he come quickly. He asked if it was Jimmy, was Jimmy ill? I didn't want to, but I had to tell him over the phone. His brother wasn't ill, he was dead.

Pat and I stayed until other members of the family arrived to comfort each other, then we drove back to the college. When I stepped out of the car in the college car park, I saw, on the tarmac where the medic team had tried in vain to resuscitate Jimmy, a surgeon's rubber glove. It brought it home to me that what had happened was not a dream; Jimmy was gone. I can only imagine how his family felt, but at the college the sense of grief and loss was overwhelming. I don't think the college ever actually recovered from Jimmy's death. In many ways, he had been the life and soul of the college. To this day, the presence of someone like him is missed in the Church in Scotland. A dimension to what it means to be a Catholic in Scotland has gone. He was no plaster-cast saint and never claimed to be, but that's exactly the point. In the following days, someone asked me if I would like to go to view Jimmy's body. I declined the invitation. I would remember Jimmy chasing me along the corridor after he had tried to purchase *Two Hot Pies* for us. That would be my memory. Jimmy never once, to my knowledge, stood up and told the establishment to shove it. Secretly, I think he often wanted to – and he quietly supported those of us who did.

That year we all went off on the annual week-long retreat. During one of the sessions, we were split up into groups of four and asked to draw what was called 'a path of life'. This entailed drawing small pictures to symbolise different stages of our lives. I think the idea was that pictures can often convey much more than words. We were then asked to share with the other three people in the group, what each picture represented. I explained that the sunshine I had drawn was the trip to the World Cup, the pint of beer represented the six years I had worked. If I had been honest, I'd have said the beer represented what was my main hobby during that time. When I had finished, I waited for the next person to begin his story. There was a silence – then a guy whom I had previously not really got on with, pointed to the black cloud I had drawn and said gently, 'Steve, do you want to tell us what that is?' For the first time, I began to explain to my peer group something of what had happened to me at the junior seminary. From that moment, instead of fearing that I would be rejected, I experienced acceptance and understanding. Again, it was a step on the road towards healing.

We were taught different methods of praying during that retreat. One of them was 'Ignatian contemplation'. It was to be an important experience for me. I had told people what had happened at the seminary and had been accepted by them. I had not, however, told God. That may again seem strange to the non-religious reader, but it was important in terms of my own self-esteem and feelings of self-worth. We gathered in the small chapel, which was lit only by candles. It was a very relaxing atmosphere. The priest asked us to close our eyes and imagine our favourite place. I imagined the place where we had camped on the banks of the River Yarrow. I could hear the sound of the river, the wind blowing through the trees. He told us to put ourselves in that favourite place. Too late, I was already there. I sat down on the pebbles and stones beside the river. The priest continued softly, 'In the distance you can see the figure of a man…He's walking slowly towards you…' In my mind's eye, I could see this man and I also knew who it was. It was Christ. He came straight up to me and stood in front of me. I sat there and stared at the stones around his feet. Then the most amazing thing happened. The priest said, 'If you are staring at the ground, look up. Look at his face…Look into his eyes…' How did the priest know that I was so ashamed, I was staring at the ground? I looked up and into Christ's eyes. They weren't condemning me. The priest then asked us to speak to Christ in our hearts and tell him whatever we wished. I told him about the abuse and the beatings then stopped, waiting for him to speak. He smiled. His lips began to move. He said, 'It's okay.' I was suddenly engulfed in what I can only describe as total love. I don't know how long I sat there, immersed in that tenderness, but when I came out of it, everyone else had left the room. The effect of those few moments on my life has been profound. The guilt and shame had gone. It was as if an anvil had been hanging over me all of my life. I had got so used to it that I no longer realised it was there. It was only when it had been taken from me that I realised the tremendous weight I had been carrying all along. After all those years, Peter Perfect had eventually arrived and saved me from the Hooded Claw.

At the seminary, I was now at the stage where I just wanted out. Not 'out' out; I wanted 'ordained' out. We had returned to the days of being required to call some of the priests 'Father' again. I found myself doing things to which I totally objected in conscience, but for the sake of being ordained, I had to kowtow. I was ordained deacon in 1989 and began to work in one of the biggest parishes in the archdiocese. It was a tremendous learning environment for me. The deacons were required to return to the college for an overnight stay once every two weeks.

During that year, I met a girl with whom I had worked at the Blood Transfusion Service, six years before. She had moved on as well. She told me that she had been in counselling for some time now so I asked her what was wrong. As she spoke, I found myself understanding exactly what she was saying. She was telling me my story. She had been going through terrible depressions and didn't know why. One night, her sister had left her in her flat, to catch the last train to Glasgow to visit her parents. When her sister had gone, she had swallowed two bottles of tablets in an attempt to take her own life. Fortunately, her sister had missed the last train to Glasgow and had returned to the flat to find her lying unconscious on the floor. This was no 'cry for help' – she had intended to end it all. It was a pure fluke that her sister had come back to the flat. She was rushed to hospital where her stomach was pumped. I asked her why she had tried to take her own life; it had emerged in counselling that she had been seriously abused as a young girl. She started recounting to me various incidents I could remember from our workdays. She was saying things like, 'Remember how I always used to take a red face, remember how I would never take anything seriously…' She told me that much of her behaviour had simply been a front. I told her that I had been doing exactly the same thing.

I came away from that meeting realising that there must be a pattern to such things. Following Jimmy's death, I'd put my own journey on hold; now, I began thinking about it again. What about the other guys who had been at junior seminary with me, who had suffered a great deal more than I had; had they too experienced depressions and so on?

The night before my ordination was my 'stag night'. (Well, I considered it a kind of wedding.) I was over the moon when friends from the past turned up at it, and was moved by the amount of good wishes that were expressed. People turned up from various stages of the whole of my life, from my earliest childhood. The only institution not represented was Saughton Prison – seemingly, they wouldn't let them out for the night.

The church was relatively small, so many people crammed into the adjoining hall, to watch the proceedings on closed circuit TV. Considering the whole carry-on I had been through from the age of eleven, I had expected to be really emotional that night. But I wasn't. I was fine. The only time I felt a lump in my throat was when I thanked Jimmy, in his absence, for all his goodness to me. I thanked the whole seminary staff, those I had got on with and those I sometimes had wanted to meet in a dark close. I had received a letter from my old spiritual director, Pat. He had advised me to look on my senior seminary training as a whole and not to retain anger or bitterness towards any one part of it; I had already arrived at that conclusion myself. I knew that the senior seminary had totally changed me as a person and had helped me in so many ways. I am, and will remain, totally in debt to the priests and students I met during those six years: those who made me want to emulate their gifts and qualities, and those who made me decide, by their actions, that I would never act like that should the day ever dawn when I became a priest. I have nothing but admiration for many priests. It was priests who hurt me, but it was also priests who saved me. It has been frustrating to read some comments about this book in which some people have attacked me for criticising the clergy. You cannot state, and I am not stating, that all the clergy are bad. Some clergy are pitiful human beings, others are brilliant. The best human beings I have ever met in my life happen to be Catholic priests. Some of the worst people I have ever met, also happen to be priests. That's life, is it not?

There was no sit-down meal for five hundred afterwards. There were a couple of speeches and a cup of tea or a glass of wine, then everyone was invited to the pub. That was my choice; I wanted it that way, although some people found it difficult to understand my thinking. I did take out for a meal all those who had worked so hard in organising the ordination. I was appreciative of what they had done and am forever grateful to them.

I had been invited to return to my primary school to say a Mass and we had arranged it for the Monday morning after my ordination. I had invited my ex-spiritual director, Pat, to concelebrate the Mass, the reason being that Pat had been born in my home town. When he had been newly ordained, he had gone back to the same school to say Mass. I had been in primary one at the time and I could remember that Mass. He had given all the kids an ordination card that was in the style of a brightly coloured stained-glass window. Two decades later, when I went to my first spiritual direction in senior seminary, I saw the same card pinned to Pat's 'rogue's gallery' on his office wall. I realised then who Pat was.

It was a weird experience to go back as a priest; a wee primary one boy was sitting on the end of the bench where I had sat in 1967 during Pat's Mass. So much had happened since I'd sat on that bench. My prayer that day was that these children would grow up free of the constraints which had caused me so much pain – obviously it was a silent prayer. My sermon was simply meant to give the kids a laugh. My aim, as it has always been with youngsters, was to leave them with the feeling that, 'That guy is a priest, he represents God and he's okay.' No need to go into an in-depth discussion of the Hypostatic Union here. The sad thing was that for three of the children sitting in the school gymnasium at Mass that day, life was to deal them a far crueller blow than it ever dealt me. Three of those children tragically died during their teenage years. I didn't know it then, but I would be attending their funerals before many years had passed. Today, that thought tends to give me a sense of perspective with regard to my own life. At least I'm still alive.

Chapter Fourteen

I was given my first appointment as an assistant priest in 1990. I didn't really care which parish I was to be sent to; my concern was more to do with which parish priest I was going to. When I found out, I was over the moon. My parish priest was to be Ben, the same guy who had greeted us, on our first day at senior seminary, with the question as to how 'shagged out' we were after our journeys. We had become good friends at seminary so I knew we would be fine in the parish. One Friday night another young student and I had knocked on the staffroom door. When Ben answered, we asked him if he would like to come out for a pint with us. He later told us how much he had appreciated that night; no one had ever asked him out for a pint before. The following year, when the other student left the college, this priest had given him £300 to see him by until he found a job. We were going to be just fine in the parish. There was a slight cloud over the whole thing: Ben was at present in hospital. He had some sort of heart trouble, but I was assured that he was going to fine.

Ben felt that there was nothing in the parish for the young adults and he seemed to think that he lacked the ability to reach them. I was to be the catalyst to get them involved in the church again. We agreed that I would run a weekend for over-eighteens. When I announced it from the pulpit, only six or seven signed up, so I went down the local pub, where I knew all the young folk were, and made them sign up for it. I was able to announce to the priest that we had about fifty names. Then I worried that some of the youngsters would take cold feet at the last minute and wouldn't turn up on the Friday night. One of them was a bit of a cool dude. He was looked up to by many of them. I knew that if he would come along, many of the others would come too, so I worked on him. Eventually he came along, and so did the rest of them.

The weekend was magnificent. I knew that in my own life I had stored up things that I was too frightened to tell others. The weekend was geared towards freeing the young people from the things that shackled them. One of the most difficult sessions was the one on sexuality. I was worried that it would be too embarrassing for them, that they wouldn't be able to cope with it and that the weekend would grind to a halt. I needn't have worried. One of the team stepped forward to start the input, saying, 'Section Seven. Sexuality.' Suddenly the cool dude in the corner said, 'Ya beauty!' The place erupted into fits of laughter. All the nervous tension was released and they settled down to what became one of the most powerful sessions of that weekend.

We had spent the Saturday digging deep into ourselves and dredging up and facing things that had hurt us. Many of the young folk spoke for the first time in their lives about things like being bullied at school, their parents' separation, and so on. The following morning, after the Masses, a number of bleary-eyed parents accosted me outside the church. They asked what on earth I was doing with their sons and daughters. They had been up all night listening to these 'new people' talking about how the weekend was brilliant and how the church was relevant after all.

The following day the parish priest, away on a visit to his mother, phoned to ask how the weekend had gone. I assured him that it had been a huge success. When he returned to the parish, there would be fifty young people seeking a meeting with the two of us to discuss how they could become involved in the Church. I knew by the tone of his voice that he was chuffed to bits. I was on a high as well. I was pleased at the generous response from the young folk.

I still had that feeling of optimism a couple of days later, when the phone rang at about eight in the morning. It was a priest I had known at seminary. He was phoning from Ben's mother's house. Ben was dead. I refused to take him seriously. His voice became more urgent. 'Steve, listen to me. Sit down and listen to me. This is no joke. I've just anointed him. He's dead.'

Still in a state of shock, I went over to the church to get ready for Mass at ten o'clock. Sometimes there were up to sixty or seventy people for a weekday Mass. How could I tell them? What words were there to explain? At the beginning of Mass, I asked them all to sit down, and just told them straight out – their much-loved priest was dead. Some people burst out crying, others gasped, others sat and quietly sobbed. I struggled to get through the rest of the Mass. He was only in his early fifties. How could this happen? It just wasn't fair.

At the weekend Masses, I made an appeal to the people: I told them what Ben had asked of me in terms of the music in the parish. He had wanted me to modernise it and have it in place one year from then. I told them how he had loved the music we had played at the seminary and that his aim had been to get that style of music introduced into our parish. He knew that he didn't have either the time or the ability to do it himself, but he knew that I had. I explained that we didn't have a year to do it now – we had four days; it was important to me that the transition to the new music be completed in time for his funeral. I asked for anyone who could play an instrument or sing to come to the church each evening at seven o'clock to prepare for the funeral; they came in their droves. The music at the funeral was tremendous. It was heartfelt and sincere, as well as excellent – some of the many priests who had turned up said so. Others criticised me for playing the guitar instead of being on the altar, which was my rightful place as his assistant priest, they claimed. The grief I felt was too much for me to give a damn what any of them said. I knew that we, his people, had given him a good send-off. That was all that mattered to me at the time.

I can't really explain how I felt in the following months. I still hadn't really recovered from Jimmy's death when Ben had died. Funerals were nineteen to the dozen in the parish, but I never once said to any of the grieving families, 'I know how you feel.' I didn't know how they felt. How could I? I didn't even know how I felt. It was difficult to move between the funerals, the happy baptisms, the visits to the terminally ill, the exuberance of the young people, the family problems and so on. It was as if I had to take a sad head off and suddenly put on a happy one ten minutes later. It came to the stage where the 'theory' about priesthood clashed headlong with the actual praxis.

One evening, I brought the remains of a man I had known reasonably well into the church. His family wanted to go to confession, as was the usual practice, to make everything right for the funeral. His widow came into the confessional box and tried to begin to tell me her sins. She just cried, unable to formulate any words. For God's sake, her husband was lying in a coffin yards away, no wonder she couldn't speak. As I sat on the other side of the curtain, listening to her sobs, I suddenly asked the question, 'What kind of a God are you? Is this really what you want, to listen to someone in such anguish rattling off a shopping list of sins?' I pulled the curtain open, stretched out my arms to the woman and told her that it was okay, God didn't want to hear about her minor misdemeanours. He wanted to hug her and somehow try to fill the void which the death of her husband had left. To this day, I have done the same thing with anyone in that position. I listen to fools going on about how the proper words of absolution have to be said or the sacrament is invalid. What utter tosh. I can hardly envisage a God who was nailed to a cross getting his undergarments in a twist over punctuation or vocabulary. It's a nonsense. Which is easier to say, 'Pick up your bed and walk,' or, 'Your sins are forgiven?'

I was in a state of inner turmoil. Instead of my life coming together after my teenage years, things seemed to be falling apart again. It all seemed like a nightmare. Every time I thought that I had come to terms with one thing, something far worse would happen. Believe it or not, the only safe part of my life was now my junior seminary days. I had faced them, come to terms with them. It seemed almost as though they were beginning to turn into a refuge for me because at least I could understand what had happened there, or so I thought. That refuge was now about to be obliterated.

Celtic were playing Dundee United in the Scottish Cup final, or semi-final, whichever it was. A friend had got me a ticket and told me to get out of the parish for the day and get away from it all. I was appreciative of his offer. Incidentally, if it had been a Rangers ticket, I would have gone just the same. I am not one of the Parkhead white-collar brigade. I travelled back home on the Friday night, went for the statutory couple of pints on the Saturday morning and then boarded the local supporters' bus to travel to Hampden Park for the match. It had been arranged that the bus would stop for an hour at the Celtic Supporters Club in Glasgow's London Road. Happy days. A few more pints would be just the tonic. A crowd of us sat at a table while one guy went to the bar to order the pints. I looked across the hall and saw a tricolour draped over a table. The flag had the name of an English city emblazened on it. The city named happened to be that nearest to my junior seminary where one of my college mates, from those long-lost days, lived. It was a chance in a million, but I thought I would go over and ask the guys if any of them knew my mate.

I greeted the group of guys and made small talk about their long journey up from England. I told them that I used to go to school in their neck of the woods and that I had played in one of the local football teams there. They knew the team. Then I asked if any of them happened to know my college mate. There was an awkward silence as they all stared at each other, not knowing what to say. The oldest of them turned to me and said, 'No, we've never heard of him.' I knew immediately that he was lying. I knew by their reaction that every one of them knew him. But why would they deny it? 'Fair enough, guys, enjoy the match,' I said, then returned to my seat.

When I rejoined my friends I looked over at the English guys and watched them closely. A heated debate was taking place. Eventually, they seemed to come to some sort of agreement. The older guy stood up and started to walk across the hall towards me. He leaned over and asked if I was a close friend of the guy whose name I had mentioned. I explained that I hadn't seen the guy for years but that, yes, we had been great friends. He apologised for denying that he had known the guy, explaining that my question had taken them by surprise. 'Why, what's wrong?' I ventured. 'He's dead. He committed suicide,' came the sombre reply. He squeezed my hand and said that he was really sorry to be the bearer of such bad news. Standing on the terracing at the match that day, I was totally oblivious to the game. Why had my mate killed himself? One-nil to Dundee United. Why did he kill himself? One-all. Why did he kill himself? Two-one to Celtic. Why? For God's sake, why?

Once my pal's suicide had sunk in, I wanted to speak to someone. This was now way out of my league. The only one alive who knew anything of the story was Pat. I needed to go to speak to him. I had visited Pat once since I had been ordained, but we hadn't talked about anything serious; it was just a social call. I phoned to make an arrangement to see him, but he was out. The next time I phoned, he had gone on holiday. So, I put the problem on the back burner. It became one of those things that you intend to do, but never get round to. Months passed, during which my own thoughts became my spiritual director.

Then one day, I had to attend a meeting at the Archbishop's house. Halfway through the meeting, the phone rang. The Archbishop said casually that he would just take this call. I watched him as he answered. His face turned white. Pat was dead. Another priest was gone, again in his early fifties. I just sat there in shock. Pat had shown no physical signs that anything was wrong. It turned out that he had had a brain tumour which had gone undetected. There was no warning, nothing. His life was just switched off in an instant.

Three of the most influential people in my life had been snuffed out in as many years, long before their time. The utter sadness of it all plagued me. Apart from just sorely missing their presence, I became conscious of the fragility of life; but I spoke to no one about how I felt inside and began to store things up again. There is a card with a few verses on it which is now used at many funerals. The verse says that, 'Death is nothing at all, I have only slipped away into another room…' I would beg to differ with those sentiments. Death is something. It's something to the living who are left behind.

As always, it was the people of the parish who lifted my spirits again. I took on a much more pragmatic approach to Christianity. Obviously, it wasn't everyone's cup of tea, but I began to take on Gospel principles and apply them. (Imagine a priest almost apologising for trying to put the Gospel in to practice!) I had spent my first few years of priesthood being approached by hundreds of people who were good, decent committed Catholics, but who, for one reason or another, had legitimate problems which tended to make them feel ostracised from the Church. The more I met these people, the more I realised that it wasn't good enough simply to pat them on the back while politely saying that there was nothing I could do for them. These were God's children. At the Bishop's Conference of England and Wales, complaints were made that Church rules were requiring priests to turn people away – people whom Christ might very well have welcomed into his own company. So I made my decision not to turn anyone away any more. If parents who hadn't been attending Mass wanted their children baptised, I would baptise them. I would make them feel welcome. I would make them want to come to Mass. If someone who had been divorced and remarried was going to the Sacraments, I would welcome them, not just turn a blind eye. I would begin to challenge those 'sinless' individuals who have a craving for pointing a judgmental finger at the 'less worthy' people in the parish. For God's sake, I knew priests who were breaking their vow of celibacy every week, yet they still preached fire and brimstone to the people. Well, as one decent guy once said, 'The judgement you give will be the judgement you receive.' To the priests I would say, it's okay to fall in love. Sleep with who ever you want to…but stop shouting at the people for doing the same! Own up – or shut up.

On one particular Sunday, the Gospel reading was the one about the Pharisees asking Jesus if it was okay to divorce your wife. Jesus realises that it is not a genuine question, they are out to discredit him. He points them in the direction of their own Law: 'What does it say?' The Pharisees state that Moses allowed them to divorce so long as they made out a writ of dismissal. Jesus snaps at them, 'It was because you were so unteachable that he allowed that.' Jesus then tells them that if they divorce their wives and take on another, they are guilty of adultery.

In my sermon that day, I told the people that I could not accept that Jesus' words were directed at the whole of humanity. They were directed at hypocrites like the Pharisees who had demanded that a woman be stoned to death for committing adultery, while they themselves could ditch their own wives and take on another at the stroke of a pen. How could Jesus possibly condemn the wife of an abusive and violent husband for walking out? How could he possibly condemn such a woman if she later found real love with another man and married him? I contended that this Gospel was being used to beat the divorced and remarried, many of whom are anything but adulterers. I added that I would never refuse communion to anyone in such a position and that if I ever heard of anyone picking on such people in the church, I would personally bounce the critics out the door.

After my sermon, I sat down for the offertory procession. When I looked up the aisle, I wanted the ground to open up and swallow me. One of the women who was bringing down the gifts was a divorcee. I felt terrible for her. Me and my big mouth had just put her in a highly embarrassing position as she approached the altar in front of a packed congregation. As she handed over to me what we believe would become Christ's body, the tears were streaming down her face. I wanted to kick my own arse.

After Mass was finished, I tried to catch her at the back of the church, but she had left via another door. Half an hour later, I got into the car and drove to her house where she invited me in. I apologised for my insensitivity to her and said sorry if I had caused her pain. I will never forget her words. She said, 'Father Steve, for ten years, ever since my husband left me, I have felt like an outcast down in that church. Today, for the first time, a Catholic priest took the risk of speaking up for people like me. My tears were tears of pride because I walked down that aisle, in front of everyone, with my head held high for the first time.' It is people like that woman who continually make me feel that what I am doing with my life is worthwhile after all. One of the greatest evils in the Church today is the treatment of women. Not only the refusal to ordain them, but the refusal to allow them to receive the Sacraments after their husbands have pissed off to go with someone else and the spurned wife has later remarried. Can we all please wake up here and stop accepting this drivel? And, I apologise if I am being prophetic here, but when there is a deficiency of male priests, suddenly Rome will discover that women can elevate a host and chalice pretty much the same as humans with testicles can. Again, I say that the present state of affairs is a nonsense.

As my time in my first parish as assistant priest drew to a close another incident was to shake me and make me question the whole structure and workings of the Church. A young woman came to see me and told me that her family had just been given a bit of a shock. Her grandmother had been ill in hospital and it had looked like her illness was life threatening. Unbelievably, the grandmother had asked to speak to a Catholic priest. I say unbelievably, because the family always assumed that the grandmother was a Protestant. A priest was indeed called in and he administered the sacrament of the sick to the old lady. She had made an almost miraculous recovery and was now back at home – in my parish. The family filled me in as best they could with what she had just told them about her past life.

In her childhood and teenage years this woman had been a regular attender at Mass. She was very much involved in the life of the local Catholic church. As a young woman, she had fallen madly in love with a young man from the town. Unfortunately, he was a Protestant. However, they got engaged and went to see the local parish priest. In those days, there was a 'None shall enter' sign above the front door of the parish house. It was invisible, but everyone knew it was there. As was the custom then, the priest arranged a meeting with the young couple in the local park. When he arrived he began the questioning: 'Young man, what are your intentions by this young woman?' The young man answered that he wanted to take instructions in the Catholic faith, he wanted to become a Catholic, he wanted to marry his fiancé in a Catholic church and he wanted to bring up his children as Catholic. The priest said that he would contact them in a few weeks and the process for his instruction and preparation for their marriage would begin. The couple couldn't have been happier.

Sadly, within the week, that young priest was moved to another parish. There were no discussions in those days about possible placements or the question of whether a particular parish would suit the priest. The Bishop cracked his whip and the priests jumped, end of story. The replacement priest, however, didn't contact the young couple. After months of waiting, they eventually approached him. When the priest found out that the young man was a Protestant, his response was along the lines of, 'Yes, I'll marry you in December – because it will be a cold day in Hell before I ever marry a Catholic to a Protestant.' The couple were understandably shattered. The young woman was left with a stark choice – her religion or her man.

Pressure was then exerted upon her to ditch her fiancé in favour of her faith. Her mother begged her not to marry this man because it would bring shame on the family if she were to marry outside the Catholic Church. They would effectively be, to use that quaint phrase, 'living in sin'. The priest contacted a convent in Edinburgh and arranged for her to get a job in the city while staying with the nuns. He didn't even ask the young woman if that was what she wanted to do. Thankfully, the young woman refused to buckle under the pressure. She married her young man…in the Kirk.

It was then made clear that she was no longer welcome in the Catholic Church. She attempted to go to Mass on a couple of occasions but became the target of cruel and wicked jibes by the 'morally upright'. Many parishioners even shunned her on the street and refused to give her the time of day. She never went back to Mass again.

Sixty-two years later, I arrived on her front door step. The door slowly opened and this white-haired, frail old lady appeared. I was wearing my collar, which I didn't do normally, so that I was immediately recognisable to her. I wondered if she would tell me to get on my bike and slam the door shut in my face. I would not have blamed her if she had. Her first words were, 'Oh, Father, come in, please come in.' At first, we made small talk. She pointed to photographs of her grandchildren, of whom she was immensely proud. She told me their names and little snippets about them. Suddenly, she went silent and bowed her head to look at the floor. She said, very quietly, 'Well, Father, I suppose you've come to give me a talking to.' I said that I had. 'Mary, I'm here today on behalf of the Catholic Church, to apologise for what happened to you. It should never have happened. What they did to you was sinful.' Still with her head bowed low, her shoulders began to shudder. The tears fell from her face on to her apron. Eventually, when she could speak, she said, 'Father, I never thought I would see the day when I would hear those words from a Catholic priest.'

We sat and spoke for at least two hours; it was the least I could do after the sixty-two years of exile she had suffered. It was the old lady herself who filled me in on the details I have related above. She told me that her husband had died twenty years ago, but that he had been a wonderful husband and dad. She showed me a photograph of him and described him with much affection. She was obviously still deeply in love with him. She explained that every night of their lives, before they went to bed, they would read together a passage from the Bible. She showed me their Bible; it had definitely been 'lived in'. I asked her about how she felt towards those supposed Christians who had treated them so wickedly. She answered that she had forgiven them years ago. She explained that she had accepted that these people were products of their time, then added with a smile, 'And anyway, they're all long since dead.' She also said that some Catholic friends and neighbours had quietly supported and loved the two of them through all those years. She then stunned me when she asked if I would hear her confession. Everything in me wanted to say, 'It's me who should be kneeling in front of you to plead for forgiveness.' I didn't though. As another priest described his mother's confession, 'It was like being stoned…with popcorn.' I told her that I would bring the Eucharist to her the following day.

When I left her house, I sat in the car for a while just pondering over what I had just witnessed. Here was a woman who had been ostracised from the Church for sixty-two years. In all that time, she had never received the Sacraments, things that we believe to be grace-filled encounters with Jesus Christ. And yet here too was a woman who displayed more compassion, love and forgiveness than I had found in many people who go to the Sacraments every week of their lives. I thought about the Book of Psalms in the Bible, a collection of some of the most insightful, powerful and beautiful texts ever written. And yet, they were written by a group of people who were in exile and who had been stripped of all their familiar religious surroundings. Their faith in God could no longer be expressed in the traditional manner, so they had to seek out God anew. The awful thought struck me that the sacramental life of the Church could be having the same effect on our people. Maybe we have so standardised and structuralised our Sacraments, that the journey to seek God has stopped. Maybe we need a period of exile ourselves, so that we can rediscover Christ. I still to this day find myself asking the question, 'What is important to us, the structure or the reason why the structure exists in the first place?'

I brought the old lady the Eucharist the next day and asked if she would like to come to Mass. I promised her that whenever she wanted to go to Mass, wherever she wanted to go, I would personally come and pick her up to take her there. She said that there was no need, her family would take her. I asked if I could tell the parishioners her story because we were having a service of reconciliation that week. She agreed. At the service, the theme was 'social sin', how we as a community can be capable of carrying out evil. There are those who perpetrate the evil and there are those who condone it by their silence. The lady had called the people who had been wicked to her, 'products of the time'. But she had also told me that some parishioners had secretly supported her through it all. These people knew that what was happening was wrong. Now, when I read the parable about judgement day, when those who are condemned bleat, 'But Lord, when did we see you naked or hungry or thirsty or sick or in prison?',

I realise that there is such a thing as 'culpable ignorance.' We have a choice either to stand beside those who are torn apart by Church structures or to say nothing and allow the structure to continue unchallenged and simply watch thousands of people being brushed aside uncaringly. For me, this has become the crux of the moral dilemma in the modern era for people who call themselves Catholic. How much longer are people in the Church going to stand idly by and watch decent Catholics who have made mistakes being pushed out by self-righteous hypocrites?

The old lady attended Mass that Sunday evening for the first time in sixty-two years. The parishioners gave her a tremendous welcome that touched her deeply. A few weeks later, my time in the parish came to an end. Hers was the last house in the town I visited before I drove off to start in pastures new.

The parish I was transferred to now, again as an assistant priest, was in the East of Scotland. There I spent one of my happiest years in the priesthood. Liam, the priest I worked under, encouraged what he saw as my qualities and turned a blind eye to my many faults. I was sad when my year there came to an end but I was just about to appointed to my first parish and I relished that challenge. A year previously I simply couldn't have faced it. I left the parish house a much more balanced and healed person than I had entered it. I had Liam and his people to thank for that

I enjoyed the transition to my first parish, my current parish, although I was very nervous. Very quickly I realised that the buck stopped with me; there would be no handing over of difficult situations to a more experienced priest. Whatever happened from here on in, I had to deal with myself. The 'parish' was actually three different parishes, with three different churches. Over the previous ten years, they had been looked after by three priests from an Order, but they had moved on to a new parish so I was to take over. Another reason for my nervousness was that there was no way that I could fill their shoes. How could I hope to achieve anything like the work of three priests? I thought that I would be doing well just to maintain what they had achieved. I must admit that for the first year, I tended to be a bit lost – the tail wagged the dog. I was priest to three parishes, chaplain to a secondary school on the other side of the city, chaplain to a college of further education, a regular contributor to two different radio stations and a weekly columnist for the *Edinburgh Evening News*. It was all becoming too much with the result that I felt that I was doing nothing particularly well. I didn't even attempt to do the college of further education. I found myself going from one thing to another all day long, then going to bed at night worrying about all the things I had forgotten to do that day.

One day, into that almost chaotic lifestyle, came what I thought at first was a perfectly innocent phone call. It was the wife of a guy who had been at junior seminary with me. I had met them both intermittently over the years but we had never really kept up. They now lived in the North East of England and wanted me to go and stay with them for an overnight. I was happy to take the break. During the journey there, the junior seminary was the last thing on my mind. I was just happy to be seeing a friend and his family again. We greeted each other at the door, then I settled down in an armchair. His wife asked if I would like a tin of beer. I gave one of those, 'Is Salman Rushdie's phone number ex-directory?', replies and she disappeared into the kitchen. I was just about to ask my mate how he was when suddenly he stood up and walked towards me. He put his finger to his lips in a gesture to tell me to keep quiet, then he put his arms in front of me and rolled up his sleeves. I looked at him in total confusion and whispered, 'What is it?' He whispered back, 'Look look.' raising his wrists to my face. I looked and saw that his wrists had been slashed. He whispered again, 'Don't ask, I'll tell you later.' He rolled down his sleeves and quickly sat back on his chair. His wife poked her head around the kitchen door and asked, 'Will lager do you, Stevie?' Still stunned, I mumbled that it would do fine. She then turned to her husband and asked, 'And what about you, Slasher?' I didn't know whether I was supposed to laugh or what. In any event, I was too shocked to do anything.

I think that the reason she had called her husband 'Slasher' and the reason that she had phoned me, was that she knew that her husband was bottling something up. He wouldn't talk to her about it, so she thought he might open up to me. She called him the name to let him know that if he didn't tell me what he had done, she would tell me; he had tried to take his own life a few weeks previously. For apparently no reason, he had slashed his wrists. When asked why he had done so, his reply was that he had been depressed. Beyond that, he didn't have a clue what was wrong. We spoke into the early hours of the morning about why he had done it. Not once was junior seminary even referred to by either of us. When I left the next day, I begged him, that if he ever felt like doing something like that again, he was to phone me and I would be there in an instant. He did promise, but it was a promise he was to break.

As I drove home, I tried to figure out why he had done it. Maybe he wasn't happily married. Maybe he didn't like his job. I still didn't make any connection between his actions and junior seminary, even though I had had earlier clues. Over the weeks and months that followed, I thought about him constantly. Then, in the space of a few weeks, I met someone who had known me and a few other guys at the seminary. He told me that one of them had become a chronic alcoholic after he left the seminary and one night had drowned in his own vomit. I then found out that another student was serving a life sentence in prison – he had exploded in temper at another bloke and battered him to death with a pole. To add to the ever-growing list, a member of another student's family told me that he had taken a massive nervous breakdown in his early twenties, but that he was better now. 'He just gets bother with his nerves sometimes now', was the way the person put it. And of course at the top of the list was my friend who had committed suicide.

I have no way of verifying whether the people who told me these things were giving factual accounts of what happened to these guys or not. But I certainly would like to know what became of every student in that college; I'm sure it would make for interesting, but tragic, reading. If the information I had been given about some former students is true, then I fear that there are many more broken human beings out there in need of healing. I hope they read this and have the courage to come forward for help. However, the practical offshoot of this information for me was the conclusion that what lay behind my mate's attempted suicide was the junior seminary.

A few months later, another phone call came. It was my mate's wife again. He was in hospital getting his stomach pumped after overdosing. I told her that I would be there as quickly as I could. She urged me to speak to him on my own as she felt sure that I had the key to unlock whatever was going on in him. It was a very perceptive comment. So, my mate and myself went for a walk together. I asked him again why he had done it. He just kept saying that he didn't know. I decided to confront him. I stopped him and faced him and asked if Bligh had 'touched' him at junior seminary. He bolted down the road away from me. I gave chase and pushed him against a wall. He was white. I asked him again, had the priest touched him? He broke down in tears and nodded. I told him to say it out loud. He wouldn't actually verbalise it, so I shook him again, 'Say it!' For the first time in his life, he told another person something of what had happened to him – he had been seriously molested. I knew he was undergoing counselling at that time because of his first suicide attempt, so I made him promise that he would tell his counsellor the details of it all. If he didn't, I would seek a meeting with his counsellor and tell him myself.

From that day on, my mate's health got steadily better. His wife phoned me from time to time to tell me that he was like a different man. It came out in the months that lay ahead that not only had a priest been abusing him, but a senior student too.

From being something that was buried deep within me for years, the junior seminary and the damage it had caused had become uppermost in my mind; never a day passed when I didn't wonder about the effects of the place on me, my friends or even on all those who had been there over the decades. I suddenly found myself wanting to return to the place. I had heard about 'revisiting', going back to the source of the pain and facing it. I decided to go back, even if it was only to spit on the place and get my anger out. It turned out to be a very weird experience.

I headed south, taking the same route that I had travelled with my dad on so many occasions as a youngster. At first, the landmarks I passed reminded me of my trip to Spain for the World Cup, and the Monty Python sketches we had laughed at then. As I got nearer the Lake District, those happy memories began to evaporate and a feeling of dread overcame me. As I neared the college, I passed through the area where one of the borstals had been. I grew increasingly uncomfortable but was aware of a feeling of being in control; I could turn the car around at any moment and go home. Nobody had the power to harm me any more. I eased my foot down on the accelerator and headed towards the college with resolve.

For the first time in twenty years, I approached the driveway to the seminary. I slowed the car right down so as to take in everything. I passed the cottage where the only lay member of staff had stayed with his wife and children; it was now a dilapidated wreck. The fences around it had been broken and the grass was up to the windows. The sight of the canal behind it sent a shiver down my spine. I continued on into the quadrangle where I parked the car. It was a miserable day, overcast and cold – just how I remembered the place. I wanted one of the priests to come out of the building so that I could have a chat with him – the type of chat that would have left him with a black eye and a fat lip – but there was nobody there now, the priests having long since departed. Many of them are dead now.

I wandered around the building. At the back of it I saw the lawn where my mate had fallen from the rope and nearly killed himself. I stopped at the stone table where the brother's lifeless body had lain. Slowly, I walked down the steps to where the canal stagnated; the pungent smell of sewage hit me. It was amazing, even my nose had a memory. Looking up to the old bridge, I remembered my initiation night. There was a constant desire in me to return to my car and get out of there, but I forced myself to stay and face it all. I walked a complete circle around the college and ended up back in the quadrangle. Then, a man wearing climbing boots and a kagoule suddenly appeared, walking from the driveway towards me. He seemed very friendly as he enquired who I was. I told him that I had been at school here many years before and that I had just been passing and wanted to see the place again. He invited me into the building to look around, explaining that the place was now used to give kids from the inner city a holiday, a kind of 'fresh air fortnight' type of set-up. I shuddered at the thought of kids being brought here for a 'break'. As soon as I stepped into the building, the smell was again the first thing that pierced my senses. The odour of Dettol still shrouded the corridors. I could almost hear the sound of mop buckets scraping along the stone floors. The only other place I had been in that gave off a similar whiff was the prison. I noticed the bare brick walls of the classrooms in the downstairs corridor. There was no plasterwork or wallpaper. The bricks had just been painted bright red. It obviously hadn't been touched since I had been there. It was also obvious that, when the original decorating had been done, no woman was involved in the planning. A priest in the distant past must have found a few tins of red paint in an old cupboard somewhere and thought, 'That'll do for the corridor.'

We slowly climbed the stairs to the dormitory. When I pushed open the door, it made the same noise I had heard a thousand times before, but had long since forgotten. The same old wooden lockers stood like sentries between the metal-framed beds. I lifted the lid of one of them and looked inside. It smelled of carbolic soap and toothpaste and still had dust and fluff in each corner. I let the lid bang down. It was again a noise I'd heard a hundred times every day when I had been there. I wondered how I could possibly have allowed myself to stay in such a place.

By this time, the guy knew that I was a priest and wanted to know if I would like to see the chapel. As always, the minute a person knows that you are a priest, they jump to conclusions. But I did want to see the chapel – for the same reason that I wanted to see the toilets or the dormitory or anywhere else. He thought that I'd like to see the chapel because I might want to say a prayer. No thanks. The chapel was neglected to say the least; prayer books were lying scattered all over the floor, which hadn't been polished with the same rigour as we had polished it. The red Sanctuary lamp was no longer lit and there was a gaping hole where the tabernacle had stood. Loads of memories flooded my mind in an instant. The goat's head floating in mid-air, the sermon about the dead priest leaning on the tabernacle, Status Quo blaring out as we shined the floor. The vestments and religious artefacts had all gone but the students' prayer books remained. I picked one up from the floor and opened it. The name scrawled on the cover was the guy who had committed suicide. I closed it and gently placed it on the floor beside the others. I thought about taking it with me but immediately changed my mind. I wanted nothing from this place in my own house.

At this point, my guide wanted to know if he could ask me a few questions; something seemed to be troubling him. I was intrigued by what he might want to know. He began stuttering and stumbling about whether I had been happy in this place and had anything strange ever happened here. I replied, 'Look mate, just come clean, what exactly do you want to know?' He began to talk specifically. He told me that it was his job to employ domestic staff to clean the place but any staff he had employed thus far had left within a matter of weeks. Those who stayed on had refused to work in certain rooms or areas of the college. I asked why, but I already knew what the answer was. The workers had claimed to have seen apparitions and heard voices. He was able to give me a detailed description of a 'ghostly figure' which kept appearing to the staff since it had been described so often to him. He accurately described one of the priests who had been found dead in his bed after the college had closed down. The figure had been appearing in a room in this priest's part of the college, and in one of the small chapels in the crypt. He invited me to come with him so that he could show me. I stopped him and said, 'No. I'll show you.' I led him up the stairs into the priests' quarters, went straight to one of the rooms, pushed the door open and said, 'In there?' The guy's face turned white as he nodded. I then led him down to the crypt, walked past most of the chapels, then stopped at one, pushed the door open and said again, 'In there?' His jaw dropped. He asked how I knew. I explained to him that the ghostly figure he had described was one of the priests who had died. I had simply taken him to his room and to the chapel where he used to say Mass.

The guy seemed more frightened than impressed by what I had told him then continued to talk about one particular part of the college that gave him the creeps. He wanted to show me. I just knew where we were going as we headed off along the corridor. We climbed more stairs, went through a side door and straight into...the old library. There was now a modern-looking desk in the middle, surrounded by all the old bookshelves. The poor guy went on to tell me that this was his office; sometimes he worked on his own here until the early hours of the morning. He said that sometimes he had heard voices as well. My last words to him before I departed were, 'Well, mate, good luck to you, but rather you than me.' With that, I headed back to my car; I had seen enough. As I drove down the drive towards the main road, I was so glad to be leaving the place behind, this time of my own free will. I was glad that I had gone back, but the further up the motorway towards Scotland I got, the more at ease I felt.

At the time, I thought that that was me 'cured'; I had gone back and exorcised a few ghosts. I could now get on with my life having faced the past eyeball to eyeball. I could put it all behind me. In actual fact, as I came to realise, healing does not come by re-burying the past. It comes in simply accepting that the past is part and parcel of the present. It was a part of who I am – and that's okay.

Life went on as normal back in the parish, or as normal as life gets in the parish. I decided to write my past down on paper, for my own therapeutic purposes. So, each evening, I would spend an hour writing down as much as I could remember. But one question kept cropping up – why hadn't I told my parents about what had been going on? That question was answered in a most unusual way. I went to the local shopping centre to get in some food for the week. As I shoved the trolley, with the statutory buckled wheel, up and down the aisles, something in the video section caught my eye. The advert on the front of one video cassette stated that the film was about the true and shocking story of a group of American children who had been systematically abused. I bought the video.

That evening, I watched the video. The story was about a group of children from a housing estate who were left with a married couple each day while their parents went off to work. The children were being abused by this couple who were telling the children that this was all just a fun game to play. However, the parents of one of the children began to notice behavioural problems with their child. They wanted to get the police in to investigate what was going on, but nobody would listen to them. Eventually, other parents became suspicious and a group of expert child psychologists were indeed called in. One child is interviewed for months but will say nothing about what had been happening. The most powerful scene in the film is where the child psychologists are interviewing the child in one room, while his parents and another psychologist are in another room watching the proceedings on closed circuit television. Suddenly, the child opens up and begins to reveal the perverse nature of what had been going on. The child's father goes berserk and begins to shout,

'Why didn't he tell us? We're the ones who love him, we would have protected him. Why didn't he tell us?' The psychologist pins the father against the wall and shouts, 'Don't you realise, don't you understand? Your son was simply trying to protect you. Don't you see that?'

Whether the father saw it or not, I certainly did. The psychologist's words jumped out of the screen at me – I was protecting my own parents. How could I tell them that these people, to whom they had entrusted their son, had treated us so wickedly. I could not take the responsibility for them turning against the Church that they loved deeply. Just knowing what had been going on in my mind, understanding my silence, helped me so much. I knew that as an adult, two decades after what had happened, I was still trying to protect them. I didn't want them to be hurt or to feel guilty that they didn't get me out of that place. I made up my mind then that, sooner rather than later, I was going to tell them. I knew it would devastate them, but it was something they would have to face.

A few weeks later, my sister came to visit me. She was going through a phase where she was questioning many of the things the Church taught about sex and sexuality. During the course of the conversation, she told me that she had been at my parents' house when a news report on television had been talking about a sex abuse case involving a priest at a junior seminary. My mum had commented, 'Oh my God, I hope that didn't happen to our Steve.' I told my sister that it had. I explained that it hadn't been as serious as the reported case on TV, but, along with other events, it had been enough to stunt my development as a teenager. I assured her that I had come to terms with it as best I could and not to worry. I told her that I intended telling mum and dad when the time was right.

That time was not too far away. My Nana was ill and was deteriorating fast. My mum was constantly by her side. After an all-night vigil, my mum had gone home and my uncle took over the vigil. He phoned me at about eleven o'clock in the morning to tell me that my Nana had just died. My immediate reaction was to visit my parents to see that they were okay. When I arrived, my dad was out. I asked my mum how she was. She said that she was fine. She explained what I already knew, that my Nana had been a tremendous human being who had coped admirably with so many hardships in life. She had 'bounced straight into heaven'. I had no intentions of saying anything at that point about junior seminary, but it just happened. I asked my mum if she had kept anything back from my Nana, if she was away to her grave leaving my mum with any regrets. My mum said that she had told everything to my Nana and that she felt at peace with her. She then asked why I had posed the question. It just came out. I told her that there were things I did not want them to go to their graves without knowing. I then told her some of the details of what had happened. She burst into tears.

I left the house later with a whole mixture of emotions. I loved my Nana. She had been one of my favourite people on the planet and I would miss her. But I felt guilty at having dropped such a bombshell on my mother's lap on the very day of her own mother's death. It felt awful to think that the cause of the tears on that day was not my Nana's death, but what I had told my mum (and my dad, when he returned to the house). Still, it was out now. When I had given relatively clear signals that I wanted out of the college, the priests had assured my parents that it was just homesickness. My parents, being faithful Catholics, had gone against their natural instincts and had trusted the Church. Families were very honoured to have a priest in the Church. They had been preached to so often about how it was their responsibility to provide 'labourers for the harvest'. If a young boy had made any mention of becoming a priest, parents would suffer guilt if they didn't act upon it. My parents now have to come to terms with their decisions at that time, and they are doing so. Many Catholics still have not learned that lesson. Why do many people still not believe that God speaks most powerfully from the pulpit of their own instincts and consciences?

By now it was obvious that I was not the only one who had emerged from a junior seminary 'slightly the worse for wear', psychologically speaking. The vast majority of the priests in Scotland had attended a junior seminary of one sort or another. I began to recognise tell-tale signs in other priests, of certain blockages in their development as rounded, balanced human beings. There were a lot of masks being worn. I had been invited to contribute a regular column to the *Scottish Catholic Observer*. So, I decided to write a piece for this paper, just to scratch the surface of the subject, in the honest belief that a huge number of Catholic men, some of them priests, have been damaged by such institutions and have not come to terms with it. I was well used to being labelled 'mad' or a publicity seeker by some readers who disliked my views, but I wrote the piece because I wanted to preach the Gospel. I was not looking forward to the irate mail and phone calls which would no doubt ensue. I wrote the article as sensitively as I could, hinting from afar that possibly all was not well at my seminary and that maybe people who had attended other seminaries might wish to reflect on how the experience had affected them. I gave the example of one student having been caned to the extent that it resulted in a bone broken in his hand. His parents had promptly removed him from the college, never to return.

From the moment the newspaper hit the tables at the back of Scotland's churches, my phone started to ring. The calls were not invitations to parties. The most significant thing for me though, was that the majority of calls came from clergy. One parish priest in the West of Scotland had previously cancelled fifty of his parish's *Observers* because he wasn't happy at the tone of my articles. He was on holiday when the article on junior seminaries was published, but his subservient young curate had dutifully cancelled the rest of the subscription in his absence, upon reading that week's page. Various other priests phoned to complain about my article. They all stated how blissfully happy they had been at junior seminary and what a treacherous liar I was. Don't forget, I had written practically nothing about the place. I had simply hinted that the experience might have been damaging. As the complaints came in, I suddenly began to realise that I had underestimated the depth of feeling there was about the subject. If these priests had had such an idyllic junior seminary life, what power was at play here, causing them to pick up the phone and complain so bitterly about me questioning the benefits of such institutions. None of them had picked up the phone to complain when I wrote questioning the Church's attitude towards the divorced and remarried. There was not a whimper from any of them when I spoke on the issues of celibacy or women's ordination. Why were they going ballistic because I had discussed the relative merits and faults of junior seminaries?

A week later, I received a letter from yet another priest in the West of Scotland. The letter began, 'It is only now I have calmed down enough to be able to write to you in any sensible manner...' The letter went on to demand that I apologise to every member of staff in every junior seminary in Scotland over the previous years. I was to examine my conscience and pray for forgiveness for such a scurrilous article. He complained about the way I had spoken about Mass when I had stated that, in those days, they spoke about Satan more than they preached the love of Christ. He said that I had no vocation to the priesthood and so on and so on. The letter was the straw that broke the camel's back. I found myself sitting weeping, yet again. What kind of people are these? What is the Church all about? Is it all just a game where we all just act things out? Don't say anything uncomfortable or too near to the bone. Keep everything at a surface level and at all costs, spare people's blushes. That letter sickened me. I spoke to a priest friend about what I should do. I was well used to simply binning such mail but he advised me to write back to the priest concerned and tell him some of the things that I hadn't put in the article.

I wrote back to him and explained, as best I could, that many of us had really suffered because of what had happened at that college. My intention had not been to destroy the Church, but to build it up by making it face some unpleasant realities. I outlined the fact that one priest had tried to fondle me during one of the letter-writer's beloved Masses. I informed him of the canings and the beltings. I told him directly that I would never apologise to the people who had treated me, and others, in such a fashion. To give this priest credit, by return of post came an unreserved apology for his letter if it had caused the surfacing of any unpleasant memories. He said that I obviously had a very deep sense of vocation if I had stayed in the priesthood after such things had happened. At the end of the letter he wrote something which typifies the attitude of the institutional Church in Scotland: 'Steve, I promise you, I will tear up and burn your letter to me. No one will ever get to know what happened in that junior seminary.' I deeply appreciated the priest's letter to me, but I wanted to scream, 'You've missed the whole point!' The reason I had written the article was to gently invite the Catholic population to reflect on the less

212

palatable things in our past and to face them, to accept them. I was being faced with a huge wall of silence. In the words of Spike Milligan, 'I know it's the truth, but just don't tell me it.'

Am I mad? Do I have a chip on my shoulder? When I look at the alternative, I'll say an emphatic 'yes' to both questions any day. I can go out and say Mass every day as a madman. Having a hundred chips on my shoulder wouldn't stop me functioning as a priest. But I couldn't even bless myself if I chose to continue in this culture of cover-up that so disfigures the Church. The saddest thing is that those who were abused by institutions within the Church as children, are being psychologically abused all over again as adults. I believe that the day is coming when those who are condoning abuse by their silence, or by their attacks on the abused who happen to speak out, are going to have to account for their actions. The following letter, which I received recently, makes me feel that that day is not far away.

Dear Steve,

I read in the papers this morning that you have written a book about the abuse you suffered while training to be a priest. Firstly, let me express regret that you have and still do suffer from that period. Sadly, as you well know, you are not alone.

I was incarcerated (!) at Langbank and Blairs and subsequently Cardross in the mid 1960's and can testify that what you have reported is but a bare sketch of the often systematic abuse suffered during those years.

I have not read your book but I can imagine the content. I can also imagine the uproar it has caused with the hierarchy, especially after recent events. To hear the squeals of clerical indignation at your book sets my teeth on edge. The hypocrisy is unbelievable if you had not witnessed events at first hand.

I too feel the effects long after my years there, they are always at the back of my mind, surfacing unbidden on good days and bad, alike. Sad to say, I have kept in touch with a few friends from that period and have an extensive insight into their, and their friends' continuing nightmares. You are the tip of the iceberg – a big iceberg.

That we have not gone public before this, is due to the abused person's guilt at being abused, fear of exposing ourselves to media scrutiny and the glare of publicity exacerbating the feelings we have. That you have chosen to chase the demons has my, and our, admiration.

The abuse we suffered was premeditated, from the priest in the showers pulling back the shower curtain to look at you, turning the showers cold deliberately and flinging you back with force, to allowing systematic bullying, to making children stand on classroom chairs, holding their hair and making them jump off. Putting their hands down the front of your shorts to 'take the pain away' of being hit at football matches.

Too often, the culture of abuse in the name of the Lord has been used to harm innocent children. I was twelve when I was first sexually abused. Looking back, I was more abused by the priests who were supposed to see to my care than I was by the older abusers in the year above. They were condoned by the priests, both in attitude [sic] that the lower form was to be seen as a lower form of unworthy life. 'Traditional' beatings were the norm as when sixth form knowingly beat the shit out of the young lads during traditional snow fights, put them in ditches, perpetrated abuse of all descriptions while hunting in packs for their victims.

Or what about the indiscriminate abuse of the discipline system where good guys were sent home because they would not acquiesce in silence? They were sent home to the (perceived) great shame of their parents, through no fault of their own, whereas those in the clique with the staff could survive anything. Those who were not had recourse to no one. What about the Spiritual Director who got his rocks off asking teenagers about their sexual dreams? Or the Form Master who was happy with groups of boys 'wrestling' with him? Harmless sounding, but you had to be there for the dread that facing these people gave you.

I could go on and on, but you know I'm not making it up. It's just the anger that comes on me after the jolly banter ends. We all feel this way, we all still talk about it as if it were only yesterday, though in reality it is today and every day. That is why we get so fucking angry when we see X's [a senior Catholic priest] face in the newspaper spouting the 'official' line.

We can't all be liars and jumping on the bandwagon, if so, there would be a sight more litigation for the Church to worry about! What about honesty, has the Church forgotten that? They know the abuse went on, they were probably abused themselves in the norm for the times. That is the worst of abuse, the abused then abuse others. The abuse lasts for life, their mealy mouthed statements which automatically address the next abused person to stand up, confirms it. They are still abusing us.

As for their attempts to set up counsellors as their sop to the abused, it stinks. Anyone who has worked in the Social Service area, as I have, knows that it is not worth the paper it is written on. Abuse is not cured by these people – yes, some good ones help, – but it is only in cleaning the house from the top down that it will stop. There must be no hiding place for abusers in the Church, no 'holidays' at retreat centres to cure abusers. Never another parish for them to go to.

I'll finish now by wishing you the best, now that I've stopped ranting. But in doing so, I offer these thoughts:

I have copied this letter to the Bishops of Scotland, I hope it makes unpleasant reading. My friends and I wish to remain anonymous for reasons already given. But I swear that if you get grief in the press from the Catholic Church that leads to your denigration or even your dismissal, we will come into the open to prove you right – even if that means more litigation against the Church. So, brethren, shut your mouths and get your house in order.

We have an idea waiting for the nod for an Internet site to attract all who have abuse stories about the Church. We joke about it now, but we will do it if you come to grief over this book.

Very finally, none of us go to church any more – very sad considering many of us were within a couple of years of ordination. But that is what abuse does, it makes you not care any more what happens to you. I would now actively discourage a boy from going to seminary – the worst indictment of the Church, isn't it? I leave you for the moment anonymously. God bless you – and watch your back.

I hope that these guys do come forward one day. They too have had the Church stolen from them.

Chapter Fifteen

One priest who had a profound influence on my life, although he doesn't know it, told me the following story. He recalled his very first theology class. A group of first-year students was sitting nervously awaiting the arrival of their priest lecturer, not knowing what to expect. The priest eventually arrived in the classroom then ordered them all to follow him. He led them downstairs, across the car park, round the back of the building and down to the farmyard. They came to a fence, behind which was the piggery. He told all the would-be priests to look over the fence. There stood a pig covered in mud and filth. The students looked at it: wondering what on earth was going on. The lecturer started, 'Theology lesson one: God has either got everything to do with that pig – or he has got absolutely nothing to do with anything at all. Lesson over.' When the priest recounted this story to me, I didn't have a clue what he was talking about. I do now. The Church needs to return to the piggery.

On a similar theme I recently participated in a documentary on BBC television called 'Frontline Scotland'. The programme's subject was 'Mandatory celibacy for all Catholic clergy' (except those married priests who have left the Anglican Church and signed up with the Catholic church!). On the programme, I argued for a relaxation of the celibacy law. Given the drastic decline in the number of priests, the numbers of priests buckling under the pressure of priesthood, I feel that celibacy should be freely chosen. What I didn't say was that I honestly believe that mandatory celibacy has caused untold misery to thousands of people – and not just those who have promised it. A married clergy could be a good thing for the Church even though it would no doubt bring new problems with it.

The programme makers told me off-camera that they had contacted nearly fifty Catholic priests and not one of them was prepared to argue for mandatory celibacy. They eventually found one priest, a relatively young man, to argue for maintaining the status quo. The priest spoke about how celibacy was right for him and for the Church. He stated that 'celibacy was the perfection of the priesthood'. I beg to differ. Celibacy is not the perfection of the priesthood – love is. I thought of something that Bishop Comiskey once said: the greatest scourge in the priesthood today is the cult of perfectionism. It is just such perfectionism that is the breeding ground for so many ills in the Church. It was such an attitude that encouraged eleven-year-old children to be taken from their families to be 'made into' priests. Such perfectionism didn't see anything wrong with that. In the seeking of perfect discipline, some priests excused themselves for caning and belting the life out of young boys. It was for the sake of the perfect image of the Church that priests who abused children were quietly shunted off to Africa, or to other parishes where they could continue to do what they liked. That was a lesser evil than having the Church's good name tarnished on the front pages of the national Press. It was such attitudes that allowed the rector of the second junior seminary to call me to his room and ask me to drop my trousers while he fondled me stating that this was simply, 'a health check to make sure my testicles had dropped'. Why, Father, in your great concern for our physical well-being, did you never get the doctor in to inoculate us against TB, as every other school kid was in every other school in the land? Why were you only interested in the health of certain parts of our anatomy? A perfect Church indeed.

A few years ago, while on holiday in France, I visited a town called Oradour. It was a particularly hot day and I could have done with a cool drink. The shops were all open but you couldn't buy anything because there were no shopkeepers. They had all been murdered along with everyone else in the village. This was a ghost town. At the end of World War II while the Germans were retreating, they entered the village and butchered everyone. They bundled the baker and his wife into their oven; they shot every adult male; they gathered together all the women and children and herded them into the church, then threw in petrol-drenched bales of hay and set them on fire. One woman climbed up to the stained-glass window and crashed her baby through it in the desperate hope that he might somehow survive – which he did. He fell into some bushes, breaking his leg in the process, but he was hidden from the Germans. She then sank back into the inferno to her death. As I stood there and stared at the melted church bell and the bullet holes in the charred wall, I swear I could hear the women and children screaming.

The baby did indeed survive. He was the man who was now taking me round the village and explaining the horrific events of that tragic day. He still walked with a slight limp. He had decided to spend his life giving visitors tours around the village and trying to instil in them a sense of the barbarity of war. As he showed me around, there were lovely tree-lined streets. But I didn't notice them really; I just saw the smashed windows and the burnt-out-buildings. The thought struck me that nobody accuses this man of having a chip on his shoulder or of having a hidden agenda. They realise that he has suffered and that out of that suffering he is trying to do something positive.

I relate this man's story because, as a priest, I have tried to do a similar thing. It would be easy to simply chuck in the towel and just walk away, to throw bitter stones at the Church, or to just not give a damn any more. But I do give a damn. I have chosen to stay in the priesthood and to challenge the 'cult of perfectionism' which wreaks so much havoc even to this day. I have attempted to combat those who would have us believe that the Church is simply a beautiful tree-lined street. I want people to see the burnt-out houses that lie behind the trees because I honestly believe that that is where Christ is to be found. For that, I have been labelled a maverick, a man with a chip on his shoulder and, of course, someone with a personal agenda. When I wrote the original, very restrained article on junior seminaries for the *Scottish Catholic Observer*, a couple of Catholic psychologists wrote to the letters page a week later stating that I was obviously a deeply scarred young man who needed professional help. There was a sense of relief from some that now they didn't have to take seriously anything I had been saying because obviously I was 'loopy'.

I would ask those same experts in 'space cadetship', what did you expect the man from Oradour to talk to me about when he showed me the church where his mother was burned alive by the Nazis? The football? French cuisine, perhaps? And what do you expect me to talk about as a priest from my background? The necessity for cassocks? A return to fish on Fridays? Of bloody course my background is going to colour my views of the Church, why wouldn't it?

Will anything change? Of course not. The institution will not change until the people within it do. If I was to sit down with the Pope and tell him my story, tell him the details of what happened to us, some of which I haven't put on paper, I'm sure he would be compassionate. He would probably even offer to get the police to some of the individuals who perpetrated the crimes against us. He would not, however, even think of changing the structures that allowed such situations to arise. 'Long live mandatory celibacy!' is the cry of the deluded. Don't they realise that by shouting this, they are also shouting 'Long live paedophilia!'? Don't they see the connection?

In his memoirs, Cardinal Daly of Ireland describes how he wept when details of Father Brendan Smith's abuse of children came to light. He says that when he thought of the suffering those poor children went through, he was broken-hearted. Well, I was one of those children, although not at the hands of Brendan Smith, and I now question the real reason for the Cardinal's tears. Does he really understand the mental torture such children go through well into adulthood? Does he understand the burden of not even being able to tell your own parents, your own flesh and blood? Does he realise that some such kids were driven to suicide in their late teens or early twenties? Alcoholism, nervous breakdowns – or becoming abusers themselves? Or becoming so possessive of their own children that they wouldn't let them out of their sight in case, horror of horrors, they became victims themselves.

No, I don't think the Cardinal wept for the children. During his time in office he must have had complaints against priests and simply moved them to another parish. He knew what was going on before the media suddenly woke up. He wept because we all love the Church and here was the Church being scandalised and made to look awful. He was crying for himself. If he really cared for those children, he would have spoken out loudly and clearly against the structures which fertilise such obnoxious behaviour. As a Cardinal of the Church, he could have stood up and opted to argue on behalf of the people against bad Church laws, as did Archbishop Romero in El Salvador. But he chose not to; obedience came first for him, the welfare of the people, a poor second. I'm sure if I told Cardinal Daly what happened to us, I would get a hug – and my bus fare home. I do not say this as idle speculation. When I told my story to my own parishioners, one woman wrote to the Church authorities stating that she expected many of the clergy to be very angry with me for exposing what had happened to us. In a sincere and heartfelt letter, she begged the authorities to show support for me. She received a curt reply:

Dear Mrs —,
Thank you for your letter of May 2nd. I apologise for the delay in replying to you. From it I gather that you are a very caring person. There is more than one opinion on this matter and I uphold your right to express yours.

With every good wish

Yours sincerely

The only members of the Hierarchy who have given me and other victims support, to my knowledge, have been Archbishop O'Brien of Edinburgh and Episcopalian Bishop Richard Holloway. I'm left to conclude that the others are more worried about bad publicity than they are about the catastrophic effects the abuse has visited upon the victims.

On the day that the first articles about the book and its contents appeared in the national Press. I waited for the beginnings of the storm. My phone began to ring during the afternoon. A priest called. He told me that he had been sexually abused by another, older priest. He said that it makes him sick that after all the approaches he has made to the Church authorities, nothing has been done. It has been covered up. He told me to keep strong and not allow people to shut me up. He was adamant that this issue must be addressed for the good of the victims and for the sake of the Church. A handicapped woman then phoned and begged me to keep going. She was the victim of abuse herself but felt powerless to do anything about it. She, too, urged me to publish. Later, another woman phoned to add her support. She was one of the many who had been brutalised in a Catholic orphanage as a child. She explained that she no longer felt the pain of what had happened to her all those years ago. What hurt her now was how so many people in the Church disregarded her story. Because she and many of her abused friends have come forward and are now going to court over what happened, they have been labelled 'money grabbers'. She cannot understand why priests and Bishops stand on altars proclaiming love, compassion, truth and so on, yet none of them have the guts to actually acknowledge the truth.

It was heartening to hear such calls of support. However, in the evening I began to receive very different calls. A 'good Catholic' phoned to tell me that he had read the reports in the national Press that day, and that he had just phoned to let me know what a low-life scum-bag I was. Another caller demanded to know what I was going to do with the money I receive for this book. 'Will you be giving it to charity?' he asked aggressively. 'No, I didn't think so,' he answered, before he had even given me the opportunity to reply.

As the evening progressed, I began to realise that the persecution I had expected had begun. I reassured myself that there was nothing to worry about, they were just phone calls after all. At ten to midnight, after the telephone calls had stopped, I went downstairs to switch off all the lights, pull out the plugs and switch on the alarm system. While I was doing this, some person or persons entered my garden quietly in the darkness. They picked up the biggest stone flower pot in the garden, filled with gravel and compost, and crashed it through the back window of my car. My golf clubs and a cheque book were in the car. They took nothing. The attack was designed to be a 'shut-up-o-gramme'. Other incidents of a threatening nature happened around that time.

A number of things sustained me at that time. Under the immense pressure of the Press coverage, I had cleared off for five days to my beloved Killarney in Southern Ireland. The people there know me and, even though they had read the reportage in the Press, which was less than flattering, they were tremendously kind to me. I appreciated their love, but I still felt very much down in the dumps. They tried to cheer me up by holding an impromptu birthday party for me. I tried my best to be thankful, but I felt depressed. A group of Kosovan Albanian refugees were staying in the town and were being fed that day by the Failte Hotel. I was invited along to meet them all and I suppose their predicament did put a bit of perspective on my problems. I must admit that I never thought that it would be appropriate to smile in front of such people, but I nearly passed out when one of the Failte's staff announced at the end of the evening, in front of all the refugees, 'Come on now, drink up, have ye not got homes to go to?' I love that innocent Irish humour.

I returned to Scotland to face the music and to hear the detailed accounts of what certain people thought about me. My auntie who runs the orphanage in Bolivia phoned to see that I was okay. I broke down yet again and told her that my parishioners were brilliant, but explained that many of my brother priests were slating me. She pointed me in the direction of that Sunday's scripture readings. I looked them up and read them.

I hear so many disparaging me, "'Terror from every side!' Denounce him, Let us denounce him!" All those who used to be my friends watched for my downfall, "Perhaps he will be seduced into error. Then we will master him and take our revenge!"
(Jeremiah; chapter 20, verse 10)

It summed up just exactly how I was feeling. The Gospel that Sunday spoke even more deeply into my heart:

"Do not be afraid. For everything that is now covered will be uncovered, and everything now hidden will be made clear. What I say to you in the dark, tell in the daylight; what you hear in whispers, proclaim from the housetops."
(Matthew; chapter 10, verse 26)

As I've said that the word of God carries both a message of consolation and a message of challenge. For me that weekend, it was, without a doubt, a consoling word. I took heart. I am not mad, I am simply trying to unpack an unpalatable truth, one which, more than any other group of people, the clergy would rather keep hidden.

One positive product of the Press coverage was that I received a phone call from one of my classmates from the first junior seminary, who is presently living in England. I knew as soon as I heard his accent just exactly what this phone call was going to be about. He had read about the contents of the book in an English newspaper. He remembered me and wanted to speak to me. For the umpteenth time in my adult life I began to listen to the horrific story of yet another of my childhood friends unfold. He told me that one of the priests (the one who had got me belted for cutting out a secret compartment in the book) had abused him. I was shocked. I had always known that this particular priest was a bit of a fascist, but I had never even suspected him of sexual abuse. The caller told me the details very openly and courageously. He had been a 'day boy', a student who attended the seminary for the education only, and went home every evening. This priest had sent a letter to his parents stating that the student could really do with some extra tuition. The priest asked that the parents allow their son to stay with him in the lodge at the end of the college drive for the weekend. The parents gave permission. During one of the 'extra tuition' sessions that weekend, the priest read him a story from a book about a man standing naked on the deck of a ship at sea. He described the waves splashing against his naked body. Unbelievably, the priest then offered the thirteen-year-old student a glass of whisky, then another one. He then asked the boy to follow him into the bathroom, where he undressed him. He asked him to stand in the bath. The priest then began to splash cold water over him, telling him that he had to experience fully what the character in the book had experienced. He also stressed the importance to the student that no one should ever find out what was going on. The priest then undressed himself and masturbated the young boy. The caller told me that he suspected the same thing had happened to many of the other students. The caller had only told this to his wife after reading the article in the newspaper about this book. He told me that he was now going off to tell his parents, knowing that they would be devastated by what he had to say. I tried to reassure him that he might find his parents were stronger than he had given them credit for.

My old friend's call came a day after I had provided the Cumbrian police with a detailed statement of what went on in that place. I had thought that I would find some sort of healing in the writing of this book. However, after the gruelling interview with the police, I realise that I am still carrying deep wounds. After they left, I broke down and wept bitterly. I experienced a mixture of emotions. I wanted to expose all of this, but I didn't see the point in just slapping various individuals in prison. I had seen what happened to sexual abusers in prison and I had no wish to see the people who had persecuted us treated in that manner. I felt awful after the interview. Then I received the phone call from my friend. When he told me the details of his abuse and added the name of yet another student who had committed suicide, I felt nothing but rage. How dare they! They put on a front about being so holy and so pious and yet, all the time, they were preying on us sexually, physically and emotionally. How dare some of the present day 'cardboard cut-out' clergy tell me to shut up. Have any of them got the guts to stand up and scream with the rest of us that this was evil? Are any of them going to show the courage to, for once, publicly question the wickedness of mandatory celibacy? Before the interview finished, the detective asked me if there was anyone I was angry with. The answer to that one is yes. I have tried to resolve my anger at the guys who did those things to us. But every time I hear a priest today standing up and stating that these things are better kept in the past, hidden, I am outraged. They are quite happy to see the Catholic Church, which they profess to love, living a wicked lie because the reality of what has gone on is too shameful for them to face.

Not long after that, yet another former abused classmate contacted me. He wanted to return to the junior seminary to face what had happened there. He asked if I would go with him. I had promised myself after I had revisited that I would never return there again. I broke my promise and returned, for the sake of my classmate. A priest mate of mine offered to drive us. During the journey south, he tried to keep our spirits up. He said that he had done this same journey the previous week. A family from India had been staying with him and they had wanted to visit the Lake District. He had packed them into the car and when they were south of Carlisle he had asked if there was any particular lake the family would like to visit. The dad had answered, 'Yes, Lake Lomond.' My mate had just about crashed the car. We laughed for most of the journey, but that began to change as we neared the college. I had done all this before so I wasn't as emotional or as nervous as I had been the first time. My classmate seemed extremely nervous though. I could see him recognising landmarks and allowing memories connected with them to surface. When we actually got to the college, he was very much on edge. As we wandered round the college, the sights, sounds and smells were obviously deeply penetrating his mind. This student had been belted, caned and abused more than most. He was actually going to each place where each incident had occurred. It was almost as if he was trying to feel what he had felt all those years ago, trying to recall vividly those terrible moments.

We walked along the banks of the canal as far as the bridge. My classmate climbed a fence and walked across a field to an old barn. For some reason he wanted to go into it and look at it. It obviously held some memory or other for him. I did not ask him what it was, neither did he tell me. While he was away, I said to my priest friend, 'You know, when you look at this countryside, it really is quite beautiful. I should be standing here recounting happy childhood memories. This should actually have been a wonderland for any youngster, instead of the nightmare it actually was.' My classmate returned a few minutes later, stood on the bridge and stated, 'You know, see when you think about it, we should be standing here saying how wonderful a place this was instead of —' I cut in abruptly and said, 'Yeah, I know. Come on, let's go.'

As we returned to the car, I had a last look inside the main corridor. There were colour photographs of children in canoes or hill walking or climbing trees. These were the kids who now come along to the place for outdoor activities and adventure weekends. The children all had one thing in common, they were all smiling and laughing and so obviously happy. The place is now being run professionally and is now achieving in today's kids what it should have achieved in us in the mid-seventies. I left the college for the last time a few moments later and I will never go back again, no matter what. I suppose it's a bit like viewing a dead body. Some people do not want to do it because they prefer to keep an image in their mind of the dead person when he or she was alive and happy. I prefer to remember the photographs of those smiling children. The other photographs, the ones which I have in my mind and which will probably never leave me, are still painful to look at. But I know now that it is only in having the courage to view them that healing can begin to take place.

The year 2001 was approaching, but no date was given for the court case. The not knowing began to eat away at me. I began to drink far more than normal to escape the anxiety. The result was me being carted off to hospital with pancreatitis. After a slow recovery, I received the phone call I had been dreading. Bligh was to appear in court to plead to the charges. That meant a long wait to see if he would plead guilty. He didn't. His defence team asked the judge for more time. After much legal to-ing and fro-ing, he eventually pled not guilty in court. The trial date was set. I was now distraught. I would have to drive back down that motorway.

The trial date got closer. I began to have nightmares about it. I wondered if I would break down in court. I began to worry that his defence lawyers would make mincemeat of me in front of the jury. (If you consider some of the things I've written in this book, it wouldn't take O.J. Simpson's lawyers to make me look a complete jerk.) I was haunted by frightening thoughts of what might happen. The Press will murder me, my parish will reject me, my family will never be able to show their faces in public again. I would be branded a liar forever. Matters were made worse by a particularly vindictive, religious zealot who had been publicly criticising me for years. She had contacted Bligh's defence team to volunteer to be a witness against me, claiming she could prove that I was an unreliable witness. She had claimed in her bi-monthly magazine that I was lying. I was raging that this poisonous puff adder, who had never even met me, was not only slagging me in public, she was now taking steps to interfere directly in my life, something that she knew nothing about.

Suddenly, when I felt at my lowest ebb, the phone rang. The CID informed me that Bligh had changed his plea. He had pled guilty. None of us would be required to go to court, there would be no trial. We were vindicated at last. It was so important to me that he had pled guilty. Now it was beyond doubt. It wasn't a jury who decided, which people could always question. The guy himself admitted it. We had not been lying.

During my sermon the following Sunday, I told the people what had happened. I got through what I had to say without breaking down. I told them that I had innocently gone to primary school, with my school bag and play-piece twenty-seven years ago. I said that I felt I had only just got home that Friday when I received the call. At the end of Mass, I also had to announce that my good friend Carl was retiring from all church duties due to ill health. He had been my right hand man since I had come to the parish. The warmth of the round of applause showed the affection the people had for him. When it came to an end, I did break down. I couldn't say the final blessing. I walked off the Sanctuary in tears. A woman stepped forward and hugged me. It was probably the most emotional moment of my life. A few parishioners took me out for a drink after Mass. I had too much to drink. A group of ex-Hibs players took me out in Glasgow that night. Not for the first time in my life, I made a complete eejit of myself. I apologised to the players on the way home the next day. I kept saying sorry to them until eventually Jimmy O'Rourke, a Hibs legend, grabbed me by the lapels and said, 'Steve, let him who is without sin cast the first stone. Forget it, it was a minor mistake and we've all had too much to drink before. We all know what you've been through, you deserved a blow out.' At that moment, he became one of my legends too.

Two weeks later, Bligh was sentenced to two and a half years in prison and ten years on the sex offenders' register. I would have preferred to see him receive professional help, but that is not my decision. He would have received a far greater sentence had he been tried and found guilty, but the judge took into account that he had not put us through the ordeal of giving evidence in court. Other former students who contacted me are extremely unhappy about the sentence, students who suffered far more than I did. One told me that he still harboured anger at the priest's Order because they have not been in touch to apologise or to offer compensation or even counselling. As far as I'm concerned, I'm not interested in hearing from them. I have written much about 'denial' in this book, but what is actually going on in the Church is something even more sinister. The Church has been forced to set up child protection schemes, and rightly so. But from what I have witnessed about actual situations of abuse and the way they are dealt with, I still fear that the abused child is never the main priority. In our case, did that Order of priests really move mountains to help us, or was it partly an exercise in moving from denial to the next stage which is 'covering one's arse'?

Certainly, correspondence from the Vatican to my own Archbishop, seems to have been more concerned with the publication of this book than with the plight of the victims. At all costs, protect the image of the Church. The initial letter from them didn't even inquire as to the whereabouts of the abuser priest, or if indeed he was still a threat to children. He was never even mentioned. The only worry seemed to be how the Church would look if I published.

I set out to write all this down for my own benefit. It then became something which I hoped would help other victims. It has also now become a direct challenge to the Church to get its own house in order. It is also an invitation to the good people of the Church to stand up for themselves and demand from the Church authorities the legacy left to them by Christ: an honest Church which serves them and doesn't lord it over them; Apostles of Christ, not religious diplomats; and, most important, a Church which listens to them more often than it pronounces at them; a Church which is more open.

After Bligh was sentenced, a letter arrived marked with the insignia of the Vatican. I drew a deep breath as I began to read the contents. I wondered what disciplinary measures were to be taken against me. Was I to be booted out of the priesthood? I was amazed at what I read. It was an invitation to come to Rome – fare paid – to meet with the head of the Congregation for the Clergy. The letter assured me that I was not to worry, the purpose of my visit was to receive whatever pastoral support the Vatican could offer me. The letter was sincere and extremely understanding.

I flew to Rome the following week, still apprehensive about the motives of the Vatican. I needn't have worried. I was shown to a beautiful apartment within the Vatican. It was explained to me by a Cardinal's secretary that I was actually in the newly built apartments which were to host the next conclave. It was five-star accommodation. I had never before stayed in such sumptuous surroundings.

That night, I met with the Cardinal. He welcomed me very warmly and asked if I was comfortable in my apartment. He then got down to business. He wanted to know what the Church could do to make up for what had happened to me. He wanted to know the names of the other victims so that the Church could help them as well. I was astonished at what I was hearing. He asked about financial compensation but I told him I wanted nothing. This was enough: the fact that the institutional Church cared was by far the most valuable compensation any of us could ever receive.

I flew home the next day absolutely thrilled at what had just happened. On the flight, I asked for a glass of champagne to celebrate. All the hurt and pain had dissipated. I actually planned a holiday in the Lake District. I could go there now and enjoy the place. I thought about my weekly column in the *Evening News* and my slot on the BBC's 'Thought for the Day'. Never again would I criticise Church authorities. I would be able to speak with tremendous affection for the Church. I could now do what I have always wanted to do as a priest. I could stand up for the Church and proclaim from the roof-tops my pride in being a member of such a caring organisation. I drifted off to sleep serenely happy and looking forward to a future filled with hope. There would be no more fights, no more letters of complaint about me to my Archbishop. I would be able to return to clergy meetings in the archdiocese. I could even go to clergy golf matches without feeling I was being talked about. I was totally at peace.

'Would you like a cup of tea, Sir?', a voice interjected. Still half asleep, I moved my body to a more comfortable position to receive the cup of tea from the air hostess. A sharp pain pierced through my belly. I opened my eyes and was horrified by what I saw. The woman leaning over me was not an air hostess – she was a hospital worker. I wasn't on a plane. I was in bed in St John's Hospital. The pain in my belly was the pancreatitis. I was shattered. There had been no visit to the Vatican, no compassionate Cardinal, no apology, no offer of help. There would be no golf outings with my brother priests. I had dreamed the whole thing.

I sipped the lukewarm, bitter tasting tea. For a brief, fleeting, magical moment, I had experienced what the Church could be like, what I would dearly love it to be. One day I hope to swap that NHS cup of tea for a glass of champagne. I will raise it high and shout out my pride in the priesthood, the Church and the Vatican. That is my dream. For the moment though, all I have is a cup of tea.